TAUNTON'S
HOME REMODELING
PLANNING · DESIGN · CONSTRUCTION

Editors of *Fine Homebuilding*

The Taunton Press

The Taunton Press
Inspiration for hands-on living®

The Taunton Press, Inc., 63 South Main Street, PO Box 5506, Newtown, CT 06470-5506
e-mail: tp@taunton.com

Editors: Joe Provey, Christina Glennon
Copy editor: Diane Sinitsky
Indexer: Jim Curtis
Interior design: Carol Singer
Layout: Rita Sowins/Sowins Design

LIBRARY OF CONGRESS CATALOGING-IN-PUBLICATION DATA
Home remodeling / from the editors of Fine homebuilding.
    pages cm
 Includes index.
 ISBN 978-1-60085-428-6
1. Dwellings--Remodeling. I. Fine homebuilding.
 TH4816.H6529 2012
 690'.837--dc23
                        2011049153

PRINTED IN THE UNITED STATES OF AMERICA
10 9 8 7 6 5 4 3 2 1

ACKNOWLEDGMENTS

Special thanks to the authors, editors, art directors, copy editors, and other staff members of *Fine Homebuilding* who contributed to the development of the articles in this book.

Contents

Value-Added Remodeling

BY FERNANDO PAGÉS RUIZ

When embarking upon a home remodel, it's often difficult to decide what jobs to tackle first. Should you make over the kitchen or replace the furnace? Paint the exterior or build a deck? A good starting point is to ask yourself the question: "How long will I be living in this house?" If the answer is only a year or two, focus on upgrades that will make the house easier to sell when the time comes. If you don't foresee a move anytime soon, choose improvements that will improve comfort and give you long-term personal pleasure.

If you plan to stay

1. SUPPRESS YOUR HOME'S ENERGY APPETITE

Energy repairs and improvements can range from simple air-sealing to a full insulation and mechanical retrofit. The first step, however, is to invite a building performance analyst to evaluate your home. The two largest organizations that train and certify energy auditors are the Residential Energy Services Network (www.resnet.us) and the Building Performance Institute (www.bpi.org). Both are good, but I prefer BPI because their inspectors specialize in aspects of building performance that go beyond energy considerations.

2. UPGRADE YOUR ENTRYWAY

Too often, we spend money on impressing others instead of making our lives easier. Upgrade the entry you use most: the side or garage door.

An updated everyday entrance or mudroom should include a welcoming, functional door (with glass if the fire code allows), as well as a place inside to drop off groceries, leave notes for family members, hang a coat, stash boots, and comfortably transition into and out of the house.

3. TAKE CUES FROM A LIGHTING DESIGNER

Most of us work during the day and enjoy our houses mostly after dark. Upgrading lights and changing bulbs yield a quick uplift to your interior while saving energy.

Use compact fluorescent light bulbs (CFLs) only where lights will remain on for at least 15 minutes, such as exterior fixtures, kitchens, and bedrooms. Use halogen bulbs where you toggle the lights on and off more frequently, such as hallways, stairs, and pantries. Halogen bulbs also work well on dimmers, which makes them ideal for dining rooms, master bedrooms, and family rooms.

4. UPGRADE THE CABINETS

New cabinets make up about a third of the cost of a typical kitchen renovation, so it pays to explore alternatives to replacement. The options include painting, refacing, and accessorizing. I like to combine all three. Paint the boxes, replace the door and drawer fronts and pulls, then refurbish the interiors with an array of organizers, shelf drawers, and rollout bins.

5. REFINISH COUNTERTOPS AND APPLIANCES

Refinishing companies such as Miracle Method (www.miraclemethod.com) specialize in resurfacing countertops. Similar companies offer services to refinish your appliances with electrostatic paint. The finish is factory tough and will make your appliances, if they work well, indistinguishable from new products.

6. BUILD A BETTER BATHROOM

Consider reconfiguring the bathroom to include double sinks and a privacy door between the lavatory and the tub/toilet area. To update a bath, use some of the techniques for kitchen cabinets and counters. Tub

and shower options include ceramic-tile refinishing and thin stone veneers that apply directly over sound surfaces, such as old tile.

7. ADD TRIM

Millwork, or trim, does not have to feature high-cost exotic woods like cherry or laborious improvements like a fully paneled mahogany library. Paint-grade crown molding, wainscoting, and casing upgrades can transform a room for relatively little cost and time.

8. INSTALL BETTER FLOORING

The flooring trend has moved decidedly away from carpet to hard surfaces. Cork, bamboo, ceramic, Forest Stewardship Council (FSC)-certified wood, plastic laminate, and vinyl are now more popular flooring options. They also wear better, so if you decide to upgrade your floors, you not only will enjoy the marked change in your home's appearance, but you'll also have a long-lasting improvement sure to provide a sale-clinching wow factor even five or 10 years from now. Choose classic floor styles.

9. UPGRADE THE SIDING

Although exterior improvements are best done right before a sale, there are some exterior improvements that are worth considering because they provide long-term practical benefits and immediate pleasure. From a cost and maintenance standpoint, don't overlook vinyl and fiber-cement products. Vinyl siding is now available in countless styles, including clapboards, shakes, and even scallops.

10. EXPAND OUTDOOR LIVING

If you need more space for entertaining, the one place where it's relatively inexpensive to add square footage is your deck or patio. It's also one of the better remodeling investments, with an 80% payback for a wood deck versus most room additions, which yield about 60% return on investment (ROI). Decks also provide the kind of homebody moments of happiness that make you want to keep your house. The average cost of a deck addition—even an extravagant one—is less than $15,000. A room addition starts at around $50,000.

If you plan to sell

1. RESTORE THE FRONT ENTRY

This is the point where prospective buyers make first contact. Make sure the threshold is clean, the door panel freshly painted, and the hinges not squeaky. If the door does not look good, replace it. Among mid-

range projects, steel entry-door replacements yield more than a 100% ROI.

2. REPLACE OR PAINT THE SIDING

New siding can yield among the best ROI of all of the home improvement options, about 80%. This does not translate into a profit, but curb appeal can result in a sale quicker and closer to your asking price.

3. UPDATE THE EXISTING BATH

A bathroom remodel may not be the best investment when selling a house, but in consideration of the buyer, picture yourself checking into a hotel room. You don't really want the bathroom to look like someone else has used it. Replace corroded fixtures, install a new toilet seat, and remove mildew. Fresh caulk and paint and clean, sparkling faucets and fixtures will make a buyer more comfortable with the prospect of moving in.

4. CREATE CUSTOM CABINETS

Give cabinets a new look by refinishing them with paint or stain, or use a glazing technique. The glazed look darkens the kerfs along door panels and molding contours, giving the cabinets a richer, albeit antiqued, aesthetic.

5. REPLACE APPLIANCES

Just as buyers prefer clean, like-new bathroom fixtures, they also like new appliances. At a minimum, change the pans on an electric stovetop, clean the oven, and consider having all the kitchen appliances refinished. Otherwise, a simple suite of clearance-sale stainless-steel or black appliances may do more for your kitchen than new countertops.

6. USE MIRRORS TO CREATE A SENSE OF SPACE

A mirrored wall or set of closet doors can enlarge the feeling of a room and throw more light into an otherwise dim environment. Natural light is essential in creating a home that feels welcoming and comfortable.

7. REMOVE A FEW KITCHEN CABINETS

Creating a little breathing room by reducing cabinet clutter can improve the feel of your kitchen, even if it sacrifices storage. When you're after first impressions, how the kitchen feels is more important than how it functions. A creative way to do this is by replacing some upper cabinets with open shelving. Remember to keep them uncluttered.

8. LANDSCAPE THE YARD

Take the time to mow the lawn, prune bushes and trees, mulch flower beds, and, if the weather allows, throw in some annual plantings. While I don't recommend spending thousands of dollars on your yard, I do encourage you to make it as appealing and

as neat as possible. Much of that can be accomplished with a little bit of sweat equity.

9. REDECK THE DECK

Another high return-on-investment project is new exterior decking. Outdoor entertainment areas are one of those things everyone shopping for a house dreams about; otherwise they would be shopping for a condo. Exterior remodeling, especially something like upgrading an existing deck surface, usually costs less than almost any type of remodeling you can do inside.

10. INSTALL LAMINATE FLOORING

Buyers want solid flooring, not carpet. Plastic-laminate flooring looks better now than it ever did and can dramatically update the look of your entry, kitchen, and living areas. Also, it costs a fraction of what true hardwood does. Snap-and-lock flooring technology makes for a fast installation. And use one floor throughout; small spaces feel bigger this way.

PART 1

Plan to Save Money

11 Essential Remodeling Strategies

BY KEYAN MIZANI

Many of us live in houses that need something. They might be cramped, confined, dated, dark, poorly laid out, or all of the above and more. If you live in an older home, it was probably designed and built to accommodate a lifestyle that has long since gone by the wayside.

Like a big Band-Aid®, additions are often proposed as the way to heal a house's ailments—and sometimes they do, but not if the core problems aren't fixed as well. If an addition really is needed, designing it in tandem with improvements to existing space can minimize its size and result in a house that functions and feels better. When my firm, eM/Zed Design, works with clients who want to upgrade their home, we focus first on identifying opportunities within the existing footprint. After all, making the most of what lies within is often less expensive and one of the greenest things you can do. The remodeling strategies we typically use are all interrelated, as you'll see in the examples shown here.

1. Look at the big picture first

This strategy is number one for a reason: It's the most important. You don't want to fix one clumsy room only to discover that it needs changing in a couple of years to solve another room's problems.

HOW TO DO IT RIGHT

- Consider your future needs and whether the current renovation either can expand to meet them or can be part of a larger overall plan that's accomplished in stages. Combining projects usually shakes loose more space, bringing better opportunities for creative rearrangement of available square footage. The project shown on pp. 8–9 illustrates this approach.

- Rearrange room locations for the best fit. For example, we've seen many poorly placed first-floor baths that act as a plug in a plan that could otherwise feel more spacious and open.

- Subdivide extra-large or underused spaces. Perhaps the living room is larger than necessary and can lend some space to form a better entry. What if the underused bedroom next to the kitchen became a family room as part of a kitchen renovation? Can you steal some space from an adjacent room to recess the refrigerator that has always been in the way?

- Design spaces that serve multiple functions. This strategy can free up a good deal of room for use in another part of the renovation. Home offices can occasionally be guest rooms, while hallways can sometimes accommodate a homework or bill-paying station. Stairways might include shelving.

CASE STUDY

A master-suite project grew to include an anticipated kitchen renovation. Working on both allowed for reconfiguration of the space separating them, which contained a short hallway and a dark basement stair that led to the laundry room. Reversing the stair direction and opening it to the kitchen made the kitchen seem bigger, brought more light to the downstairs family room, and eliminated the short hallway. Removal of the hall provided space for a pantry and a larger master closet. All this fine-tuning allowed us to shrink the size of an expected addition to a 2-ft. bump-out under the existing roof, as shown in the "After floor plan" on the facing page.

1   BEFORE

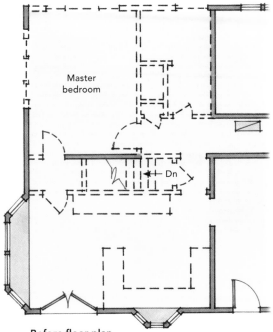

Master
bedroom

Dn

Before floor plan

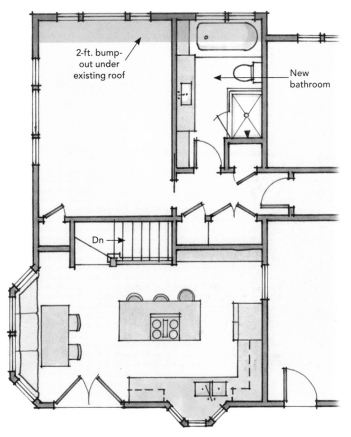

2-ft. bump-
out under
existing roof

New
bathroom

Dn

After floor plan

1 NEW BATHROOM

2. Remove pieces

Never assume that all parts of an existing building should be retained, especially those added over time. Poorly positioned bays, bump-outs, and additions can detract from the function of a home, especially if they are in disrepair. A typical small-scale example is the prefab bow window applied to a large wall. Removing it can create opportunities for a wider expanse of windows that enlarges the feeling of the room without an appreciable loss of usable space. In other situations, removing larger portions of a house can have a surprisingly beneficial effect (photos at right and below).

CASE STUDY

This hillside house lacked a direct connection to its beautiful backyard. A poorly conceived addition (foreground lower level, "before" photo) restricted views to the yard, blocked yard access, and contributed little to an already spacious lower-level family room. The addition was removed and replaced with a deck and a stairway to the yard. New, large windows and a full-lite door offer expansive outdoor views and provide more daylight to the family room. The rest of the back facade also received a face-lift to enhance its proportions.

3. Improve circulation

Circuitous circulation is great in a Japanese garden but not in your house. On the other hand, while efficient circulation is the goal, it also should be enjoyable and a way to experience the unfolding of a home's interior.

HOW TO DO IT RIGHT

- Establish a clear hierarchy between public and private areas. Openings to private spaces should not compete with those that lead to communal areas.
- Make the width of the path feel generous to impart a sense of spaciousness. Long corridors should be wider to help offset their depth.
- Preserve space for furniture by placing through-room pathways along the edges instead of through the center of rooms. Most early-20th-century kitchens are common offenders, guaranteed to have at least three to five doorways with zigzagging paths to and fro interrupting the middle of the space. Eliminating some doorways and moving circulation to one side of the kitchen can provide more wall area for cabinetry, an undisturbed work area, and a clear path through for family and friends.
- Convert a dreadful, dark corridor into a welcoming one that shares light and air between rooms. At the end, either a window or an interior feature can serve as a pleasing focal point. Think: No cheap hotel corridors allowed.

This house has a deep footprint with a 20-ft.-plus distance between the entry and the living/dining area. The original corridor was jumbled and uninviting, presenting a wide-open view of the laundry and a partial view of one side of the fireplace. The reconfigured corridor frames the new fireplace with two pairs of columns, frame-and-panel wainscot, and decorative lighting that leads the eye inward. The laundry is now behind closed doors.

3 AFTER

AFTER

4. Resurface instead of demolish

Sometimes one unattractive element can overwhelm a space. Your first impulse might be to remove it, and although sometimes this is necessary, first consider resurfacing it. If something can be resurfaced, the project will likely be less expensive and will lead to less waste. Don't like the texture of the 1970s-era brick-wall fireplace in your living room? A cement skim coat can change the wall and its texture entirely. Similarly, kitchen cabinets can be partially reused by replacing tired drawer fronts and doors.

BEFORE

CASE STUDY

A cement skim coat gave new life to this old fireplace. The new smooth-painted finish creates a dramatic monolithic appearance and covers peeling paint ill-applied over unattractive stone. A mantel of reclaimed Douglas fir adds warmth. The new opening beyond the fireplace connects the kitchen to the dining area and shares light and views.

5 AFTER

5 BEFORE

5. Revisit the stairs

Moving or reversing a stairway is not for the faint of heart, but there are times when it is well worth the effort. If a stairway is in the wrong place, it can eat up much more space than necessary; relocating or modifying it can yield significant square footage and a better overall floor plan. Stair position and direction also affect circulation patterns on all levels of a house. Poorly placed stairs often have a ripple effect and cause more space to be wasted because of inefficient circulation to and around them.

HOW TO DO IT RIGHT

- Position a stair for a centrally located landing rather than at one end of the house, where it would require a long hallway. The goal is to have spaces pinwheel off the landing (floor plans on p. 14).
- Stack stairwells. If the stair to the basement is not located under the stair to the second floor, it probably should be, especially in an efficient floor plan. In one recent project, this change afforded enough space in the kitchen for a cozy eating nook.
- Don't be afraid to change stair direction. This low-impact fix sometimes is all that's needed when a stair arrives in an unfortunate place and can be flipped. This solution usually maintains existing floor framing and just requires new stair framing (floor plan on p. 9).
- Open up the stairwell. Houses with stairs crammed between walls are passing up an opportunity to add drama and intrigue to adjacent spaces. Whether moving the stairs or not, consider opening up walls to create two-story glimpses, shared light, attractive railing details, and a greater sense of spaciousness.

5 | NEW ENTRY FOYER

Relocating the stairs in the house shown here and on p. 13 made a two-story rear addition on a small lot unnecessary. Cutting through the middle of the 1920s plan, the original walled-in stairs consumed prime real estate, were steep and narrow, and created wasteful circulation. Moving the stairs closer to the front entry and tucking them under the slope of the roof yielded enough space for another bedroom on the second floor and for a more spacious kitchen. A small, landlocked, first-floor bedroom right off the entry was sacrificed to accommodate the new stair and a better-organized plan—a worthwhile trade-off. The new stair with a detailed railing and a skylight above creates a more open, graceful, and bright entry foyer. The foyer also gained a walk-in closet (white door in photo) from the former bedroom.

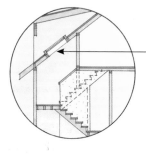

The skylight increases perceived headroom. The new stairway takes advantage of the sloped space.

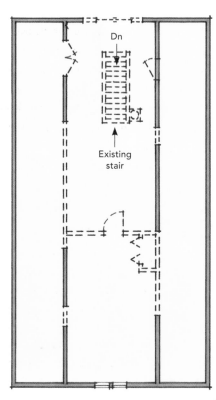

Dn

Existing stair

Second floor before

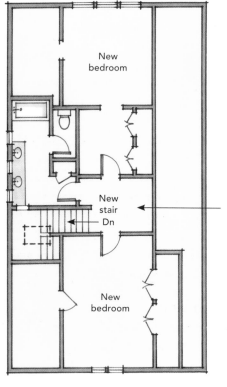

New bedroom

New stair
Dn

New bedroom

A centrally located landing takes up the least space.

Second floor after

6 AFTER

6 BEFORE

6. Add more natural light

Almost every client's wish list calls for more natural light and for good reason. Abundant daylight makes spaces seem larger, brings inside the drama of ever-changing weather and seasons, lifts spirits, and reduces the need for artificial lights. In the presence of daylight, details come alive, like the play of sun and shadow passing through a stair railing or the long reach of reflected sky across a floor near tall windows. In all cases, window and skylight placement relative to overhangs, trees, and solar orientation should be evaluated first.

HOW TO DO IT RIGHT

- Widen windows, especially those in need of replacement. Adding width to openings admits more light and enhances views.
- Raise window heights. This change has even more impact because the higher you raise the win-

dows, the deeper the light reaches into the house. Although it depends on factors such as overhangs, trees, and the room's reflective surfaces, generally daylight can reach at least twice the window height into a room.

- Use stairwells to deliver light. Skylights and/or dormers can enliven the stairway and bring natural light into adjacent spaces.
- Bounce light off walls. A wall or plane placed perpendicular and adjacent to a window will be illuminated by daylight and will bounce it inside. Light, reflective surfaces distribute natural light; dark, absorptive surfaces absorb it. Merely changing a living-room floor from carpet to wood can result in a brighter space.
- Share light through openings between interior spaces.

CASE STUDY

Bringing in more daylight became an important way of making an attic master suite seem larger and lighter (photos above). Two existing dormer windows that previously occupied a low storage attic along the front of the house were connected to the new suite via niches that extend forward to meet the windows. Although the windows are not large, they provide another exposure, helping to balance daylight within the room and creating bright focal points with character.

7 AFTER

7 BEFORE

7. Improve access to the yard

In climates where outdoor living can be enjoyed for at least part of the year, direct access to the yard can extend the apparent boundaries of a house and add more square footage without more building. In addition to doors, improved yard access includes having enough well-positioned windows so that you can appreciate the views from inside. For families with children, being able to have kids playing in the yard in full view from inside allows parents to continue with other activities while maintaining supervision. The kitchen is one important room that can benefit from this strategy. Improving the connection between kitchen and yard facilitates outdoor dining and enjoyment of the yard from the hub of the home.

CASE STUDY

A relatively small maneuver results in a huge pay-off. In a house that had no direct connection to its backyard, replacing the dining-room windows with French doors and sidelites opened the interior to the exterior. A simple paver patio beyond the doors provides a convenient outdoor dining area. Rerouting major circulation to the yard through the dining room also relieved the kitchen of an intrusive travel path to an exterior side door.

8 | AFTER

8 | BEFORE

Reorganizing a kitchen can create opportunities for opening it to adjacent spaces. In this kitchen, the refrigerator, ovens, and most upper cabinets were relocated to another wall, making way for a new opening that connects to a renovated living and dining room. Although generous, the opening preserves the surrounding wall area that defines the kitchen and adds layering between the rooms. The extended diagonal sightlines between rooms and the rows of windows beyond make an enormous impact on the interior's brightness and overall sense of spaciousness.

8. Create appropriate openings between interior spaces

Although most new houses have open floor plans, older homes typically do not. Houses with walls separating every room no longer fit contemporary lifestyles. Private kitchens, separate living and dining areas, and back halls can feel confining. Open floor plans allow everyone in the family to feel connected, even when engaged in different activities. Openings between spaces can also share daylight and views, thereby brightening a room or hallway, expanding the sense of interior space, and providing additional views of the outdoors. When aligned, openings between several rooms can greatly enhance the feeling of depth and interest in a home.

Open floor plans allow everyone in the family to feel connected.

HOW TO DO IT RIGHT

- Consider the opening carefully. Although completely removing a wall is sometimes the right solution, there are situations where it is not. Walls with carefully proportioned openings can create spatial definition between areas, the absence of which can make spaces seem smaller. The answer could be to enlarge a space by moving a wall and then adding an opening in it.
- Maintain a private space. In most situations, there should be at least one common room in the house that is either completely private or able to become so via closed doors. This can be where the TV lives if it is not part of the home's open spaces, or where family members can go to have a quiet conversation, read a book, or work on a project.
- Don't block daylight. Where visual and acoustic privacy is needed but light can be shared, consider adding frosted doors or windows, sliding screens, or other translucent materials. For example, adding frosted French doors to a home office allows it to be open to surrounding spaces at times and to share light even when the doors are closed.
- Open up hallways. Dark corridors and stairwells often have much to gain when surrounding walls are partially or fully removed. This change also allows for better ventilation. Matching the openings to common rooms on both sides of a hallway can create an interesting cross axis and expand the apparent size of a house.

9. Use areas under sloped ceilings

Many houses have unused real estate under low portions of the roof. These attic areas can be annexed to the floor plan in a variety of ways, depending on their location.

HOW TO DO IT RIGHT

- Make room for little people. Bed nooks or play spaces for kids are great uses of low-ceilinged areas. Children love spaces that aren't big enough for grown-ups and delight in creating forts under sheltering sloped ceilings.
- Fit furniture under the roof. Nooks under sloped ceilings can accommodate the head of a bed, a sitting area, or a desk for people of all ages (top photo on p. 15).
- Tuck in convenient storage. Under-roof space shouldn't go to waste. Storage can be created using doors, drawers, and recessed shelves. In very low areas, drawers are the most functional way to retrieve stored items.
- Relocate a stairway. In some cases, a stair can rise up parallel to the roof, making use of low space.
- Squeeze in a small bath. Bathrooms can be expanded or added to areas under a sloped roof as long as code-required head heights are maintained above showers and tubs and in front of toilets and sinks. However, the depth of sinks and toilets can usually extend into lower spaces. Showers also can extend into lower spaces, provided a bench or other barrier is present. In some cases, a fixture with a noncompliant head height might be grandfathered.

9 | BEFORE

9 | AFTER

CASE STUDY

A child's tight bedroom was transformed by carving into adjacent attic space. The new bed nook creates a cozy sleeping berth and expands the width of the room. The nook is also sized so that the twin bed could be replaced with a full-size bed whose headboard tucks under the skylight. Additional attic space was used to improve storage, including new recessed shelves, drawers, and an adjacent closet. The new window and skylight brighten the space and provide more outdoor views.

JUST ENOUGH HEADROOM FOR AN ATTIC BATH

Mirror between the rafters

A skylight well can give the lavatory mirror a lift.

Toilet against a low wall

Codes allow the ceiling to slope downward if it meets the minimum standard at the front of the toilet.

Skylight solves headroom problem

A shower under a sloped roof gets positively expansive with a view of the sky.

10. Consider a face-lift

The appearance of our houses influences our feelings about them and about ourselves. If you are unhappy with the face your house presents, there are ways to improve its looks and your outlook. Ideally, a home's curb appeal should be more than skin deep; it should express parts of what and who are within. Begin by evaluating which elements of the facade are trouble spots and which are worth keeping.

HOW TO DO IT RIGHT

- Make a dramatic impact with new windows. If the existing windows are poorly proportioned, too few, or in the wrong places, consider new proportions, enlarged openings, or complete relocation. Changing the width of a window requires a new header, in which case a raised head height also can be considered.
- Consider a minor change to the roof to make a big difference. For example, framing a simple shed pop-up over a group of windows can lift an other-wise low roof. Adding dormers is another way to introduce detail and rhythm to the roof.
- Make the front door easy to find. The entry should be visible and welcoming, and, in most climates, some roof cover if not a front porch is a necessity. Either way, the process of getting to and through the door should provide an interesting transition from outside to inside.
- Modify siding, trim, and paint colors, but beware of superficial fixes such as changing the siding on only the front of the house. Different types of siding and trim, however, can be used effectively to emphasize separate parts of the house. For color changes, always apply at least 4-ft. by 8-ft. test samples before making a decision.

CASE STUDY

Low roofs, small windows, and drab colors gave this house a brooding appearance. The roofs received a lift with the addition of two shed pop-ups atop the existing roof framing. Although ceiling heights were unchanged by these pop-ups, raised eaves allowed the head heights of the expanded windows to be raised 6 in., contributing more daylight to the interior and better proportions to the exterior. A new front walk, a projecting gable roof, and Douglas-fir door and sidelites create a welcoming entry that holds its own against the more prominent garage. More trim, new siding, and better colors add greater detail and interest.

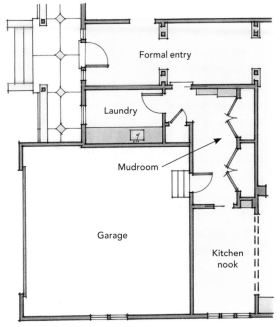

11. Increase storage

Every home needs to have dedicated storage for the stuff of modern life, or it will overflow into living spaces and make them feel cramped. Rooms free of clutter always appear more spacious and inviting.

HOW TO DO IT RIGHT

- Add a mudroom to create a family entry with places for shoes, coats, and backpacks. You also can include shelves for cell-phone chargers, keys, and other gadgets best left near the door. Either in the mudroom or elsewhere, include spaces for recycling bins and a place for the vacuum, broom, cleaning supplies, step stool, and flashlights.
- Establish a command center. This HQ (usually near the kitchen) offers a place for the phone, the family calendar, bill-paying supplies, take-out menus, and messages. It can be compact. Occasionally, a big closet can be downsized or a kitchen cabinet converted to carve out just enough space for this vital function.

CASE STUDY

Same doorway, very different room. The door on the left leading to the garage originally opened into the kitchen, providing no transition space and meager storage for a family home. Relocating a landlocked dining room (beyond the pocket door in the "before" photo) and redesigning the kitchen created space for a mudroom that connects to the kitchen, the formal entry (beyond), and the garage. Two long closets keep most items organized and out of sight; a bench provides a place for putting on shoes; and open shelving and hooks accommodate everyday items such as cell phones with chargers, purses, shoes, and backpacks.

How to Afford an Architect

BY DUO DICKINSON

When David and Nancy Stein came to see me about designing a house, their biggest concern, like that of most clients, was cost. Their house had just burned down, and they had to rebuild. They would be reusing most of the original foundation, and they had a builder, Clark Sellars, lined up. But they wanted to know whether they could hire me to design the new house and still stay within their budget.

The Steins' budget was limited strictly to the insurance check. If the project came in over budget, they wouldn't have the money to pay for it. Given their insurance settlement and the house's footprint, they could afford about $115 per sq. ft., including design and structural-engineering fees. Although I knew completing the project on this budget was possible, I wouldn't be able to provide a full scope of architectural services. The Steins, however, were willing to roll up their sleeves and become actively involved in the design process.

Because this extra work required the clients' time, this approach might not be for everybody. All told, my firm's design fee was about 5% of the total construction cost. This figure is extremely low, even for the strictly limited work that we did. The Steins' experience, therefore, is a case study of the ways involved, conscientious homeowners can reduce an architect's fees.

Design options and detailed drawings are expensive

Architects most often charge some form of a fixed fee, either a certain percentage of construction costs, a dollar amount per square foot, or a lump sum. Regardless of the mechanics of billing, a client really is paying for the architect's time. If you can plead your case to an open-minded architect, explain that you will diligently limit his or her time, and take on added responsibility, there is a good chance that you can weave the cost of a creative, innovative, and (you hope) beautiful design into your construction budget.

Involved, conscientious homeowners can reduce an architect's fees.

My own firm charges all fees on an hourly basis, but we offer two different service levels: a full-service option and a consultant option. Under the full-service option, my firm serves as the architects of record and provides a full scope of architectural services, including weekly site visits during the construction of the house. In this scenario, we typically present five or six design options to the client and react to his or her feedback. Once the client and I have

MODEST BUDGETS DEMAND STRAIGHTFORWARD SHAPES AND SPACES. Part of an architect's job is to design a house that can be built on budget. For these cost-cutting clients, that meant simple framing (a basic roof shape) and simple materials (clapboards, T-111 siding, and asphalt roof shingles).

come up with a consensus design, my firm draws a complete set of construction and shop drawings, generally somewhere between 60 and 80 drawings. On average, this full-service approach costs between 16% and 18% of the total construction budget.

Saving money means making more decisions yourself

With clients like the Steins, for whom limiting costs is the primary concern, I recommend our other service option. In this scenario, my firm limits the services we provide to make the project buildable for the minimum possible fee, thereby providing maximum savings to the client. We essentially serve as consultants. The client supplies explicit guidelines and design criteria. I deliver a minimum number of drawings for an accurate bid and a viable permit application. The drawings provide critical dimensions rather than complete dimensions, and the builder gets performance standards rather than product specifications.

To reduce my involvement, the client takes on greater responsibility to interpret designs and to intercede with the builder to specify materials and finishes. In this client-architect relationship, it's important that the client and the builder have a good relationship and that the builder be involved early in the design process.

Although I'm billing an hourly rate for my time, this type of consultancy contract generally translates to a fee of between 11% and 14% of the construction budget. However, the more that clients know what they want, the less they'll spend on design services.

With this house, we were able to reduce fees to 5% because the Steins had such a clear idea of what they wanted. David Stein had sketched a rough floor plan before we met. My firm presented the Steins with two options, and they readily approved one of them.

The Steins also took steps to reduce the time I spent on their project. For instance, they cut back on my travel time by coming to my office for design meetings and by requesting only two site visits dur-

MORE THAN A DECK. The family's outdoor life revolves around a backyard that is several feet above the first floor. To avoid an awkward traipse around the house and up the hill, a bridge from the second floor links the house to the yard. The entry from the bridge ties neatly into a landing on the house's central stairs, complete with a small office space. The location and general style of the bridge were shown in the plans, but the builder worked out the specifics on site in consultation with the owners.

SIMPLY APPEALING. To build a house for $115 per sq. ft., the Steins and their builder relied on drywall and flat stock trim as a way of limiting costs. A taper added to the fireplace shroud makes these common materials expressive.

ing the construction phase. They also were willing to make a million decisions on the fly as the construction of their house progressed.

For a house of this size and complexity with a moderate design budget and this level of design service, my firm typically would produce 25 to 30 drawings. The Steins received just thirteen 24-in. by 36-in. drawings. One reason we were able to get by with so few drawings is that the Steins had chosen a builder before hiring me, and he could weigh in on the design process.

Working from so few drawings meant that many features were lightly drawn, showing limited detail. The homeowners, then, had to be willing to answer dozens of questions about things like tile patterns, stair-railing details, paint colors, and hardware choices, often at the last minute. On average, they said this involved about two hours a day of research and returning calls.

FEWER DRAWINGS MEAN A SMALLER BILL

LABOR-INTENSIVE DRAWINGS account for a large part of an architect's billable hours. For the Steins' house, my firm drew about 80% fewer drawings than we'd typically do for a full-service project. Of course, this means the homeowner and the builder have much less detail to guide them. How much less?

For the Steins, who used our consultant-service option, the staircase was lightly drawn with all its details shown in a cross section of the house (top drawing at right). The notes indicate the headroom required, critical framing details, and stair location. By comparison, a client with a similar staircase who used our full-service option received multiple detailed drawings showing all elevations of the stairs (bottom drawings). The plans included all dimensions and trim details, including the baluster design and placement—something that was left up to the builder and the homeowners in the Steins' case.

LIGHTLY DRAWN STAIR PLANS

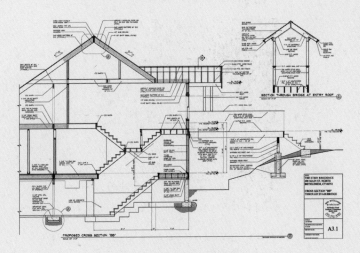

DETAILED STAIR PLANS

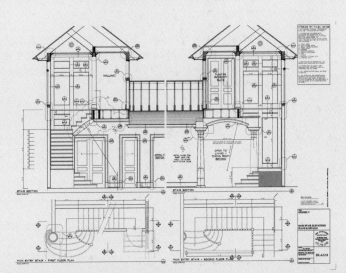

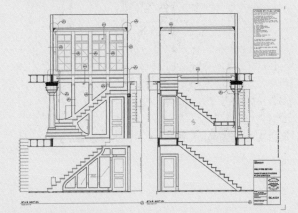

TEN STEPS TO REDUCE DESIGN FEES

NOBODY NEEDS AN ARCHITECT. The fact that only 2% to 3% of new homes are architect-designed proves this. A well-designed house, though, should be comfortable to live in and should save you money. That's because the details and specifications of a carefully considered design prevent unnecessary, ongoing maintenance while creating a more efficient, smaller home with lower utility costs and, perhaps, a lower property-tax assessment.

That's a lot to ask and, consequently, an architect's services aren't cheap. But there are things you can do to make the architect's job easier and less costly. It all comes down to taking on responsibilities that you could avoid with higher design fees. Working on dozens of projects like the Steins', I've learned a lot about what homeowners can do to reduce the number of hours I bill. Here are the 10 with the biggest bang for the buck.

1. EDUCATE YOURSELF
Before you begin interviewing architects, dedicate yourself to becoming a home-design and building nerd. Learn everything you can about design, the construction process, and available materials by watching TV, reading back issues of *Fine Homebuilding*, and buying boxes of books about houses.

2. KNOW YOUR BUDGET
You need to know exactly how much money you have to spend and what that budget must cover. If you want landscaping or particular appliances or furnishings for your new house, you have to factor that into the budget.

3. DON'T EXPECT LOVE AT FIRST SIGHT
Interview as many architects as necessary to find the right one. (And you should never hire your brother-in-law until you've considered hiring pretty much everybody else.) You should look for an architect whose aesthetics match yours and whose design process inspires you and reflects what you value, whether it's aesthetics, green design, natural materials, or wild sculptural details.

Remember: Architects are like leopards; spot-changing is not likely. Regardless of the style you want, make sure the architect has done work you love. Don't accept an architect's promises to change from what he has done in the past so that he can meet your specific needs.

4. BE VERY CLEAR ABOUT YOUR NEEDS
The more precise you are about the physical requirements of the structure and the more precise you are about what appeals to you before the design process starts, the less time an architect will spend on your project and the less time will be spent in design development. Less time equals less money.

5. GET YOUR BUILDER INVOLVED EARLY
The best-case scenario is to have a builder whom you can trust on board during the design process. The builder can head off structural approaches that he is either inexperienced or uncomfortable with. He also can offer an immediate reality check on the cost of your and the architect's ideas. Involving the builder in the process means he won't find any surprises when he gets the construction drawings. That means few, if any, revisions caused by the builder's reactions to the design, the detailing, or the structural approach.

Your architect can refer you to a builder, but never accept only one referral. Interview three or four builders, and find the one who fits you best, independent of the architect's recommendations. Then bid out the project to the leading contenders to establish a budget, and negotiate the architect's final scope of work and design based on the builder you've chosen.

6. DON'T CONTRACT FOR SERVICES YOU DON'T NEED
When you meet with the architect, plainly state what design services you need. If you don't require a full-service architect, say so. Then make arrangements with him or her for specific services.

7. ENGAGE IN THE DESIGN PROCESS
Demand full explanations of all the elements of the design as it's being presented. Don't sit back and take it. Actively seek the logic behind the architect's choices so that you understand why your house is designed the way it is.

8. DIGEST EVERYTHING BEFORE MAKING DECISIONS

Thoroughly review the architect's proposals before you provide feedback. You don't want to make a snap decision and then have a change of heart once the architect has incorporated your feedback into the design. Take the time for discussion with your family to arrive at a mutual decision. The more time an architect spends on revisions, the more you'll end up paying.

9. SEND AN EMAIL

Use email instead of scheduling meetings to discuss the design. It's easy to scan drawings into either a PDF or JPEG format and email them to the architect to establish a dialogue, rather than spending time and money on meetings. Regular email exchanges allow you to maintain close contact and to short-circuit an architect's normal tendency to present "perfected" proposals. This should prevent him or her from spending too much time developing a design that is off-track.

10. BUY A DIGITAL CAMERA

Take site photos during construction, and email them to the architect every day or two as construction progresses. It's a lot cheaper than a site visit. Not only will this satisfy the architect's urge to see his or her brainchild take form, but it also might improve the project. Regular photo updates can head off misinterpretations by the builder. An architect working on a tight fee simply cannot explore all the possible design ramifications, so photo updates also might lead him or her to suggest improvements that can be incorporated during construction.

A reduced design fee still means a quality house

When designing a house without the resources to spend time drawing every detail and specifying every material and construction method, there is potential for some miscommunication and gaps in the information conveyed in the drawings. In the Steins' case, though, the process was remarkably smooth. The vast majority of the house was built exactly as drawn by my colleague Brian Ross, and those areas (the fireplace, the bridge to the backyard, and the lofts above the upstairs bedrooms) that had to be figured out in the field turned out well. Figuring out these lightly drawn areas is where an experienced, thoughtful builder makes all the difference.

When I walk through the finished house, I see that the office area on the stair landing is smaller than I anticipated and that a few interior-trim details aren't exactly as envisioned. When I look at the code-compliant, standard stair rail, I think that it would have been fun to design a more expressive one because the stair is a central feature of the house. But these are small points.

As built, the house turned out to be both an exceptional value and an extraordinarily apt reflection of a family's values and lifestyle. Most important, the project was finished on budget and more or less on time. Obviously, my firm helped to make that happen, but in truth, the builder is almost always the hero when time and money issues are resolved satisfactorily. In this case, his diligence, thoughtfulness, and can-do attitude very much enabled the project to be a success for everyone concerned.

Design an Addition that Looks Right

BY LYNN HOPKINS

As needs change and decisions must be made about whether to move or to stay put, homeowners should begin by asking questions about their current residence. Where can we make room for a growing family by adding a couple of bedrooms? Can we carve out space for a home office? Will some artful reworking of the exterior make it more appealing to a potential buyer?

As an architect specializing in residential design, I've spent years addressing these questions for my clients. Adding square footage to a house can transform a poorly laid-out plan into something that perfectly suits the occupants, often with just a modest amount of new space. A construction project that recasts the exterior shapes of a house is an excellent opportunity to fix problems such as clumsy rooflines, poorly conceived entries, and missed opportunities for outdoor spaces.

Here, I'll take a look at an assortment of houses that have been improved with additions both large and small. In each case, the addition not only provided the desired space, but it also enhanced the look of the house.

Should you build up, out, or both?

Every addition begins with a fundamental question: Where should it go? A variety of conditions influence the answer.

Whether to expand a home upward instead of outward depends on the kinds of spaces you want to add, the configuration of the lot, and the restrictions imposed by the building department. As a general rule, most public-space additions, such as living rooms, family rooms, and kitchens, are outward expansions, while most private spaces reach upward. But conditions such as views, height restrictions, physical needs of the occupants, setbacks, and terrain can trump the general rule.

Going-up considerations

- Rooms with similar functions should be near one another. For instance, bedrooms want to be close to each other and to bathrooms. The living room wants to be close to the dining room and the front entry. And almost every room wants to be close to the kitchen, especially the family room, the dining room, and the garage, mudroom, or wherever groceries enter the house.
- Upward additions with dormers can improve existing rooms by adding headroom and natural

1 AFTER

light, or they can transform former attic or storage spaces into habitable rooms if the ridge is high enough. Because these additions fit within the confines of an existing roof, the volume of the new space they can provide is limited. In an average-size house with a 10-in-12-pitch roof, the usable dormered space on the floor directly below the roof is generally about half to two-thirds that on the lower full floor.

- A new upstairs bath or bedroom that opens directly off the stair hall is ideal. If this is not possible and you have to walk through an existing bedroom to get to the new space, consider changing the existing room to something more public—a study or a TV area, for example—or creating a hallway with storage closets. Although having access to a bath from an adjacent bedroom is a common arrangement for master suites, walking through one bedroom to get to another should be avoided.

1 BEFORE

- Going-up additions can be built without additional foundation work or loss of precious outdoor space, but they are the most disruptive. It can be best to move out for the duration of the project.

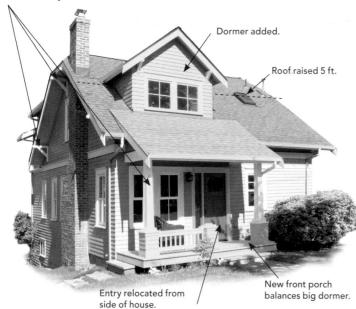

Brackets and tapered porch columns add Craftsman style.

Dormer added.

Roof raised 5 ft.

Entry relocated from side of house.

New front porch balances big dormer.

BORROW FROM YOUR NEIGHBORS, BORROW FROM A STYLE

The original house, a small, nondescript bungalow, had a cramped entry and odd windows ("before" photo on p. 29). In the walk-up attic, the roof's ridge was so low that a person could stand fully upright in only the very center of the space. When Seattle architect Jim Rymsza designed a second-floor addition ("after" photo on p. 29) with two bedrooms, a bath, and a home office, the original roof was removed and a new one built with the ridge about 5 ft. higher. Besides improving headroom on the second floor, the new roof respects the low-to-the-ground character of other bungalows in the neighborhood. This house still looks like a one-story home.

The new roof also borrows a half-hipped roof detail from an adjacent home. Deep eaves and an overhanging rake were part of the original house, a handsome and practical characteristic in rainy Seattle. New eave brackets play up the deep eaves and rake, transforming the home from a forgettable tract house into an exemplar of the neighborhood's prevalent Craftsman style. The tapered porch posts sitting on low, shingled pedestals further elaborate on this style.

Double-hung windows with a two-over-two muntin pattern, typical of the Craftsman era, replace the soulless casement windows of the original house. The foursquare lite pattern of the dormer windows adds another important level of detail and refinement.

The addition of a wide front porch not only creates a much more inviting and useful entry, but it also cleverly balances the addition of a large dormer. Imagine how top-heavy this dormer would look if the porch weren't there. When expanding a house upward, it is important to consider how the new will affect the old. Often, it's necessary to make changes on the first floor as well so that the entire house hangs together as a coherent whole.

Going-out things to consider

- Building out might make it possible to nestle a new family room into a leafy corner of the yard, simultaneously creating a protected area perfect for a terrace.
- Building out can block a less desirable view and provide privacy to part of the yard.
- Rooms that serve multiple people simultaneously, such as a family room, a living room, or a dining room, generally function best when they are close to the kitchen. When these rooms are also adjacent to outdoor living areas, they provide convenient circulation for guests during social functions. These desirable connections argue in favor of a going-out addition for public rooms.
- Going-out additions substantially affect the existing room or rooms where the new construction attaches to the house. Windows likely will be eliminated and circulation disrupted, making it necessary to compensate for these losses. For example, if a new family room attaches next to the kitchen, then the kitchen should be configured so that people can access the family room without disrupting kitchen workflow. Often, it's desirable to open the wall between the two rooms so that the kitchen can borrow light and views from the family room, effectively making it an extension of the new room. Another strategy is to put func-

2 AFTER

2 BEFORE

Circular window, table, and paving tie the house and yard together.

Axis encourages long views.

Windows in clusters of three establish an underlying order.

tions that don't require natural light in these now interior spaces, such as closets, a pantry, a laundry, or a powder room.

- Although going-out additions require new foundations and result in a loss of outdoor space, they are typically the least disruptive to living in the house while construction proceeds.

CASE STUDY 2

LET THE ADDITION CREATE AN OUTDOOR LIVING AREA

The original house ("before" photo above) ignored the backyard. With the addition of a master suite, this corner of the house now defines an exterior space. Low stone walls, plantings, and paving that take their design cues from the house further define the outdoor room. For instance, the sitting area carved into the garden is on axis with a bay window and takes its circular form from a circular window above. The walls of the house establish the edges of the paving. Features from the addition, such as the circular window, the overhanging rake trim, and the cottage-style windows pulled together in groups of three, were added to the original house to improve existing rooms and to unify the old with the new.

3　AFTER

Consider going up and out

The most cost-effective projects often combine both upward and outward expansion, generally with a family-room addition/kitchen expansion on the first floor and a master-suite addition above. This type of project adds the spaces missing from many older homes: a large room with good access to the outside connected to an updated kitchen, plus another bedroom with generous closet space and an additional bathroom. The living, dining, and sleeping spaces of the original house remain relatively undisturbed.

3　BEFORE

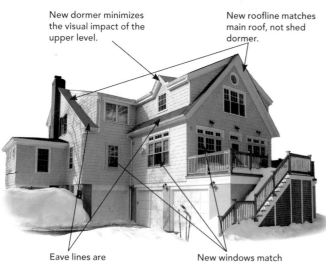

New dormer minimizes the visual impact of the upper level.

New roofline matches main roof, not shed dormer.

Eave lines are maintained.

New windows match height of existing windows.

A CLASSIC SOLUTION OF PUBLIC SPACES TOPPED WITH A MASTER SUITE

A two-story addition at the back of the house, built by a previous owner, ignored many of the architectural features of the original house. The pitch of the roof on the old addition looked squat because it matched the shallower pitch of the shed dormer, not the steeper pitch of the main roof ("before" photo above). Also, the addition's picture windows and tall casements differed in scale, proportion, and type from the double-hung windows on the rest of the house. The heads of the taller casements on the rear of the addition didn't align with the heads of the double-hung windows right around the corner. The entire structure seemed precariously balanced on a skinny post.

The first addition was retooled with one that preserves the steeper roof profile of the original house ("after" photo on the facing page). Eave lines are maintained on both levels, which keeps this three-story structure from becoming overpowering. The uppermost level is treated as a dormer, minimizing its visual impact. The ceiling of the new addition is taller than elsewhere in the house. Transom windows take advantage of the additional height, while double-hung windows directly below the transoms maintain the head height and muntin configuration of the windows in the rest of the house.

CASE STUDY 4

ROOFS UNIFY THE EXTERIOR

At some point in this vintage home's history, a previous owner doubled its size by grafting another house to the back of it ("before" photo at right). The partnership certainly increased floor space, but it didn't improve the home's looks or circulation. Judiciously adding another 7 ft. by 35 ft. to the front and side of the house solved several problems ("after" photo at right). It provided room for an upstairs hall that doesn't have to pass through an office to get to the bedrooms, and it gave the downstairs parlor and sitting room a little more space for furniture and a piano.

On the outside, the rooflines of the new addition improve things in two ways. As it wraps around the corner of the porch, the low roof breaks up the tall, monotonous facade, lowering the perceived height of the house. The low roof dies into the side of the gabled portion of the addition, which disguises the fact that the eaves and ridges on the front and back do not align. The existing roofline is maintained but now includes a third-floor dormer to accommodate a new attic bedroom. The face and sidewalls of the dormers are covered in wood shingles to match those on the roof, further disguising the fact that this is a three-story structure.

4 | AFTER

4 | BEFORE

ADD A FOCAL POINT WITH CONTRASTING MATERIALS

This house has a bold, contemporary form; a pair of shed roofs sweeps continuously over three floors from peak to eave. However, the base of this form had been chopped out, leaving a forbidding cavelike entry with a front door hidden somewhere deep inside ("before" photo at left). The windows seemed puny in relation to the house, and the semicircular window had nothing to do with the geometry of the house. The siding was unrelenting, with no details to provide scale and interest.

Finding the front door is no longer a challenge ("after" photo at left). It has emerged from the cave and now stands proudly on the front wall, protected by a shed-roofed canopy that echoes the shapes of the larger roofs. Cedar shingles visually tie the door, windows, and canopy together into an entry bay that contrasts with the more subdued vertical siding on the rest of the house. This two-story entry bay is sufficient in scale and detail to serve as a focal point among the simple, bold shapes of the house. Other details add refinement, such as the wide-narrow-wide horizontal pattern of sidewall shingles, the upstairs window muntins, the V-groove front-door paneling, and the standing seams on the metal canopy roof.

DON'T LET THE GARAGE DOMINATE THE HOUSE

The street front of this postwar Cape had been disfigured by an insensitive addition above the garage ("before" photo on the facing page). The garage's blank front wall, squat side windows, and odd roofline all combined to disrupt and overpower the modest charm of the original house.

Lowering the ridge of the garage made it subordinate to the house ("after" photo on the facing page), and filling in the missing piece beneath the cantilevered room allowed the garage to grow enough to accommodate a car and simultaneously

6 AFTER

to look more rooted to its site. While building out the front entry not only made the home more welcoming, it also put the emphasis back on the house. The divided-lite proportions of the multi-paned windows over the garage door and next to the front door further unify the street view.

6 BEFORE

AFTER

BEFORE

BY THE WAY, A LITTLE TRIM MAKES A BIG DIFFERENCE

A SHED DORMER ON THE BACK of the house gave the side of the building an odd shape (bottom photo). The addition of rake trim with a generous overhang restored the simple gable profile of the original house (top photo). Now the dormer looks like a dormer. Gable trim and overhangs on the addition continue the theme of simple peaked roofs, keeping the new in scale with the old.

7 BEFORE

7 AFTER

CASE STUDY 7

GIVE A CRAMPED SPACE A LITTLE BREATHING ROOM, AND MAKE A GOOD ROOM BETTER

Although a realtor might have called the existing space a bedroom, it was barely large enough for a bed, and it didn't have a closet. Adding a 5-ft.-deep bump-out provided that much-needed closet, as well as sufficient space to walk around the bed and room for a chair in the corner.

Directly below this bedroom, the first-floor living room was large enough, but the connection to the backyard was circuitously routed through a screened porch ("before" photo above). And the only place for the homeowners' piano was in front of some built-in shelves. The new arrangement of French doors and high windows provides light and access to the backyard and also creates a place of suitable importance for the piano. The columns that support the second-level bedroom extension create a nice porch off the living room and a gracious transition between indoor and outdoor living areas ("after" photo above).

CASE STUDY 8

EXPAND A ROOM WITH A SITTING BAY

In densely populated towns, zoning laws can make it tough to add floor space to a house by bumping out a wall if it extends into the required setback from the lot lines. But in many of these same jurisdictions, bays that do not add floor area and that extend no more than 2 ft. beyond the exterior wall plane are exempted from square-footage calculations. Thus, sitting bays offer expansion possibilities for zoning-tight projects.

In this example, Bay Area designer Lance Alden Johnson enhanced a kids' playroom by adding a comfy nook for cushions, bordered by multipaned

7

windows. This inviting focal point, awash in daylight, amounts to a major expansion in both feel and function.

The bay is 2 ft. deep by 5 ft. wide. It is supported off the wall by angled brackets wrapped in an envelope of stucco-coated ogee-shaped architectural foam (photo below).

REPLACE ONE WINDOW WITH TWO

Windows and wall cabinets battle it out in many older, smaller kitchens. Homeowners want more light in the kitchen, especially at the sink, but they don't want to sacrifice wall space where upper cabinets can often provide the most convenient storage. An oriel window can be the solution. This triangular bay window doesn't take up any more wall width than a conventional window, yet it almost doubles the amount of light in the room and provides views in two directions instead of just one.

A Contract that Makes Everybody Happy

BY ROBERT KNIGHT

In terms of making clients happy, the most important events in a custom residential project are picking a builder and structuring a contract.

There are two common ways of hiring a general contractor: at a fixed price or on the basis of time and materials. At my firm, we aren't fond of either approach, but we have found a third option that's fair to both builder and client. First, though, let's take a look at how the two industry standards work.

A fixed-price contract usually is awarded after competitive bidding. A group of builders receives a complete set of construction documents, and they return some weeks later with proposals to build the house for a set amount of money. The job normally goes to the low bidder.

Although the builder is the one taking the risks, potential problems also exist for the client. First, in a hot market where demand for builders is high, there's no guarantee they will price their work aggressively. They may come up with a rough esti-mate, add a very high profit, and figure if they get the job, then they'll be well covered. Even the lowest bid may not be a good deal.

Second, fixed-price contracts require complete construction documents, which can cost approxi-mately 5% of the project total. If the bids are too high and the drawings need to be revised, the architect typically doesn't have enough information from the bidder to know exactly where to change the plans.

Finally, a subtle but nevertheless important adversarial quality exists in the relationship between client and builder. The moment a contract is signed, the client wants to get a bit more for the money, while the builder wants to provide a bit less. That's just human nature.

Time-and-materials bids

The other standard is a time-and-materials contract, abbreviated as T&M or cost-plus. A builder is hired on reputation, availability, good chemistry, and possibly on what he guesses the building will cost. The client pays an hourly wage to all workers, which includes a markup over their actual cost to the builder. The builder also adds a percentage to the cost of materials. In Maine, where my firm is located, the markup usually ranges from 12% to 17%.

In a perfect world, there's nothing wrong with this type of contract. It's flexible and easy to administer. Assuming the builder is competent and honest, the client gets a house for exactly what it costs, plus a known markup for overhead and profit.

However, the contract's flaws are obvious. The builder makes a profit on every dollar he spends. At some point, especially if the job is over budget, the

client may start to feel taken advantage of.

Shopping for an estimate when using a cost-plus contract is never a good idea. The worst decision a client can make is to pick a builder based on what he estimates the cost of the job will be and then sign a contract that doesn't obligate him to that number. If clients must shop for a builder based on price, they should bite the bullet, pay for the drawings, and put out the job for a fixed-price bid.

Cost-plus-a-fee contracts

If there were a contract that solved every single problem, it would be locked in a vault at the American Bar Association along with the lawyer who wrote it. In fairness, it was my lawyer (who hates lawsuits) who put me onto the cost-plus-a-fee contract, and I think it balances risk and reward at about the right point. Unlike a time-and-materials contract, this one has a fixed fee that contains all of the overhead and profit.

Let's take a hypothetical $460,000 house. In a fixed-price contract, the builder bids $460,000. If the house ends up costing more, the builder eats the

The moment a contract is signed, the client wants to get a bit more for the money, while the builder wants to provide a bit less. That's just human nature.

overage; if it costs less, he gets an additional profit.

In a time-and-materials contract, the builder estimates the house will cost $400,000 plus $60,000 (a 15% markup). If the house ends up costing more, the builder's fee goes up, too.

With cost plus a fixed fee, the client signs a contract for the $60,000 plus the cost of construction, which is priced at the builder's actual out-of-pocket cost. Whether the house costs $350,000 or $500,000, the client still pays $60,000 for the builder's overhead and profit.

The advantages are obvious. If the cost exceeds the estimate, the builder isn't making a fatter fee. Getting the job done and moving on to another one will be to his advantage. However, the builder will not be taking such a bath that he is likely to walk off the job or go bankrupt, a real risk for smaller builders.

What are the disadvantages for clients? They can occur in the estimating process. The client needs assurances that both the estimate and the fee are reasonable. In my office, we compare the costs and the fee against a database of jobs. If it appears the builder has inflated the cost of construction to justify a proportionately higher fee, we encourage the client to move on to another builder.

Clients can dicker over the fee, but it's really chump change compared with the total cost of the job. Why not give the builder the fee he wants and get him on your side? He may be more inclined to go after reducing costs because he'll still get the same fee.

Risks for the builder, too

Disadvantages for builders arise when they estimate from incomplete documents, and the client/architect team subsequently inflates the building's quality and complexity as the drawings are completed. The builder could end up building not the $400,000 house he was shown but the $600,000 house the owner and the architect were dreaming of—all for the same markup.

The solution is for the builder to insist on change orders, including an adjustment to the fee when the scope of the work is altered. Generally, that means anything that makes the project take longer, but the change also may include substantial quality upgrades in materials that increase the builder's liability. Being rigorous about change orders and their effect on the bottom line is to everyone's

> Clients can dicker over the fee, but it's really chump change compared with the total cost of the job.

advantage. If builders insist on it, this kind of contract can make for a good deal all around.

In our office, we usually recommend an old contract (A117-1987) from the American Institute of Architects (AIA). Over the years, my lawyer added annotations that we believe offer more protection for both our clients and their builders.

The current AIA contract designed for cost of the work plus a fee is A114-2001. The only drawback with this form may be that it incorporates the 40-page A201 "General Conditions," which many people find to be too much material.

To quote my attorney: "I would use the A114 when (a) an actual copy of A201 will be attached to it and will be read and understood by both the owner and the contractor (not to mention the architect); and (b) the parties will actually follow the A114/A201 procedures and requirements instead of the simpler requirements of the old A117. A super-duper contract that people don't actually follow is worse than a so-so contract that people take seriously as a guide to their conduct and relationship."

Talk to your attorney. You are signing an important contract.

PART 2

Make the Most of Every Space

The Well-Designed Walk-In Closet

BY LYNNE HEINZMANN

As an architect, I often see poorly designed walk-in closets added to floor plans as an afterthought. There often seems to be no regard for horizontal and vertical dimensions, the type of door or its location, or adequate lighting.

Besides, a walk-in closet doesn't necessarily work in every home. On the contrary, I think some designers and homeowners need to face the truth: A walk-in closet might not belong in a cramped floor plan. To be useful, a walk-in closet needs to be at least 4 ft. deep, with full ceiling height and no obtrusive bump-outs. Anything less than that, and you might be better with a reach-in closet.

Then again, if adequate attention is paid to key details, a walk-in closet can offer tremendous flexibility in the storage spaces it can provide. It can be outfitted with multitier closet rods, open shelves, built-in drawers, or specialized storage for specific types of clothing. A room that's used every day deserves to be well designed.

Choosing the right location

The first crucial design decision for a walk-in closet is its location relative to other features of the bedroom. There are seven principles I like to consider, and although it's not always possible to satisfy all of them, the more the better.

- Create a circulation zone. As shown in the floor plan on p. 44, it's best to group doorways in the bedroom suite to keep the circulation zone separate from the furniture zone.
- Plan for a proper entrance. Don't put the closet behind the bedroom door or the bathroom door, a frequent mistake. A walk-in closet is its own room and requires its own unimpeded entrance.
- Plan for the door swing. A proper closet entrance won't be much good if the door can't open all the way. Don't place the bed or other furniture too close to the closet entrance. If the bedroom is too small to allow room for a proper door swing, consider a different door option or even none at all.
- Consider the exterior impact. When deciding whether to place the closet on an exterior wall, consider the overall appearance of the house. Unless the closet will contain a window, locating the room on an exterior wall will result in a blank area on the house's facade.
- Avoid a direct line of sight. A closet tends to be messy, so don't draw attention to it. Locate the closet entrance so that it is not in the sightline from the bedroom entrance.
- Use closets for sound control. A closet can provide an effective sound barrier. Take advantage of this quality by placing the closet between bedrooms.

- Locate a closet near the bathroom but not in it. Some architects might disagree, but I don't place a closet entrance in a bathroom. It seems convenient, but I think the steam and humidity of a shower or tub is harmful to some types of clothing and fabrics.

Good lighting is key

The most overlooked element of a walk-in closet is lighting. Anyone who has fumbled around in a dark, crowded closet can tell you just how important good lighting truly is.

There are three standard choices for hardwired lighting. Surface-mounted or recessed ceiling fixtures are generally the least-expensive lighting option and the easiest to install. If mounted in the center of a walk-in closet, these fixtures provide an even level of ambient light. Because of shadows that are cast by hanging clothing, however, items near the floor tend to be in shadow.

Wall sconces are mounted at eye level and are better than ceiling fixtures at illuminating shoes and other clothing stored on the closet's lower shelves. Because sconces require a blank wall area for installation, though, they tend to be reserved for larger walk-in closets.

Relatively new to the market and still relatively expensive, lighted closet rods (www.luciferlighting.com and www.outwater.com) are rapidly gaining in popularity. Installed in place of standard clothes bars, they are either hardwired or are plugged in to an outlet and cast light directly on the hanging clothing and items stored below. Of course, items stored on shelves would require another means of illumination.

Each of these three lighting styles has its own strengths, but their weaknesses ultimately mean that the optimal solution for lighting a walk-in closet usually involves using a combination of two or more types of fixtures.

Although the proper light fixtures can provide a nice, even level of artificial light, I prefer to use natural light whenever possible. If a walk-in closet is on

A ROOM THAT'S USED EVERY DAY DESERVES TO BE WELL DESIGNED. The right location, layout, lights, and storage make a walk-in closet a more useful part of your house.

the exterior wall of a house, natural light can come from windows located so that sunlight does not shine directly on the clothes, which could damage them. Because the sun never shines from the north in our hemisphere, north-facing windows are ideal in closets. If north-facing windows are not possible, window treatments and wall placements can be used to protect clothing from fading.

If you can't spare the wall space to install windows, consider using traditional skylights, or even better, tubular skylights, which use reflective tubes to channel natural light from the roof to the closet ceiling. Then again, if you get dressed before the sun comes up, you will still require a backup light source.

START WITH LAYOUT, LOCATION, AND ENTRY

Layout is driven by the size of the space.

Dimensions and details for the three most common walk-in closet layouts are shown below. Larger walk-in closets feel more luxurious, so to a certain extent, the bigger the better. But when space is at a premium, the layout needs to be scaled appropriately so that floor space is adequate and storage isn't too cramped.

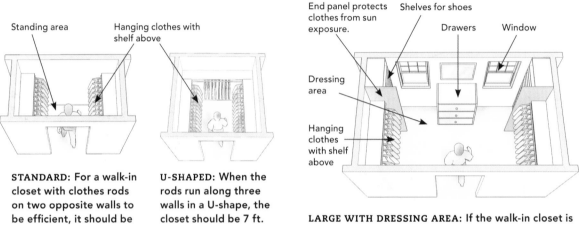

STANDARD: For a walk-in closet with clothes rods on two opposite walls to be efficient, it should be a minimum of 7 ft. wide and 4 ft. deep.

U-SHAPED: When the rods run along three walls in a U-shape, the closet should be 7 ft. wide by 7 ft. deep, minimum. These dimensions allow for a 3-ft.-wide area between racks of clothes.

LARGE WITH DRESSING AREA: If the walk-in closet is also to be used as a dressing area, the standing area's width is increased to 5 ft. Of course, customized elements (shelving, drawers, and so forth) will alter the size and shape of the closet.

Group the doorways together

Smooth the flow of traffic and eliminate the need to walk around furniture by grouping the bedroom, bathroom, and closet doors in the same area.

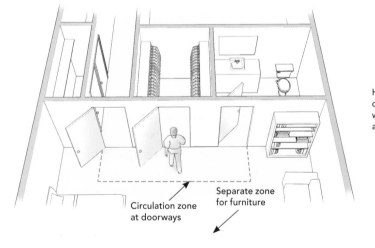

The best door might be no door at all

Consider eliminating the door by designing the closet entrance to block sightlines to the interior.

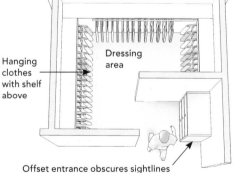

STANDARDS ARE GREAT FOR PLANNING STORAGE

Dimensions and clearances that work

Architectural standards offer the common heights, widths, and lengths necessary to provide adequate storage.

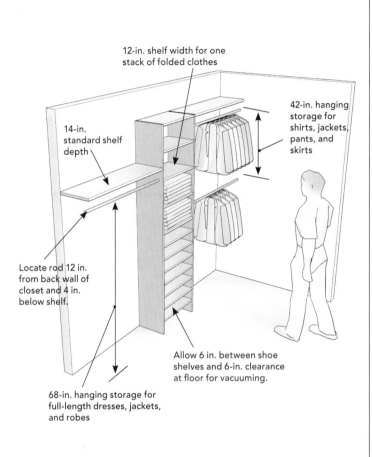

12-in. shelf width for one stack of folded clothes

14-in. standard shelf depth

42-in. hanging storage for shirts, jackets, pants, and skirts

Locate rod 12 in. from back wall of closet and 4 in. below shelf.

Allow 6 in. between shoe shelves and 6-in. clearance at floor for vacuuming.

68-in. hanging storage for full-length dresses, jackets, and robes

Dealing with corners

Corners are notorious space-eaters, but here are two ways to solve the problem.

Solution 1: Boxed-out corner

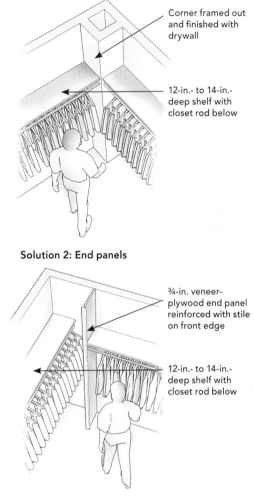

Corner framed out and finished with drywall

12-in.- to 14-in.-deep shelf with closet rod below

Solution 2: End panels

¾-in. veneer-plywood end panel reinforced with stile on front edge

12-in.- to 14-in.-deep shelf with closet rod below

Storage is dictated by needs

Closets should be designed to accommodate the types and amount of clothing you have, but should make allowances for future storage needs. When building a walk-in closet, you can incorporate many different types of storage units into the design (sidebar on pp. 46–47). If you plan to customize the closet yourself, consider specialized storage areas for shoes, ties, and other specific types of clothing. Other customizing products include benches, stepladders, rotating clothes trees, and cedar closet linings. Whatever plans you have for customization, pay attention to standard clearances to ensure a proper use of space (drawings above).

When you're finished with the tough decisions, your well-designed walk-in closet should have adequate lighting, the appropriate type of door, proper customization, basic minimum dimensions, and correct placement within the bedroom suite. When all these criteria are met, a walk-in becomes a useful tool for the homeowner, organizing clothing into easily visible and reachable areas.

CUSTOM CLOSETS CAN USE PREFAB COMPONENTS

CLOSETS DON'T HAVE TO BE OUTFITTED with site-built shelving and storage to qualify as custom. In fact, several manufacturers make prefab components that can be incorporated into a walk-in closet without sacrificing function or style.

WIRE SHELVING

The most economical option for customizing a walk-in closet is to use coated-wire shelving. This type of shelving offers several advantages. It is economical, it is readily available, and a whole-closet kit can easily be installed in just a few hours. On the negative side, wire shelving can leave sweaters with gridlike imprints, the components are not as durable as other types, and the overall appearance is somewhat utilitarian.

Rubbermaid®'s Configurations® line of products includes closet kits with available add-on products such as shoe shelves, a tie-and-belt organizer, and a pants rack. Each kit contains all the hardware and brackets needed to create the chosen closet configuration, which simplifies purchasing and installing the system. Rubbermaid also recently modified its product so that the wire racks no longer need to be

cut to fit the closet but instead telescope in or out as needed.

ClosetMaid® sells coated-wire shelving systems on its Web site or at most home-improvement stores. With five different kinds of wire shelving, ClosetMaid offers a great range of products, including whole-closet kits and closet accessories such as a two-drawer kit, a sliding tie-and-belt rack, and an expandable shoe rack. For a small fee, this company offers a custom-design service online. Simply send in your closet dimensions and storage requirements, and a design consultant will help you to customize your closet.

PLASTIC-LAMINATE SHELVING

For a slightly more substantial look, consider components made from plastic laminate. Durable laminate shelving is usually available in a wider variety of component options than coated-wire shelving units. On the downside, a plastic-laminate closet system is generally more expensive and is more difficult to install than its coated-wire cousin.

Easy Track offers $5/8$-in.-thick melamine-coated pressed-board shelves in white, maple, and cherry. The Easy Track system is installed by hanging components from a thin steel ledger strip mounted 76 in. above the closet floor. Ledger strips can be cut to length with a hacksaw and need to be fastened to studs. The 3-D design tool available on

Easy Track's Web site is easy to use, and once you finalize the closet design, you can email the company to order the components.

Laminate components from EasyClosets are made of either ¾-in. medium-density fiberboard (MDF) covered with a thermofoil wrap or ¾-in. high-density particleboard with a melamine surface. Both come with a lifetime guarantee. Because of the thicker material, EasyClosets says that an 8-ft. section can hold up to 1,200 lb. The company's user-friendly online 3-D design tool calculates the total price of the closet as it is being designed so that the relative costs of different components can be compared.

SOLID-WOOD SHELVING

If you want a beautiful closet that doesn't need to be hidden behind closed doors, solid-wood shelving is a good way to go. This stain-grade finish carpentry can be custom-made from solid wood or hardwood plywood.

If you're interested in a factory-made version, check out the John Louis Home brand. This closet system features shelves and panels made from solid-wood slats fastened together with metal hardware. John Louis Home closet components are surprisingly affordable. For an upscale look at a reasonable price, solid-wood closet components can be an option.

SOURCES

CLOSETMAID
www.closetmaid.com

CONFIGURATIONS
www.rubbermaid.com

EASYCLOSETS
www.easyclosets.com

EASY TRACK
www.easytrack.com

JOHN LOUIS HOME
www.johnlouishome.com

Make Any Room a Great Home Office

BY MARK DUTKA

I n the 15 years that I've been designing home offices, I've yet to come across two projects that come even close to being the same. No two are alike, and no two are used in the same manner. Some home offices are for full-time work; others are for occasional bill-paying. Some clients use them as part-time guest rooms or as multimedia spaces, accommodating one or two people or perhaps a whole family. And, just like their occupants, they come in all shapes and sizes.

Your perfect office is going to be a reflection of the way you plan to use it and any special equipment it will take to make that happen. All good home offices have some things in common, such as good ergonomics, thoughtful hardware management, adequate storage, and functional flexibility. I'll offer some guidelines to help you get those things right.

It all starts with ergonomics

Ergonomics is the science of adapting the work environment to the needs of each worker. It plays a role in everything from desk height to the selection of the right chair. To ignore ergonomics is to tempt fate. Over time, poor ergonomics can lead to back, wrist, spine, or neck pain, affecting your productivity and quality of life.

1. USE MONITOR AND DOCUMENT HOLDERS

To minimize neck strain, the monitor always should be centered in front of you, never to the side. Place it about an arm's length away, with the top of the screen ideally located on a slight downward angle from your eyes. The objective is to prevent looking up at the screen, which can contribute to neck problems. This is why it's a bad idea to place the monitor on top of a horizontal CPU.

Glare on a monitor screen can cause eyestrain. If possible, the monitor should be perpendicular to a window to minimize glare. If positioning the monitor in front of a window is the only solution, use a bottom-up shade to allow natural light into the room above eye level while blocking light on or behind a screen.

MONITOR MOVEMENT. A monitor arm allows you to move the screen quickly for multiple viewers or easy access to the desktop.

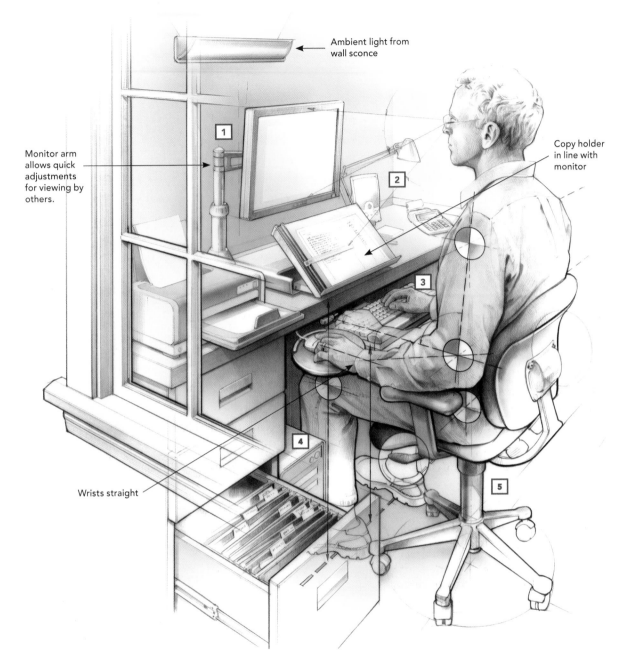

Ambient light from wall sconce

Monitor arm allows quick adjustments for viewing by others.

1

2

Copy holder in line with monitor

3

4

5

Wrists straight

A monitor arm delivers both practical and ergonomic benefits. It allows you to move the screen quickly for easy access to the desktop, which is especially useful in tight spaces where a multitude of noncomputer tasks need to be performed. An arm also allows easy screen adjustment for quick viewing by others who may not be seated directly in front of the monitor. A good monitor arm adjusts vertically,

has an arm sufficient in length to move the screen out of the way, and supports the weight of the monitor.

To prevent neck pain and eyestrain, it is also important to place the document holder in front of and not to the side of the monitor. Adjustable holders that don't block the screen are on the market ("Sources" on p. 55).

2. AVOID EYESTRAIN

Correct lighting includes ambient light, which is a combination of natural and artificial light, and task lighting to illuminate a specific work area.

Ambient light from a track or ceiling fixture should be slightly behind you but not far enough back to reflect onto your computer screen. That will cause eyestrain.

Instead of a ceiling light, try using an uplight that bounces light off the ceiling, bathing the room in soft, ample light. You can do this with a wall-mounted fixture or a torchiere floor lamp. Dimmers are a plus. Choose a task lamp with a multidirectional head or polarized lens to direct light so that it won't bounce off the work surface and into your eyes.

3. GET IT AT THE RIGHT HEIGHT

The typical desk is 29 in. high. If you are of average height, this is probably the wrong height for your keyboard; a keyboard height between 24 in. and 27 in. is more comfortable for the average-size adult. The goal here is to keep the wrists in a neutral position. You don't want them bent upward, which can lead to carpal-tunnel syndrome. Ergonomics research at Cornell University suggests that a keyboard that slopes slightly away from the user maximizes correct workstation posture. A keyboard drawer, a lower desk, or an adjustable keyboard tray with a tilt option (see www.humanscale.com for a wide selection of trays) can help you to dial in the right combination of dimensions. The keyboard should be positioned so that your forearms are parallel to your thighs when your feet are flat on the floor.

The mousing surface should be adjacent to the keyboard tray. It should not be on a higher desktop, which would necessitate overreaching and twisting of the shoulder, arm, and wrist.

LEAVE THE LAPTOP FOR LAPS. Using a laptop with a docking station turns it into a CPU that is controlled by a full-size keyboard and is viewed on the desktop monitor.

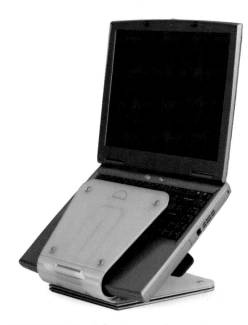

LAPTOP UP TOP. A laptop stand gets the screen to a better elevation for extended use. A separate keyboard controls the keys.

4. DOCK YOUR LAPTOPS

Designed for mobility, laptops can be ergonomic nightmares if used on a permanent basis in a home office. Not only do they have small monitors that strain the eyes, but the keyboard and mouse also are at the wrong height when placed on a desktop. If you are working from a laptop, consider using it as a CPU in lieu of a bulky tower, and connect a separate monitor, keyboard, and mouse (photo below).

Another option is a laptop stand, which will allow you to get the screen to a more comfortable height (photo above).

Leave a 2-in. gap at the back of the cabinet for wires to hang vertically.

Ambient light reduces eyestrain by reducing contrast with monitor.

Pullout shelves keep bulky stuff at arm's length. Heavy-duty full-extension drawer slides support the weight of a deep file drawer and a shelf for the printer in this armoire-style cabinet.

5. CHOOSE THE RIGHT CHAIR

A chair is a major investment. The wrong one will contribute to poor posture and low productivity.

LOOK FOR THE FOLLOWING IN AN OFFICE CHAIR:

- Height and seat-pan adjustability. Eliminate any chair that will not allow your feet to rest securely on the floor.
- Tilt forward-and-back mechanism.
- Adjustable armrests that allow your forearms to remain horizontal while you're typing with elbows close to your body.
- Adjustable lumbar support for your back. If the lumbar support is not adjustable, make sure the chair provides support in the right places for long-term sitting.
- Casters for ease of movement and the capacity to swivel.

Managing your equipment

POWER SUPPLY RECOMMENDATIONS

A typical home office needs a 20-amp circuit at 120v. That's enough power to run a CPU, a monitor, a fax machine, a copy machine, a printer, and a charging station for cell phones and other battery-powered devices. Putting a home office on a dedicated circuit minimizes the chances that someone in an adjacent room will overload a shared circuit and cause a data loss.

An uninterruptible power supply provides backup power for your CPU (or anything else plugged into it) should there be a blackout. It ensures that information not yet saved on your computer at the time of the blackout will not be lost. I've had good luck with the backup power supplies made by APC ("Sources" on p. 55).

Desktop outlets are helpful for the occasional plug-in item. They rise above the desktop for use, then retract behind a low-profile cover plate. Doug Mockett and Häfele are two sources.

Protect your computer against the occasional voltage spike with a surge protector. Power strips frequently, but not always, include surge protection. A clever one that does is called the Socket Sense®, manufactured by Ideative™. It expands to accommodate bulky transformers next to one another.

An energy-saving surge protector by Belkin (BG-108000-04) uses a remote control to turn off equipment that would otherwise be wasting energy on standby mode while not in use.

A Zip-Linq® retractable extension cord is a useful way to hook up a power strip in a charging drawer. You can open and close the drawer without worrying about the cord bunching up when the drawer is closed.

ELECTRONIC COMPONENTS IN CABINETS

Whether they want to minimize clutter or just keep the cat away from the printer, my clients have lots of reasons for wanting to keep various pieces of office equipment behind closed doors.

When searching for cabinetry, you will find numerous sources at many price points. Look for products that can be partially customized to suit your needs. They range from the budget-conscious items found at Ikea®, to the midprice offerings produced by companies such as the Closet Factory, to higher-end options represented by Jesper®. Custom cabinets by qualified cabinetmakers can be the most expensive, but they also can be the most satisfying.

RISING POWER. A pop-up power grommet from Doug Mockett is handy for plugging in the occasional additional electronic item but is usually out of the way.

BECAUSE ONE SIZE DOESN'T FIT ALL. The Socket Sense power strip expands to allow tubby little transformers enough space to fit next to one another.

UNDER CONTROL. Select outlets on Belkin's surge protector can be turned off and on with a remote.

A RETRACTABLE EXTENSION CORD. Zip-Linq's product is just the ticket for a drawer full of battery-powered gadgets at the charging trough.

TAKE IT FROM THE TOP. A CPU holder from Doug Mockett frees up desktop workspace without compromising ventilation.

DIRECTING TRAFFIC. Wire channels mounted under a desk keep the cables from turning into a tangled mess. Rip-Tie® touch-fastener cable ties stick to the cabinet sides.

HERE ARE SOME TIPS FOR STORING EQUIPMENT IN CABINETS:

- Put equipment on full-extension pullout shelves to allow access to all sides of any component for ease of maintenance and connectivity. There should be a 2-in. gap between the back of the shelf and the back of the cabinet for wires.
- Provide adequate ventilation for each machine. There are plenty of variables here, depending on the type and the number of components. One rule of thumb is that the interior cabinet temperature should stay within a range between 55°F and 90°F. Dell advises that a CPU in a cabinet should have 4 in. of clearance above and on all sides and that at least 30% of the cabinet-door area be open. This is a good place for a decorative grille as a door panel. Another way to keep the equipment in the right temperature range is with fans. Cool Components is one source.
- Although it doesn't exactly hide the CPU, suspending it under the desk frees valuable work surface space.
- Design cabinets for equipment bigger than the devices you currently own to accommodate new equipment in the future.
- Create a charging drawer for small items (MP3 players, cameras, PDAs, cell phones, smart phones) that need regular charging. Inside the drawer, attach a surge protector connected to a retractable extension cord. This is a surefire way to keep desktop clutter to a minimum.

ORGANIZING AND CONCEALING WIRES

The wireless revolution is upon us, but even in this era of Bluetooth® technology and wireless keyboards and mice, we have not completely eliminated annoying cables. Your challenge is organizing and hiding wires while still retaining accessibility.

HERE ARE SOME TIPS FOR HANDLING UNRULY WIRES:

- Look at the equipment you intend to house on top of the work surface. Examine their power and connectivity requirements. Select the number and location of grommet holes you want to accommodate these needs. The diameter of each hole is determined by the number of wires it will hold. Grommets come in various sizes, shapes, finishes, and materials. Doug Mockett and Häfele are good resources.
- Grommet holes either feed wires from the desktop to outlets below or into wire channels affixed to the underside of the desktop and the sides of the cabinet (top photos above). The channels then feed the wires to an outlet or into an adjacent cabinet. This minimizes the unsightly wires that are so often visible hanging at the rear underside of the desk. Channels come in various lengths, configurations, and colors, and they are easily cut.
- Touch-fastener cable ties are invaluable for wire management (bottom photo above). They make it simple to group and label wires for ease of movement and identification.

RECOMMENDED DIMENSIONS FOR OFFICE FURNITURE ARRANGEMENT

WHEN YOU START ARRANGING FURNITURE, keep the following dimensions in mind to make your home office efficient and ergonomically sound.

DON'T PUT THE MONITOR IN A CORNER. This will create wasted space behind the monitor, and you'll be sitting at least 4 ft. into the room from the corner. An L-shaped solution (with the computer workstation on one leg and the ancillary work surface on the other) makes a better use of space.

TO KEEP CABINET DOORS FROM GETTING IN THE WAY, it is a good idea to "pocket" doors that will remain open for long periods. Add 3 in. to the interior width of a cabinet to allow for each pocket-door mechanism. The pocket-door width should not be much more than the cabinet depth, or the door may protrude too far into the room when it is pocketed.

To retract fully, articulating keyboard trays require a depth of at least 21 in. under the desk.

At least 36 in. of space is necessary beyond the extended keyboard tray to fit a chair comfortably.

Allow a width of 30 in. for a keyboard and mouse tray in front of your desk. When extended, the tray will protrude about 11 in. beyond the front of the desk into the room.

A single letter-file drawer is 16 in. side-to-side (exterior dimensions), while legal-file drawers are 18 in. wide. The exterior height of a file drawer should be at least 12½ in. to allow for Pendaflex® files inside. Use full-extension slides on all drawers. Ensure that your file-drawer slides are heavy-duty and can support the anticipated weight.

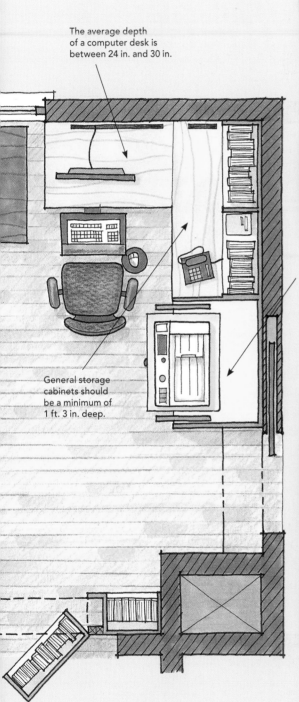

The average depth of a computer desk is between 24 in. and 30 in.

General storage cabinets should be a minimum of 1 ft. 3 in. deep.

ARMOIRE CABINETS USUALLY REQUIRE MORE SPACE than other cabinets because they typically house multifunction printers, which can be quite deep. Determine the depth of your printer (including protruding wires), and add at least 4 in. That should yield the exterior dimensions for your cabinet depth.

MOST OPEN BOOKCASES ARE NO MORE THAN 12 IN. DEEP. If you want to accommodate standard binders, shelves at least 13 in. deep are necessary. Remember to provide some extra-deep shelves for oversize books. Make adjustable as many shelves as possible.

SOURCES

FULL-EXTENSION DRAWER SLIDES
www.accuride.com

BACKUP POWER SUPPLIES
www.apc.com

SEMICUSTOM CABINETS, DESKS, STORAGE SOLUTIONS
www.closetfactory.com

CABINET-VENTILATION PRODUCTS
www.coolcomponents.com

GROMMETS, POP-UP POWER OUTLETS, WIRE TRAYS, CPU HOLDERS, ACCESSORIES
www.mockett.com

MONITOR ARMS, WIRE CHANNELS, KEYBOARD TRAYS, GROMMETS, ACCESSORIES
www.hafele.com

KEYBOARD TRAYS, WIRE CHANNELS, CHAIRS, COPY HOLDERS, MONITOR ARMS, ACCESSORIES
www.humanscale.com

LOW-BUDGET DESKS, WORKSTATIONS, CHAIRS
www.ikea.com

WORKSTATIONS, STORAGE, CHAIRS, ACCESSORIES
www.jesperoffice.com

TOUCH-FASTENER CABLE TIES
www.riptie.com

Finish Your Basement with a Durable Wood Floor

BY CHARLES PETERSON

If you need more living space but don't want to move, you've got a couple of options. Either you can build an addition, or you can put the space you already have to better use. The latter option often means finishing the basement. It's a good option, too, because it can cost a fraction of what an addition might cost. Also, the basement is isolated from the main traffic paths of the house, so it's an ideal setting for entertaining guests or relaxing with the family.

To me, nothing makes a basement feel more finished than a wood floor. It adds a sense of warmth and refinement that drastically changes the utilitarian feel of a space at or below grade. However, basements—and any concrete slab, for that matter—are notoriously moist, and moisture is responsible for more than 90% of all wood-floor failures. Installing a wood floor in a basement or on a slab so that it looks good and will last means controlling moisture, assembling an appropriate subfloor, and choosing the best engineered-wood flooring you can afford.

A floating subfloor is the best option

Wood flooring can be glued directly to a concrete slab or attached to a fabricated subfloor. Glue-down applications are intensive, and the best-performing adhesives are expensive. That's why installing wood flooring over a subfloor is typically a better option.

There are many ways to build a subfloor. Plywood can be screwed to 2x4 sleepers that have been fastened to the slab on 16-in. centers. Plywood can be scored, glued, and nailed to the concrete, or it can be installed so that it floats over the slab without attachment.

The most cost-effective method, and the one that I and most professional flooring contractors prefer, is the floating-subfloor approach. A floating subfloor is less labor intensive, doesn't rely on expensive adhesives, and can be integrated with a vapor retarder more seamlessly than other subfloor assemblies.

Install a class-I vapor retarder

Wood-floor manufacturers recommend that concrete slabs be tested for moisture content before their products are installed. If the moisture content of the slab is too high, the manufacturer specifies the use of a vapor retarder. This suggests that a vapor retarder doesn't have to be used if the slab has a low moisture content at the time of testing. The problem is that testing represents just a snapshot of the concrete's moisture level and does not factor in potential moisture levels. A class-I vapor retarder (commonly referred to as a vapor barrier) should always be

Two layers of ½-in. or ⅝-in. exposure-1 plywood

15-mil polyethylene vapor retarder

Concrete slab

installed no matter what the manufacturer's recommendations about its use.

When you're installing a wood floor over a concrete slab, the vapor retarder should be placed under the plywood subfloor. This installation contains the moisture in the slab, increases the subfloor's stability, and helps to keep the finished floor from swelling, buckling, or cracking. Because a floating subfloor isn't fastened to the slab, no fasteners are poking holes through the vapor retarder. The moisture in the air is another important consideration. Most wood-flooring manufacturers recommend that their products be installed in an environment that is a constant 60°F to 80°F with a relative-humidity level between 30% and 50%.

Use the highest-quality materials available

When it comes to selecting vapor retarders, plywood, fasteners, and flooring for a basement, don't skimp on quality. The basement will expose the flaws in inferior products quickly.

I've used close to every vapor retarder on the market. When it comes to a floating floor, I always recommend at least 10-mil polyethylene sheeting.

(Continued on p. 61)

CONTROL MOISTURE WITH POLY SHEETING

A PROPERLY CONSTRUCTED CONCRETE SLAB— one poured over a capillary break of 6 in. to 8 in. of gravel and a vapor retarder—should stay relatively dry. However, to be sure that your floor isn't dam- aged by excessive moisture, you have to install a vapor retarder under the subfloor, and you have to install it properly. Use 10-mil to 15-mil polyethyl- ene, which has a perm rating of 0.1 perm or less.

OVERLAP AND TAPE THE SEAMS. The vapor retarder should extend to a point just below the top of the baseboard on the wall. Seams should be lapped by 1 ft. and be sealed with waterproof tape.

DETAIL PENETRATIONS WITH A BOOT. Cut the vapor retarder to fit around the base of the support as closely as possible. Although you can tape the penetration, it's better to create a boot out of excess material with splayed tabs. Tape each tab to the vapor retarder, then seal off all edges with the tape. The tape and the vapor retarder secured to the post can be trimmed with a utility knife to the proper height once the subfloor and flooring are installed.

BUILD THE SUBFLOOR WITH TWO LAYERS OF PLYWOOD

A FLOATING SUBFLOOR is the best way to install a wood floor over concrete. Two sheets of ½-in. or ⅝-in. exposure-1 plywood can be fastened without risk of penetrating the vapor retarder. With any plywood assembly, proper spacing and orientation are crucial. *Safety notice:* Proceed with caution and proper ventilation when working with flammable adhesives and pneumatic nailers. Combustion is not likely but possible.

GIVE THE SUBFLOOR ROOM TO MOVE. Leave a ⅛-in. gap between all plywood sheets, and hold each panel ¾ in. from every wall and support post. You can use a tape measure or make a spacer block to speed things up.

INSTALL A SECOND LAYER. The second layer of plywood should be oriented 90° to the first layer. If the subfloor is spanning multiple rooms, orient the second layer at a 45° angle to avoid troublesome joints in doorways. Glue, then screw, nail, or staple the second layer of plywood to the first every 6 in. at the perimeter and every 12 in. in the field.

HOW TO CHOOSE THE BEST ENGINEERED FLOORING

Engineered-wood flooring is the best option if you want to install a wood floor in the basement or on a slab. However, engineered-flooring products are assembled in different ways, which affects the floor's functional and aesthetic role.

To get the best floor possible, assess each component and the way it was manufactured.

THE THICKER THE WEAR LAYER, THE LONGER THE FLOOR LASTS

The top veneer on engineered flooring, considered the wear layer, can vary in thickness from $1/32$ in. to $3/16$ in. Floors with a $1/32$-in.-thick wear layer cannot be sanded if they have to be refinished. A professional wood-flooring contractor might be able to sand a $3/32$-in. wear layer once or twice but that's it. To get the longest life out of a floor, I recommend flooring with a $3/16$-in.-thick wear layer.

SAWN VENEERS LOOK THE BEST AND LAST THE LONGEST

Manufacturers use one of three milling methods to produce top veneers. These thin pieces of wood are either rotary-peeled, sliced, or sawn.

Rotary-peeled veneers show a dramatic, wild graining that looks more like plywood and less like solid wood. Rotary-peeling yields the most material from the log, so it's relatively inexpensive. The veneers, however, have the weakest grain structure and tend to face-check. Floorboards made with rotary-peeled veneers have an extremely thin wear layer.

A sliced veneer is stronger than a rotary-peeled veneer but still tends to develop small cracks and checks in its surface. However, it has more natural-looking grain patterns and looks much more like solid wood. Sliced veneers are generally less than $3/16$ in. thick, so they don't create the longest-lasting floor.

The logs used to make sawn veneers are traditionally milled. The boards then are graded, sorted, and dried. They are later resawn to the thickness needed for the veneers. Sawn veneers are the most expensive to produce but have the strongest grain structure and are typically thicker than peeled or sliced veneers.

SUBSTRATES AND MILLING TOLERANCES ARE IMPORTANT

On this project, I used flooring made by Owens, which has since ceased production. My favorite flooring is made by Quarter-Sawn Flooring. The company uses 11-ply, quality birch plywood to create the backing substrate. Other manufacturers, particularly those that source or create their products in Asia, make substrates by sandwiching small fillets of wood between two wood veneers.

Manufacturers use this construction because it's difficult to source quality plywood in Asia. Also, fillets are made of waste wood, so it's inexpensive. This construction is considered old technology and is less stable than plywood.

Many manufacturers of engineered flooring have a maximum board length of only 4 ft. Quarter-Sawn Flooring and a few other manufacturers sell flooring that's as long as 12 ft. I prefer longer boards so that my floors don't end up looking like butcher blocks.

The best engineered flooring has tighter milling tolerances, too. The American National Standards Institute (ANSI) specifies over-wood tolerances between 0.012 in. and 0.025 in. for engineered flooring, depending on its grade. ("Over wood" is the difference in height between pieces of flooring when they're installed.) Always try to find out what the manufacturer's tolerances are because the national standard is not mandatory.

A 6-mil product is standard, but it isn't as durable. I use Fortifiber®'s Moistop Ultra® 10 and Ultra 15 (www.fortifiber.com).

For the subfloor, I use two layers of ½-in. or ⅝-in. exposure-1 plywood when possible. Exposure-1 plywood is exterior grade—perfect for a concrete application. Pressure-treated plywood can be used as well, but it must be kiln-dried. Pressure-treated plywood straight off the yard can have a moisture content as high as 18%, which is high enough to destroy any wood flooring installed over it.

I assemble a floating subfloor with 18-ga. staples and construction adhesive. You can screw the sheets together, too, but stapling is faster. Be sure the fasteners are long enough to secure the sheets together but short enough so that they don't penetrate through the bottom layer of plywood. Heavy-duty construction adhesive—PL 375, in this case—strengthens the bond between plywood sheets.

When I'm installing a wood floor in a basement, I always opt for engineered flooring because it's more stable than solid-wood flooring. However, not all engineered-flooring products are created equal, so choose carefully (sidebar at left). Some manufacturers say that you can use their solid-wood flooring over concrete. I encourage you not to heed this claim. When a problem with a solid-wood floor does arise, the manufacturers will blame it on moisture issues, not their product, and you'll be solely responsible for the repair or replacement of the floor.

Plumbing a Basement Bathroom

BY MIKE GUERTIN WITH
CONTRIBUTION BY PAUL MURRAY

Adding a bathroom in a basement might sound like a complicated project, but the plumbing part of the job isn't much different from any above-grade bath. It's simple and straightforward to bring in the small-diameter supply lines for hot and cold water. Cutting the slab and digging the trench for the waste lines are the tasks that set this project apart. I work with my plumber, Paul Murray, to map out the best fixture layout, and we then divide the tasks required to complete the project. I tackle the slab work, and he lays the drain and supply piping. Of course, the sewer-outlet pipe on most of my projects is above the basement-floor elevation, so we have to install a tank to collect the sewage and a pump to send it up to the level of the sewer outlet. The rough-in process takes several days for us to complete; then we can schedule the inspections.

Plan the drain layout first

Rather than completely breaking out the concrete slab in the prospective bathroom, I cut trenches where the drains will run. This saves me from having to move lots of broken concrete and then repour the slab. I chalk a proposed fixture layout on the concrete slab, then meet with Paul. We review options, and he recommends layout changes that minimize my work and simplify his drain- and vent-pipe arrangement.

He also identifies suitable locations for the sewage-ejector tank and draws the final trench layout.

The bathroom in this project is typical and includes a toilet, a pedestal sink, and a one-piece shower stall. Other plumbed fixtures, such as a washing machine, a utility sink, a kitchen sink, and a dishwasher, can be tied in to the same drain system.

Open the floor

Before I start breaking up the concrete slab, I make cardboard templates of the drain-riser positions for the shower and the toilet. The templates register to the adjacent wall plates or wall layout lines, so after the slab is removed and the trench is dug, Paul has a guide for installing the drains.

The largest drainpipe will be 3 in. dia., but the trenches need to be wide enough to be shoveled out. I usually make them 10 in. to 12 in. wide to leave extra working room for fittings. To cut the slab, I use an old worm-drive saw fitted with a $40 dry-cut diamond blade; it must be plugged into a GFCI-protected outlet. The blade cuts only 2½ in. into the slab, which typically is 3 in. to 5 in. thick, but that's deep enough to give me a good, clean fracture line. A gas-powered concrete saw would cut all the way through the slab, but the exhaust inside a poorly ventilated basement would be overwhelming and would migrate into the living space above.

As the saw cuts, I flood the blade with water to cool it, as well as to speed the cut and to minimize dust. I pour a puddle of water on the floor and use a brush to sweep it to the rear of the blade. The blade draws the water forward into the cutting action. The water can be pushed back into the blade until it becomes thick slurry. After every few feet of cutting, I collect the slurry in a bucket or a shop vacuum and start a fresh puddle.

A few whacks with a 10-lb. sledgehammer crack the concrete between the sawcuts; I use a prybar to pop out pieces of the slab. Once a hole is started, the pieces come out easily. A word of caution: Some slabs are placed over plastic vapor retarders. When I encounter them, I try to be careful not to damage

A TEMPLATE MAKES LOCATING DRAINS EASIER. During layout, I make a cardboard template for the drain locations. Marks on the template are registered to marks on the adjacent walls. When it's time to place the drain flange, I put the template back in its spot. I've found that it's easier to cut the slab exactly rather than remove and then repour the entire area. Chalklines guide the sawcuts.

EVERYTHING FLOWS DOWNHILL TO A TANK

THE KEY TO A BASEMENT PLUMBING system is a tank with a pump that raises gray water and sewage to the main waste line, where gravity can take over. To keep everything flowing properly to the sewage tank, the drain lines from the fixtures should be pitched ¼ in. over a 12-in. run. Here, the fixture farthest from the tank, the toilet, determines the tank's vertical position.

AN ECONOMICAL (AND FRIENDLIER) WAY TO CUT CONCRETE. I outfit an old worm-drive saw with a dry-cut diamond blade. To cool the blade and to reduce dust, I puddle a little water near the line and sweep it behind the blade as it cuts. The saw must always be plugged into a GFCI-protected outlet.

Main vent stack

Main waste line

2-in. vent stack

Vent for tank

¼ in. per ft. of pitch

Shower drain line

Check valve

Toilet flange line

3-in. main drain line

Vanity sink drain/ vent combination

3-in. to 2-in. T-connector

Garage wall

Sewage tank and pump

TAKE OUT ONLY AS MUCH AS YOU NEED. Scored by the sawcuts, the slab is easily broken out with a sledgehammer, then carted away in chunks.

KEEPING IN PITCH. As the plumber lays out the drains, he continually checks his work using a torpedo level equipped with a pitch vial.

the plastic. I slice it down the middle of the trench and fold back the sides so that I can reuse it when backfilling.

Pitch the trench downhill

I use a 3x3 (3-in.-dia. by 3-in.-dia.) elbow fitting to establish the starting depth at the farthest point in the drain run from the ejector tank—in this case, the toilet (drawing on facing page). To accommodate the 3-in.-dia. elbow, I start the bottom of the trench about 4 in. below the bottom of the slab. This leaves enough space above the drainpipe for the slab to be repoured to its full thickness. The trench needs to be pitched at ¼ in. per ft. I use a 6-ft. level with a pitch vial to gauge the slope as I'm digging. Any tangent trenches from incoming fixture drains need to be sloped at the same pitch, starting where they meet the main trench level. The area directly beneath the shower drain needs to be dug several inches deeper than the trench level to accommodate the trap.

The drain line terminates at the sewage-collection tank. These tanks are usually made of thick plastic and have an inlet hole drilled in the side. The pit for the tank needs to be excavated deep enough so that the bottom of the inlet hole matches the bottom of the trench. This level might cause the top of the tank to be beneath the slab level if the drain runs are long. It's important to let the trench level establish the level of the tank and not just position the tank flush with the top of the slab, or there might not be enough pitch in the drainpipes for the sewage to flow properly. On this project, the tank top needed to be 2½ in. below slab level.

Don't forget the vent lines

It takes me half a day to break out the slab and to dig the trenches. Then Paul returns to install the drains. Using the cardboard templates, he dry-fits, then glues together the pipes and fittings, running them into the sewage tank. A rubber bushing seals the pipe to the tank.

SEWAGE EJECTOR: THE GUTS OF THE SYSTEM

THE SEWAGE-EJECTOR PUMP sits inside a plastic tank. It has a float-controlled switch that activates the pump when the sewage level reaches the discharge height. The sewage is pumped up and out through a 2-in.-dia. pipe to the main waste line, where the sewage flows naturally (due to gravity) rather than under pressure. A check valve mounted on the discharge pipe prevents the sewage in the discharge pipe from flowing back into the tank. In the event of a pump failure or a maintenance check, the pipe can be disconnected beneath the check valve, and the sewage inside the pipe above the valve will not leak out.

Many pumps, including the one I installed, can be serviced only by removing the tank cover and disconnecting the drain. My plumber recommends a pump by Liberty Pumps® (www.libertypumps.com) with a cover-mounted panel (photo below) that allows easier access to the switch. All ejector pumps are powered by regular household current; the power cord plugs into any nearby GFCI-protected outlet. The cost for a tank and pump can run from $300 to $900.

PATCHING THE SLAB IS A SMALL BUT INTENSIVE JOB

ONCE THE DRAINS ARE IN PLACE and I've backfilled, I like to compact the fill with water 1 ; any resulting low spots are filled and compacted again. Before I pour concrete 2 , I isolate the drain risers with a wrap of cardboard, which gives me room to adjust the drain after the concrete is set. After mixing a small, stiff batch of concrete and packing it into the trench with a wooden float 3 , I finish by running a vibrator (I use an Arkie Wall Banger) on a nylon cutting board 4 and, finally, by using a magnesium float and a steel trowel.

Once all the pipes have been laid, we backfill about three-quarters of the way around them to keep the pipes from shifting. The top of the trench is left exposed for the rough-plumbing inspection. If I'm working in an area that has a high water table, I fill the tank to the inlet, or I weight it with rocks to prevent it from floating if the groundwater level rises.

While the drain lines are exposed, Paul installs the plumbing vents. Proper venting is required by code and is necessary for the drains to work. The vents equalize air pressure inside drains and prevent traps from being sucked dry. Ideally, we run a vent pipe to the exterior of the building or tap into an existing vent pipe in the floor above. A vent pipe can be run through a wall above, can be concealed in a closet, or can be run on an exterior wall. On this project, we tapped into a vent pipe on the first floor as part of a more-extensive remodeling project. Although air-admittance valves are an alternative for venting difficult locations and can be used to vent fixtures in a basement bathroom, don't use them to vent the sewage tank itself. We have run into problems with both odors and poor pump flow when we've used air valves in the past. Pumps perform much better when they are vented atmospherically.

Leave yourself options after patching the slab

After the inspector's approval, I backfill around the pipes. The cardboard templates are used to position the shower, sink, and toilet risers precisely. While the backfill is still loose, the pipes are easy to shift a little to match the templates.

I then wrap the risers with strips of corrugated cardboard or surround them with a piece of larger-diameter pipe. The toilet stub, for instance, is left unglued to the fitting below so that it can be trimmed later to match the finished-flooring level when the toilet flange is mounted. The spacer keeps the concrete away from the pipe so that the stub later can be cut to length and glued. The spacers also leave a little wiggle room for fine-tuning the drain risers

ISOLATE THE TANK LID BUT NOT THE TANK. I use a ring of cardboard as a form around the sewage tank's lid so that the repoured patch sits on top of the tank rim but doesn't interfere with the removal of the lid. In some regions, seasonally high water tables can lift the tank right out of its hole if it's not secured.

to match the fixture outlets. This is especially important when you're installing a one-piece shower.

Once the pipes are positioned, I flood the area several times with water to ensure that the backfill is packed tightly around them. The water helps to consolidate the soil and to fill in any gaps. The soil often settles when it's flooded, so I add more dirt flush with the bottom of the old slab and then flood the area again. Finally, I cover the trench with 6-mil plastic as a vapor retarder and tape it to the existing plastic vapor retarder when it is present.

The slab patch usually doesn't require enough concrete to warrant bringing in a ready-mix truck, so I either mix concrete in a wheelbarrow by hand or in a portable mixer. I mix the concrete to a stiff consistency and then pack it into the trench. Next, I run a concrete vibrator over a plastic cutting board and finish up by going over the surface with a magnesium float and a steel trowel.

After the concrete cures for a couple of days, Paul returns for a few hours to install the supply tubing and to mount the shower mixing valve. I install the subfloor panels, the drywall, and the finished flooring before Paul's final visit to set the toilet and install the sink.

Trimming a Basement Window

BY CHRIS WHALEN

Finish carpentry is the art of making rough stuff look good. Even trimming a window can be a challenge because it's usually complicated by poorly aligned framing or uneven drywall. If things go well, you can tenderize the drywall with a hammer or shim the window into alignment. If not, the window jambs might need to be planed, the casing tweaked, or the miters back-beveled at odd angles. In the end, a bead of caulk is often needed to disguise the solutions.

Multiunit windows in thick walls, such as the basement windows featured here, are prone to even more problems. For starters, even if the windows were installed plumb, level, and square, they might not be parallel with the finished wall surface, meaning that the side jambs need to be tapered. Second, the individual units might not be installed in a straight line, meaning that the stool needs to be tapered. Third, access between the window and the interior-wall framing could be limited, which reduces options for attaching extension jambs.

SAFETY NOTE: Chris usually wears safety glasses when using a nail gun, but he forgot to wear them for this photo. Please don't make the same mistake.

REMOVE THE NARROW STOOL EXTENSION, AND BUILD A DEEP ONE

THE STOOL NEEDS TO BE WIDE ENOUGH to get past the drywall while leaving room to scribe the final fit. To get the stool deep enough, glue and biscuit an extension to the profiled stool, keeping the two parts flush on top.

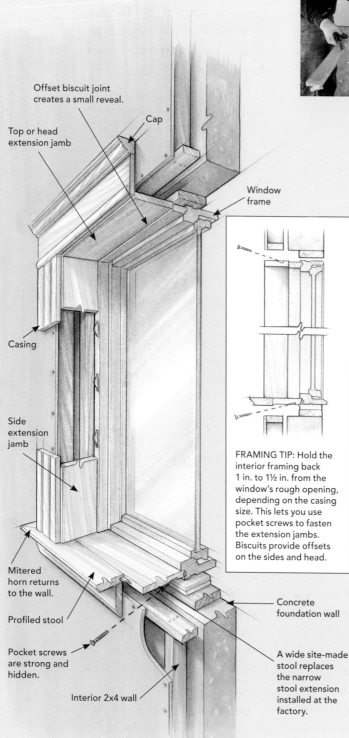

Offset biscuit joint creates a small reveal.

Cap

Top or head extension jamb

Window frame

Casing

Side extension jamb

Mitered horn returns to the wall.

Profiled stool

Pocket screws are strong and hidden.

Interior 2x4 wall

Concrete foundation wall

A wide site-made stool replaces the narrow stool extension installed at the factory.

FRAMING TIP: Hold the interior framing back 1 in. to 1½ in. from the window's rough opening, depending on the casing size. This lets you use pocket screws to fasten the extension jambs. Biscuits provide offsets on the sides and head.

ASSEMBLE THE TWO-PIECE STOOL. I use biscuits and glue, then clamp the stool assembly overnight, making sure the tops of these two pieces are flush.

RETURN THE PROFILE TO THE WALL. I miter the returns at the end of the stool using two biscuits (stacked), glue, and blue painter's tape as a clamp.

Identify the problems

The three window units here are in an 8-in.-thick concrete wall. A 2x4 wall covered with drywall sits inside. Before casing is applied to a window like this, the jambs and the stool need to be extended.

The first thing I do is determine how the window sits in relation to the drywall. With a multiunit window such as this one, I place a long straightedge along the top and bottom jambs to determine if the units are in the same plane and at the same elevation. In this case, the windows were at the same height, but the center unit was pushed out in relation to the flanking units. Next, I straddle the corners of each window unit with a short straightedge on the drywall and measure from the window jamb. This tells me how wide the extension jambs will be and if tapering is required. For reference, I write the measurement on the drywall along the edge of the opening where the trim will cover it later. If the variation is less than ⅛ in., there's no need to worry about tapering the extension jambs or stool. This discrepancy can be taken up by tipping the casing slightly. If the difference is greater than ⅛ in., the jambs need to be tapered.

Solutions start with the stool

Many windows have factory-applied 2-in. extension jambs that make the window suitable for a 2x6 wall. For basement walls, you need to extend the side and head jambs even more. I do this with a simple offset biscuit joint (more on that later). This offset joint looks good on the jambs, but it's impractical for a stool. That's why I carefully remove the factory-applied stool extension and replace it with a new full-depth stool.

The new stool needs to fit between the rough opening in the framed wall while extending past the side casings. The overall length of the stool is the sum of the distance between the side jambs, the width of the casings, the casing reveals (typically ¼ in.), and the amount of overhang beyond the casings. After cutting the stool to length, I miter the ends so that the profile returns to the wall. The

extension is biscuited and glued to the back of the profiled stool. When this assembly is dry, I scrape excess glue, sand, fill gaps, and sand again, making it ready to install.

Set the new stool in the opening, and check its fit. The width will probably need adjustment. Because the three individual window units weren't perfectly in line on this project, I needed to taper the stool in addition to notching around the mullions. I use a square and a scribe to measure and mark the notches and the ends of the stool extending past the window. After removing excess material with a jigsaw, I slide the stool into position again for final scribing and planing. Finally, I bore for pocket screws, clamp the stool into position, and screw it to the window frame. I use a lot of screws (every 6 in. to 9 in.) because someone is going to sit on this window stool sometime in the future, and I don't want it to break.

Install jamb extensions

For the head and side jambs, I add a piece to the factory extensions using an offset reveal of about ⅛ in. The head jamb needs to be long enough to pass the side jambs, but it does not have to be fit to anything else. I cut it slightly longer than the overall length of the window. To scribe the head jamb, I set it in place with bar clamps and shims. Next, I measure at a few spots to determine what needs to be removed from the jamb stock, and I set the scribe and mark along the length of the jamb. I cut to the scribe line with a small circular saw, then use a power planer, a block plane, and a sanding block to adjust until the fit is acceptable. As with the stool, the process takes a couple of fittings.

At this point, I use a biscuit joiner to create a consistent offset or reveal between the extension jamb I'm making and the one applied by the factory.

On the project here, because there wasn't as much clearance between the window frame and the rough framing on top of the window as there was on the stool, pocket screws wouldn't work. Instead, after applying glue and inserting the biscuits, I shimmed

(Continued on p. 75)

FIT THE STOOL

WITH THE DEEP STOOL ASSEM-
BLED, scraped, puttied, and sanded,
I turn to fitting. Ultimately, the stool
needs to be tight to the window
frame and drywall, and notched
around the mullions. This begins with
positioning the stool exactly parallel
to the window and ends with a slight
back bevel on the final cut. Rough
and final scribing, cutting, and fine-
tuning come between.

2. ROUGH-CUT

THE FIRST CUT IS THE DEEPEST. I use
a jigsaw to cut the notches and horns,
and a small circular saw to cut the
length of the stool. The notches will be
covered with trim later, so give yourself
some wiggle room. The horns will be
mostly covered but not where they
return to the wall.

1. ROUGH-SCRIBE

MARK THE MUL-
LIONS AND
HORNS. The depth
of the notch and
the amount I cut
off the horns is the
distance between
the window frame
and the stool. I
square the notch
lines at this depth
and scribe the
horns accordingly.

3. MAKE THE FINAL FIT

POSITION FOR FINAL SCRIB-ING. With the rough-cut stool back in place, I set my scribes to the widest gap. Next, I scribe the entire length of the stool, including the horns. This should make a perfect fit.

SOME CUTS MATTER MORE THAN OTHERS. The back edge of the stool is most important because it won't be covered by trim. To get a tight fit, I cut near the line with a saw, and then I ease the cut over to the line and back bevel with a block plane or sanding block.

4. INSTALL WITH POCKET SCREWS

BORE MANY POCKET HOLES. I put a screw every 6 in. to 9 in. on window stools for a strong connection because people often sit or lean on them.

GIVE YOURSELF ROOM TO WORK. With space between the rough open-ing and the window frame, you can attach the stool extension with pocket screws.

FIT THE TOP AND SIDE JAMBS WITH AN OFFSET

FOR A GREAT-LOOKING JOINT that's fast to fit, I use a biscuit joiner with a clip-on offset plate. A ⅛-in. offset adds a shadowline to the profile and eliminates all the fussy fitting, sanding, and patching that a flush fit can require.

⅛-in. offset

CLAMPS PROP THE TOP JAMB FOR SCRIBING

Just like the stool, the top extension jamb needs to be scribe-fit to all three window units. Don't get bogged down trying to get the exact length; it just needs to be long enough to land on the side jambs. What's important is that the top extension is parallel to the interior-wall surface when you scribe **1**. Scribe the back edge along the window frame **2**, setting the scribes to the biggest distance that the front edge of the jamb sticks out past the drywall. Because the framing wasn't held back enough from the window, I had to face-nail the head and side extensions into the framing **3** rather than use pocket screws. The side jambs need to fit tightly top to bottom and also along their width **4**. If the framed wall isn't as plumb as the foundation wall (or as out of plumb), the board needs to be tapered. To get a tight fit top to bottom, I measure in two steps. First, I make a mark 20 in. up from the stool. Next, I measure down to the mark, and I add the two numbers together. This is more accurate (and faster) than bending my tape into a corner and guessing at the exact measurement.

The Lamello Top 10 biscuit joiner has a clip-on offset plate.

and nailed the head-jamb extension in place, making sure it was square to the side jambs.

The only difference in installing the side jambs is that the length needs to fit precisely between the new stool and head jamb. Rather than bending my tape measure into a corner, I measure in two steps: up from the stool 20 in., then down from the head to the 20-in. mark. I then add the two numbers together. I cut the jambs to length and then to width according to the numbers written previously on the drywall. Finally, I fit the pieces and then biscuit, shim, and nail them in place, making sure they are square and tight to both the head jamb and the stool.

The rest is standard procedure

The last few steps of the process aren't much different than regular window trimming: Apply the mullion trim, casings, cap, and apron. I start with the mullions and work my way out. Using the same two-step measuring technique as I did with the side jambs, I measure the mullions, then cut and nail them in place.

I cut side casings to length, making them ¼ in. longer than the distance between the stool and head jamb, thereby creating a reveal at the head. After nailing them in place, I measure, cut, shim, and install the head casing and cap. Before installing the apron beneath the stool, I permanently shim and block the stool so that it is level, straight, and solid. I then make an apron with mitered returns on the ends the same length as the head casing, and I nail on the apron so that its ends are in line with the outside edges of the side casings.

Whether you're trimming a basement window or one in a double-stud, adobe, straw-bale, insulated-concrete-form, or any other thick-wall structure, these techniques ensure a quality installation for an appealing assembly.

COMPLETE THE ASSEMBLY

THE TRIM DETAIL here was dictated by the trim in the existing house. I begin with the mullions, which need to fit tightly between the stool and the head extension. The side casings are cut ¼ in. long to establish the reveal for the head casing. The apron is installed last.

LONG HEAD CASINGS ARE A BIT TRICKY. I clamp the head casing in place and adjust the reveal to the head extension before nailing it off. I use a finish nailer with 2½-in. nails to attach the casing to the framing, and a brad nailer to fasten the casing to the extension jambs.

TIGHTEN THE STOOL. I use 2x blocks and shims to clean up the joints and make a solid stool. Last, I install the apron with mitered returns.

A Skylight Cheers Up an Attic Bath

BY SCOTT DONAHUE

Of all the rooms in this old house, built in 1916, the third-floor bath had the worst layout. The room measured less than 5 ft. wide by 11 ft. long, and the tub was tucked between floor-to-ceiling sidewalls. Getting to the toilet required squeezing through a 14-in.-wide passageway between the tub and the sink.

I wanted to improve circulation and bring some light into this dark, cramped bath. The partition walls flanking the bathtub had to go, and I considered replacing the built-in tub with a freestanding claw-foot model. But no one was wild about having a shower curtain as the centerpiece of the bathroom. The only alternative was tucking the tub into the adjacent attic.

I took some measurements and discovered there was just enough headroom under the roof for a tub where a person of average height could shower comfortably. Compared with the cast-iron alternative, the lightweight acrylic tub (BainUltra®, jetless Meridian® 55; www.bainultra.com) was considerably easier to carry up three flights of narrow stairs.

Capping the alcove with a skylight went a long way toward brightening the room. Almost as an afterthought, I decided to make the skylight operable, which added more headroom. When it's fully open, whoever is in the shower has an unimpeded view of the sunrise over the Oakland Hills in California.

SMALL EXPANSION, BIG PAYOFF. Centered between the existing rafters, a 30-in. by 55-in. operable skylight provides ventilation, daylight, and adjustable headroom in this tub/shower alcove tucked into unused attic space. Shelves for towels and a narrow bench made of cedar 2x4s on edge frame the tub.

BATHED IN LIGHT

FLOOR-TO-CEILING WALLS flanking the built-in tub made this narrow bathroom seem even smaller, and getting to the loo meant squeezing past the sink. Tucked into the adjacent attic, the new bathtub frees up space for a sink with a wedge-shaped counter that contributes to the room's open feeling. An operable skylight above the tub maximizes headroom and natural light. Access to attic storage is maintained via a new hatch on a bedroom wall.

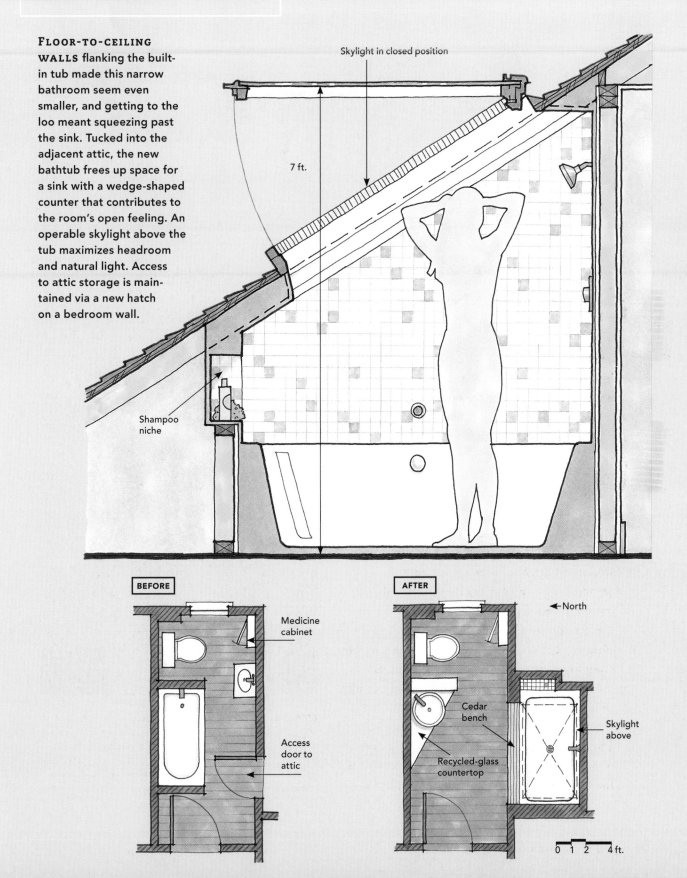

Skylight in closed position

7 ft.

Shampoo niche

BEFORE

Medicine cabinet

Access door to attic

AFTER

←North

Cedar bench

Recycled-glass countertop

Skylight above

0 1 2   4 ft.

Give Kitchens and Baths Special Attention

How Much Will My Kitchen Cost?

BY JOHN MCLEAN

"How much will it cost?" is almost always one of the first questions that clients ask. And it's a good question, because the true costs of their dream home—or in this case, dream kitchen—may not jibe with their budget. Uncovering any disparity before design begins is a good idea.

To the surprise of some people, kitchen remodels are one of the most expensive building projects. They may have seen a kitchen that they liked on television or at a neighbor's house but were left with unrealistic impressions of what it cost. What you see when you visit a new kitchen often doesn't reflect the complexity of construction. The cabinets, countertops, and floor in one house can cost more or less than the same items in another. The difference may be based on a number of factors from difficulty of demolition to region of the country (see "Regional Cost Adjustments," p. 86).

For these reasons, I often use the following charts to project the initial cost of a kitchen remodel at the first meeting with new clients (see "The Checklist: How to Use It," p. 80). When I arrive at an estimated cost for the potential remodel, we compare it with the client's budget. If we're over budget and the client can't or doesn't want to spend more money, we take a look at each item and try to cut costs. If the estimate is less than anticipated, we may consider upgrades, or the client simply may appreciate the savings.

In my experience, the cost of new construction and the cost of remodeling are similar. Therefore, these charts are viable whether renovating an existing kitchen or building a new one.

Once you've arrived at an estimated cost per square foot, multiply it by the total square footage of your kitchen. Changes to adjacent spaces need to be considered as well. For example, if you are removing a 10-ft. wall between a kitchen and a dining room, you likely will incur collateral costs for moving outlets and switches or patching the floor or ceiling in the dining room. To incorporate these costs into the estimate, I consider at least 2 ft. into affected adjacent spaces in the total size projection. For the example I just mentioned, I would add 20 sq. ft.

THE CHECKLIST: HOW TO USE IT

THE CHECKLIST CONSISTS OF THREE CHARTS. Each focuses on a chapter in a kitchen remodel, from demolition to fixture installation. The items in the chart affect the cost of a remodel in different ways. For each item listed in the left-hand column, five project levels are listed in the columns to the right. They progress from the simplest construction and least expensive materials to the most complex construction and most expensive materials. To use the chart, highlight the choices that most closely match your situation and preferences. Total the number of choices in each column, and move to the next chart. If a term is unfamiliar, skip it until you can get an explanation. If an item doesn't apply, don't highlight any level of that particular item.

To illustrate the charts in action, I've highlighted items for a kitchen remodel in San Francisco: a 235-sq.-ft. second-story kitchen in the back of the house. The room has two exterior walls that need new windows, one interior wall to be removed, and one to be given a 7-ft.-wide opening, adding 65 sq. ft. of collateral costs to the size of the renovation (now 300 sq. ft.). The new kitchen will have cabinets along both exterior walls and an island with a breakfast bar that seats three.

KITCHEN ACCESS
Direct access to the kitchen from a parking/loading area speeds debris removal and material delivery.

FLOORING REMOVAL
Sheet flooring is light and usually easy to remove. Tile and wood take longer to pry up and dispose of. Removing strong adhesive is labor intensive.

WALL REMOVAL
Removing load-bearing walls is expensive, requiring temporary support and a new post-and-beam system.

CEILING REMOVAL
Low ceilings and flat ceilings are easy to reach. Removing plaster is messy and requires diligent dust protection.

WALL CHANGES
Working with interior partition walls is almost always less expensive than working with load-bearing walls. Exterior wall openings require flashing and exterior finish work.

NEW WINDOWS
Fixed and sliding windows are less expensive because they are simpler to fabricate than casement and double-hung windows. Choose standard sizes and common colors to keep down costs.

NEW EXTERIOR DOORS
Standard-size aluminum and clad-wood swinging and sliding doors are produced in large quantities, are readily available, and often fit existing openings. Larger doors may require new framing and exterior finish work.

NEW INTERIOR DOORS
Standard-size prehung doors keep down costs because they require the least time to install. Prefinished doors tend to cost less than site-finished doors. Custom doors take much more time and money to build and install.

NEW CEILINGS
Ceilings are expensive when additional framing is needed, which is why drywall ceilings attached to existing rafters or joists are the least expensive option for both flat and sloped ceilings. Curved and plaster ceilings take longer to build.

CHART I: DEMOLITION AND STRUCTURAL CHANGES

	EASY AND INEXPENSIVE			HARD AND EXPENSIVE	
ITEM	1	2	3	4	5
KITCHEN ACCESS	Direct; less than 3 ft. above grade	Direct; one story above grade	Indirect; less than 3 ft. above grade	*Indirect; one story above grade*	Indirect; more than one story above grade
FLOORING REMOVAL	Flooring to remain	*Remove sheet vinyl or linoleum*	Remove tile on mortar bed	Remove wood flooring	Remove any floor installed with tenacious adhesive
WALL REMOVAL	All walls to remain	1–2 partition walls	*1 load-bearing wall replaced with beam below ceiling*	2 load-bearing walls replaced with beams below ceiling	1–2 load-bearing walls replaced with beams above ceiling
CEILING REMOVAL	Ceiling to remain	Remove 8-ft. to 9-ft. drywall ceiling	Remove sloped or tall (more than 10 ft.) drywall ceiling	Remove flat wood or complex drywall ceiling	*Remove plaster ceiling*
WALL CHANGES	No changes	1 opening in interior partition wall	*1 opening in interior load-bearing wall or new partition*	1–2 openings in exterior wall or a new curved partition wall	More than 2 openings in or 2 new exterior walls
NEW WINDOWS	None or 1 new aluminum slider, mill finish	1–2 new aluminum or economy-grade white vinyl	1–2 white vinyl or inexpensive wood in standard sizes	2 good-quality wood, standard sizes, primed or clad color	*More than 2 top-quality clad wood or steel*
NEW EXTERIOR DOORS	*No new doors*	1 site-finished wood or metal; or aluminum slider, mill finish	1 prefinished door, wood or metal; or wood slider, primed	3-panel wood slider; or 1 pair site-finished French doors	2–3 pairs French doors; premium hardware
NEW INTERIOR DOORS	None or 1 paint-grade hollow-core prehung	1 stain-grade, hollow-core prehung	1–2 paint-grade, solid-core wood doors	*1–3 paint- or stain-grade, frame-and-panel doors*	1–3 custom frame-and-panel or glass doors
NEW CEILINGS	None or an 8-ft. flat drywall ceiling	9-ft. flat drywall with soffit above cabinets	*10-ft. flat or sloped drywall attached to rafters*	Sloped drywall at different angle from roof rafters	Multiangle or curved drywall, or flat plaster
SUBTOTAL	1	1	3	2	2

PLUMBING CHANGES

Moving water and drain lines is inexpensive until the framing has to be modified; then cost rises quickly. New plumbing vents must extend to the roof, so unless the line is placed on an exterior wall, a new vertical space (a chase) has to be built. A second sink requires a second set of drain and vent lines.

HVAC CHANGES

Changing supply-register positions is not expensive as long as the new duct run serving the register does not entail extensive framing changes. It may be cost-effective to install a new small furnace close to the new kitchen being served. Updating the entire heating system is generally not cost-effective for just a kitchen.

ELECTRICAL CHANGES

If an existing panel has sufficient capacity, the cost of adding kitchen circuits is minimal. Bringing an old kitchen up to modern codes may require new circuits, and increased load on an electrical system may require a new panel or subpanel.

LIGHTING CONTROLS

Automated and electronic lighting controls are innovative, convenient, and very expensive. Dimmers for incandescent lights are readily available and less expensive than those for fluorescent lights. Dimmers for the latter must be high quality to be reliable.

LIGHT FIXTURES

Replacing surface-mounted fixtures with similar fixtures may require only a new junction box in the wall or ceiling. Standard-voltage recessed fixtures, while relatively inexpensive to buy, may require framing, mechanical, or plumbing changes. Low-voltage fixtures, requiring step-down transformers, are more costly.

CHART 2: MECHANICAL CHANGES, SURFACE FINISHES, AND TRIM

EASY AND INEXPENSIVE

ITEM	1	2	
PLUMBING CHANGES	None	Relocate sink and dishwasher supply and drain lines less than 3 ft. from present location; use existing vent pipe	
HVAC CHANGES	None	*Relocate 1 supply-air register and duct within 3 ft. of present location; connect to nearby supply duct from furnace*	
ELECTRICAL CHANGES	None	Minor wiring to relocate 1–2 switches and/or receptacles close to existing locations	
LIGHTING CONTROLS	Use existing switches	Replace switches with decorator-style (rocker) switches; install 1 new rotary or slide dimmer for incandescent fixtures	
LIGHT FIXTURES	No changes	Replace surface-mounted ceiling fixtures with new midrange-quality surface-mounted fixtures	
FLOORING	No new flooring	Vinyl or linoleum sheets or tiles; floating laminate flooring	
WALL FINISH	½-in. drywall with medium or heavy texture	½-in. drywall with light texture or sufficiently smooth for flat paint	
CEILING FINISH	½-in. drywall with medium or heavy texture	½-in. drywall with light texture or sufficiently smooth for flat paint	
TRIM AND DETAILING	Common paint-grade moldings for door casings; drywall-cased window openings; vinyl baseboard	Common paint-grade moldings for door casings, window casings, and baseboard	
SUBTOTAL	0	1	

FLOORING

More flooring options are available at better prices. Installation costs, though, remain unchanged, which explains the high cost of tile and hardwood floors. Floating floors and sheet flooring can be installed quickly.

WALL FINISH

High-gloss paints and smooth surfaces require better craftsmanship because they show imperfections much more than flat finishes. Textured wall finishes are less expensive and help to hide poor framing and drywall work. Tile and wood wainscot and plaster are expensive and complicated to install.

3	4	5
Relocate sink and dishwasher supply and drain lines more than 3 ft. from present location, with new vent pipe in existing vertical chase	Add new sink and dishwasher supply and drain lines and new vent pipe in existing vertical chase	Add supply, drain, and vent lines for 2 sinks and dishwasher, requiring considerable reframing of walls and floor; construct vertical chase
Relocate 2 supply-air registers and ducts more than 3 ft. from present location; connect to nearby supply duct from furnace	Add new supply-air registers, duct, and return-air grille and duct to and from new furnace; add cooling capability to heating system	Replace or supplement existing heating system with new hydronic radiant-floor system; install solar-heating system
Wiring for up to 6 new switches, receptacles, and/or light-fixture junction boxes with 1–2 new circuits from existing panel	*Wiring for more than 6 new switches, outlets, and/or light-fixture junction boxes, requiring 3 or more new circuits from existing panel*	Replace all existing wiring; install new panel; upgrade electrical service to higher amperage
Replace all switches with rotary or slide dimmers for incandescent fixtures	*Install new touch dimmer controls (incandescent and fluorescent types) and motion detectors*	Install programmable electronic light-control system
Replace surface-mounted ceiling fixtures with midrange-quality recessed ceiling fixtures	*Install new low-voltage recessed fixtures and undercabinet task lighting*	Install new low-voltage recessed fixtures, wall sconces, cove lighting, and undercabinet task lighting
Engineered wood, solid-wood parquet, or floating linoleum	Prefinished or site-finished hardwood	*Ceramic or stone tile*
½-in. drywall with smooth finish for any paint gloss level	⅝-in. drywall with smooth finish; painted wood wainscot	Full-height plaster finish; ceramic- or stone-tile wainscot
½-in. drywall with smooth finish for any paint gloss level	*½-in. drywall with smooth finish on many ceiling planes*	Plaster with cove detail or clear vertical-grain wood
Common stain-grade moldings for door casings, window casings, baseboard, and crown	*Paint-grade, built-up moldings for door casings, window casings, baseboard, and crown*	Custom stain-grade trim details including wainscot; or contemporary minimal trim with reveals to separate adjacent flush surfaces
1	6	1

CEILING FINISH

Working overhead is difficult. Thin, light drywall is the easiest ceiling material to install. Installing wood paneling or a coffered ceiling is labor intensive. In any case, the complexity of the ceiling increases the cost.

TRIM AND DETAILING

A trim package can be as simple as stock door casings, drywall around window openings, and vinyl baseboard. Wood molding profiles used alone or in combination increase installation time and cost. Stain and clear finishes require more expensive wood. Wainscot, built-up casings, and crown molding increase material and installation cost. Contemporary details (without surface trim) require detailed planning and precise craftsmanship.

CABINET CONFIGURATION
Galley-style kitchens may not be the most efficient working arrangements, but straight runs of cabinets are easy to install. Inside-corner cabinets have less convenient storage, are more expensive to purchase, and may require undesirable spacers between adjacent cabinets.

CABINETS
Prices are based on case and finish material, construction type, and the quantity and quality of hardware. Large manufacturers offer economy-grade cabinets. Custom cabinets are appropriate for unusual kitchen configurations and unique owner preferences.

COUNTERTOP AND BACKSPLASH
Plastic laminate is inexpensive to buy and easy to install. Stone is expensive, requires careful fabrication, and must be installed over an even, properly supported substrate. Color choice, thickness, and edge profile affect the price of solid surface.

PRIMARY SINK
Stainless-steel sinks rise in price as thickness and quietness increase. White cast-iron sinks are as much as 25% less expensive than neutral colors, and 45% less expensive than dark colors. Regardless of material, drop-in sinks are less complicated to install than undermount sinks.

SECONDARY SINK
These sinks are a good idea in large kitchens with multiple workstations or as a convenience. Because a secondary sink often is a significant distance from the primary sink, they may not be able to share water, vent, and drain lines.

CHART 3: CABINETS AND APPLIANCES

EASY AND INEXPENSIVE

ITEM	1	2	
CABINET CONFIGURATION	Linear (galley) base- and wall-cabinet plan	L-shaped base- and wall-cabinet plan	
CABINETS	3-in. modular widths, economy-grade carcases and drawers, pressed-wood doors and drawer fronts with lipped (standard offset) design; prefinished; ¾-in. extension slides; exposed hinges; no cabinet accessories	3-in. modular widths, midgrade carcase and drawer construction, pressed-wood doors and drawer fronts, flush overlay; melamine finish; three-quarter ⅝-in. extension slides; concealed hinges with minimal adjustment	
COUNTERTOP AND BACKSPLASH	Plastic laminate with square edge; 4-in.-high splash	Plastic laminate with bullnose edge; 4-in.-high coved splash	
PRIMARY SINK	8-in.-deep single or double bowl, drop-in; 20-ga. stainless steel or white enameled steel	8-in.-deep single or double bowl, drop-in or metal frame; 18-ga. stainless steel or white enameled cast iron	
SECONDARY SINK	None	N/A	
FAUCET	Two-handle, swivel spout, brass construction, rubber washers, polished chrome, utilitarian design	Single control, swivel spout, brass construction, ceramic-disk valve, polished chrome, hand-spray, utilitarian design	
APPLIANCE GROUP	Bargain brand or economy line in white: small fridge with top freezer, electric range, recirculating hood, base model dishwasher, ⅓-hp disposal	Brand names in white: small fridge with top freezer, electric or gas cooktop, ventilating hood, wall oven, microwave, midrange dishwasher, ½-hp disposal	
SUBTOTAL	*0*	*0*	

FAUCET
A tall, swiveling faucet with an integral spray handle is a useful convenience that may outlast its inexpensive counterpart. Single-control valves are more expensive than dual controls, and finishes other than polished chrome add 15% to 50% to the cost.

APPLIANCE GROUP
Selecting white appliances with few bells and whistles usually provides the highest value. Extremely energy-efficient and quiet appliances tend to cost more initially. As the number of appliances rises, so does the cost of the necessary mechanical work.

3	4	5
U-shaped base- and wall-cabinet plan	U-shaped base- and wall-cabinet plan with raised eating counter	*Perimeter base- and wall-cabinet plan with island cabinet in center*
3-in. modular widths, midgrade carcase and drawer construction, wood frame-and-panel doors and drawer fronts, flush overlay; clear finish; full-extension slides; adjustable concealed hinges; some accessories	Custom widths, screwed plywood and fiberboard carcases, slab or frame-and-panel doors and drawer fronts, flush overlay; full-extension slides; fully adjustable concealed hinges; many accessories	Custom widths and heights, screwed plywood carcases, slab or frame-and-panel doors and drawer fronts, frameless or inset; special finishes; top-quality hardware and cabinet accessories
Solid-surface material in neutral color with 1-in.-thick square edge; 4-in.-high splash	Solid-surface material in dark color with full 1½-in. bullnose edge; 4-in.-high coved splash	*Stone, quartz, solid surface, concrete, or stainless steel with slab or tile backsplash more than 6 in. high*
10-in.-deep double bowl, drop-in or undermount; 18-ga. stainless steel or neutral-color enameled cast iron	10-in.-deep double or triple bowl, undermount; 18-ga. stainless steel or dark-color enameled cast iron	Triple bowl, commercial-type work center; undermount or apron front; 16-ga. stainless steel, any color enameled cast iron, bronze, or copper
N/A	*Bar sink, 18-ga. stainless steel or neutral-color enameled cast iron*	10-in.-deep single bowl; 18-ga. stainless steel or any color enameled cast iron
Single control, angled swivel spout with pullout spray, ceramic-disk valve, finish other than polished chrome	Single control, high-arch swivel spout with pull-down spray, washerless ceramic valve, finish other than polished chrome	Single control, very-high-arch swivel spout with pull-down adjustable spray, washerless ceramic valve; or articulated long-reach spout
Brand names in most colors: side-by-side fridge, electric or gas cooktop with ceramic or glass top, 300-cfm hood (or downdraft), convection wall oven, microwave and dishwasher with presets, ¾-hp disposal	Quiet, excellent-grade stainless-steel appliances with electronic controls: side-by-side fridge, 5-element or -burner cooktop, 600-cfm hood, double wall ovens, microwave and dishwasher with presets, quiet ¾-hp disposal	Quiet, commercial-grade stainless-steel appliances with electronic controls: 24x36 fridge, 6-burner range, double convection ovens, 1,200-cfm hood, large microwave, 2 dishwashers, 1-hp disposal
4	1	2

TOTALS

ONCE YOU'VE HIGHLIGHTED THE APPROPRIATE BOXES, you can add up the subtotals from all three charts. Chances are, all your choices haven't landed in the same project-level categories. Find the average by following the equation demonstrated below.

PROJECT LEVEL						
	1	**2**	**3**	**4**	**5**	
EXAMPLE	1	2	8	9	5	Total items 25
Total items x Project level	1 x 1 = 1	2 x 2 = 4	8 x 3 = 24	9 x 4 = 36	5 x 5 = 25	
Item values	1	4	24	36	25	Total item value 90

Divide total item value by total items: 90 ÷ 25 = 3.6

Now find the unadjusted square-footage cost in the chart below. In our example, the item-value average is 3.6, putting it at the high end of $450 to $600 per sq. ft. We'll figure $600 per sq. ft. (remember, these are San Francisco prices). Next, we make an adjustment to the cost by subtracting $75 per sq. ft. from our projection because the homeowner is using a small, two-person construction company. Our adjusted ballpark number is $525 per sq. ft., bringing our reality-check cost projection to 300 sq. ft. x $525 = $157,500.

PROJECT COST PER SQUARE FOOT					
	1	**2**	**3**	**4**	**5**
SQ.-FT. COST	**LESS THAN $300/sq. ft.**	**$300–$450/sq. ft.**	**$450–$600/sq. ft.**	**$600–$900/sq. ft.**	**$900 AND UP/sq. ft.**
ADJUSTMENTS TO COST					
Kitchens more than 300 sq. ft.	N/A	N/A	N/A	Subtract $50/sq. ft.	Subtract $100/sq. ft.
Kitchens less than 100 sq. ft.	N/A	N/A	N/A	Add $50/sq. ft.	Add $100/sq. ft.
Small crew	N/A	Subtract $50/sq. ft.	Subtract $75/sq. ft.	Subtract $100/sq. ft.	Subtract $125/sq. ft.

Pierre, SD 82%
Boston, MA 95%
San Francisco, CA 100%
Austin, TX 83%
Atlanta, GA 88%

REGIONAL COST ADJUSTMENTS

A dollar's worth of building in San Francisco would cost 82¢ in Pierre, S.D. That's according to HomeTech, an information service that keeps tabs on construction labor and material costs. You can customize your educated guess with the help of its website, www.costestimator.com. Simply key in the details of a project with San Francisco's ZIP code (94102), and print out the results. In a new browser (very important), key in the exact same project for your ZIP code. Divide the number for your area by the San Francisco estimate. The result is your regional adjustment percentage.

Rethinking Kitchen Design

BY JANE K. LANGMUIR

In 1935 a federal task force working on behalf of President Herbert Hoover set the standards used to design most kitchens. Hoover's aim was to pump some life into the depressed economy by putting American men to work building kitchens for American women. Standardized cabinets and appliances were at the core of the idea.

The result was the demise of the traditional unfitted kitchen, in which individual pieces of furniture comprised a kitchen's storage space and work surfaces. In its place, the fitted kitchen emerged, with its linear runs of built-in base and wall cabinets separating the triangle of sink, stove, and refrigerator. For decades, the only things that changed were colors, trim styles, and materials. But there are signs that era is over.

The kitchen is now the most-used room in the home. It is everyone's domain. It is the place for nurturing body, mind, and soul. It is communication and food central—ground zero for planning and scheduling, the center for social contact and information, and last but certainly not least, the workplace with the engines that prepare our meals.

Beginning in 1993, I directed a five-year study at the Rhode Island School of Design that eventually included more than 100 students and faculty members. Our goal was to identify the reasons that

kitchens are typically bastions of poor design. All too often, our kitchens make us bend, stoop, retrace our steps, and work in poor light at counters that are too high or too low. Based on what we learned in our studies and on the lessons I've learned as a designer, I offer these 10 ways to help move your kitchen into the 21st century.

A GATHERING SPACE AMID THE ACTION. Surrounded by counters of different heights, this kitchen has a breakfast table at its heart. On the far wall, a long, shallow prep sink is topped by a slatted pot rack.

1. Consider the comfort zone

For a kitchen to be your own, it has to fit your comfort zone. What's a comfort zone? It is the space defined by the comfortable reach between one hand raised above your head and the other dropped to your side (drawing below). This range applies to both sitting and standing; the key is that everybody has a different comfort zone. This means you should adjust a kitchen's components to fit its primary user.

TO THAT END, START BY:

- Getting rid of upper cabinets, or pulling out the counter a bit and bringing the cabinets down to counter level (photo on the facing page)
- Storing less essential tools, dishes, cookware, and foodstuffs in tall, pullout storage units or in pantries away from work zones. Everybody can find their comfort-zone range within either of these storage options.

FIND THE COUNTER HEIGHT THAT'S RIGHT FOR YOU

The primary work height is the height of the counter that is best for most food preparation. Calculate it by resting your palms on a horizontal surface with a slight break in your elbows. Then measure the distance from the surface to the floor.

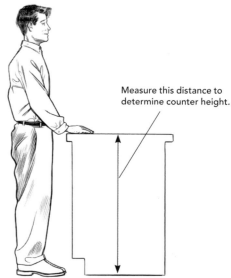

Measure this distance to determine counter height.

STORE KITCHEN SUPPLIES IN THE COMFORT ZONE

The comfort zone is the space defined by the comfortable reach between one hand raised above your head and the other dropped to your side. Use these measurements to locate storage areas for your most frequently needed supplies and utensils.

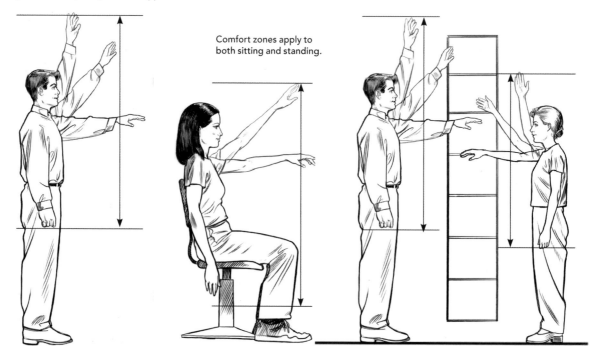

Comfort zones apply to both sitting and standing.

PUT ESSENTIALS WITHIN EASY REACH. Bringing the upper cabinets down to counter height makes it easy to grab frequently needed supplies. As a bonus, lowering the upper cabinets makes room for a row of windows. Open shelves below the cooktop provide ready access to pots and pans.

2. Who needs a 36-in.-high counter?

The standards set back in the '30s called for a 36-in. counter height. It was set to meet the ergonomic needs of the average homemaker. She was 5 ft. 4 in. to 5 ft. 5 in. tall and fully able. Today, we are designing for a much broader population range, and we need to acknowledge that everyone's needs are different. In fact, each person should have a minimum of three different counter heights for performing kitchen tasks.

First, you want to establish the primary counter height by resting the palms of your hands on a horizontal surface with a slight break in your elbows (top drawing on the facing page). Next, have someone measure the distance from the floor to the surface. This counter height is best for most prepping.

At the sink, the height of the counter should ideally be 3 in. to 5 in. higher depending on the depth of the sink. For cooking, the counter height should be 2 in. to 3 in. lower so that you can easily see in

the cooking pots and so that you can have increased reach with a utensil in hand.

3. Shrink the kitchen triangle

The triangle has been the basis for organizing the kitchen footprint since the beginning of fitted kitchens. The theory is that the work areas should be inside a triangle that connects the refrigerator, sink, and stove. This arrangement supposedly yields the most efficient work flow. But over time, this triangle connection has been undermined as kitchens have grown. Contemporary kitchens often have more counter space between the three points of the triangle. An island in the center of the kitchen will further impede traffic between the stove, the sink, and the refrigerator.

We conducted time and motion studies in our kitchen project and concluded that you can reduce by half the time taken to prepare a simple meal by eliminating unnecessary walking. The way to do this is to make sure you have the essential elements for

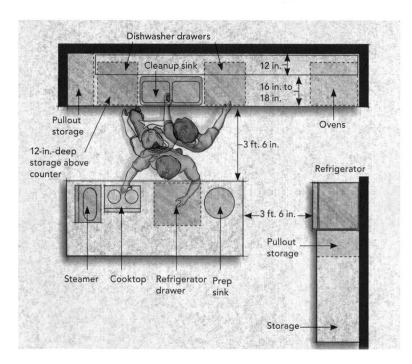

The best way to conserve time and motion in the kitchen is to have everything you need for food preparation and cleanup within easy reach. This type of plan, which has an island cooktop adjacent to a work counter with wall storage, is especially efficient when coupled with the new dishwasher and refrigerator drawers. Countertop work zones are no more than 18 in. deep. Anything deeper is hard to reach.

Diagram labels: Dishwasher drawers · Cleanup sink · 12 in. · 16 in. to 18 in. · Ovens · Pullout storage · 12-in.-deep storage above counter · Refrigerator · 3 ft. 6 in. · 3 ft. 6 in. · Pullout storage · Steamer · Cooktop · Refrigerator drawer · Prep sink · Storage

preparing a meal within reach of your work zone. Frequently used foods and condiments, water, utensils, pots, pans, and a cooktop should all be within reach. A good layout for a kitchen is an island backed up by a work and storage wall (drawing above).

4. Water, water everywhere

There is not one task in the kitchen that doesn't require water. So isn't it odd that there is usually only one sink or water source in a kitchen? For food preparation, I prefer a long, troughlike sink that isn't too deep—4 in. to 5 in. at the most (top photo on the facing page). I don't know of any commercially available sinks like this. We had the one shown here fabricated by a local metal shop out of stainless steel.

Keep in mind the cleanup sink should not be used as a holding dishwasher. Instead, consider the dishwasher as a holding sink. This usage frees the sink, or sinks, for prepping and cleaning, ready for the next task.

5. A cart offers flexibility

A cart with a work surface can serve several functions in the kitchen (bottom photo on the facing page). It can act as a ferry between two work surfaces, allowing for easy conveyance of hot, heavy pots. It can become an additional work surface when necessary.

More elaborate versions can be made with adjustable-height work surfaces, or even refrigeration or cooking capabilities.

The cart shown here serves yet another function: It has twin trash receptacles that ride on heavy-duty drawer slides. And trash/recycling/composting space in the kitchen is right up there with water in importance. When not in use, the cart should slip under a counter out of the way.

POTS AND PANS AT THE READY. Above the prep sink, a pot rack is purposefully positioned to let freshly washed cookware drain harmlessly into the sink. Pans rest on teak slats in their own cubbyholes.

A FLEXIBLE PREP SINK. Long and shallow, this custom-made stainless-steel sink is designed specifically for preparing food. Generous drain boards and a pair of chopping blocks make additional work surfaces.

6. Watch out for the doors

It would be a great boon in the kitchen if doors could disappear at the click of a switch or on the command of a voice. Alas, we are not there yet.

HOWEVER, THERE ARE SOLUTIONS TO GET RID OF THE KNEE AND SHIN BANGERS.

- If at all possible, don't place the oven below the counter. A wall oven within your comfort zone is much better.
- Raise the dishwasher 6 in. to 10 in. off the floor. This placement will save your shins and a lot of unnecessary bending.
- Eliminate all door-and-drawer combinations. You will save the doors from getting banged around and also the time it takes to accomplish two operations. Whenever possible, a drawer below counter height is a better option than a cabinet shelf.

CARTS PROVIDE STORAGE AND WORK SURFACE. A rolling workstation such as this one can expand counter space as needed or act as a truck to ferry heavy, hot pots from one part of the kitchen to another. This cart is outfitted with trash bins on heavy-duty drawer pulls at each end.

ABOVE: PULLOUT FRIDGE. Sub-Zero's refrigerator drawers let you strategically place fresh foods near kitchen work zones.

TOP RIGHT: A COMPACT DISHWASHER. A drawer full of dirty dishes will get clean if they're in Fisher-Paykel's dishwasher drawer.

BOTTOM RIGHT: A BUILT-IN STEAMER THAT'S EASY TO CLEAN. Mounted in a counter, Gaggenau's electric steamer expands a cook's options and frees up cook-top space. The steamer can be hooked up to a drain for easy cleanup.

7. Appliances that make it work

There are several great appliances that make work-ing in the kitchen a dream. They are still a bit pricey, but if you can afford them, they're worth it. And as they gain acceptance, competition will likely force down prices.

HERE ARE A JUST A FEW:

- Sub-Zero's 700 series refrigerator drawers (www. subzero-wolf.com) can be placed under the coun-ter in your work zone, bringing fresh produce to the task at hand (left photo above).
- Fisher-Paykel's drawer dishwashers (www. fisherpaykel.com) can be placed under the counter in the prep or cleanup zone. They provide easy, visible access with no bending or shin-cracking doors, and they are great as holding sinks until

you are ready to run a cycle of dishes (top right photo above).

- Two-burner cooktops and individual grills and griddles (photo on the facing page) such as Wolf's 15-in. gas cooktop (www.subzero-wolf.com), have several advantages over conventional cooktops. First, you can turn the units 90° so that you don't have to reach over hot burners. Second, you can select different fuel options, such as a high-Btu gas burner for wok cooking or an electric burner for boiling water. And third, you have the option of placing different units for different tasks wherever you like.
- Another modular appliance that can add con-venience to your kitchen is Gaggenau's built-in steamer (bottom right photo above). At approxi-mately 20 in. by 12 in., the unit takes up little space. You can cook a variety of foods in it, from rice to fish to vegetables. And it can be hooked up to a drain line for easy cleanup.

8. Use materials that combine beauty and durability

There are a number of interesting new materials flooding the marketplace, but none can beat the inherent qualities of natural materials for their efficiency, durability, sustainability and beauty.

Wood is excellent for all surfaces: counters, cabinet doors and drawers, and floors. Whether painted or left natural, it brings warmth and color. Wood can easily be refurbished and lasts a lifetime.

Stainless steel, as a countertop material, is easy to clean and nonporous, withstands hot and cold, and lasts a lifetime.

Glass panels in cabinet doors are a delight in a kitchen, especially if the cabinets include glass shelves and are lighted from within. Either transparent or translucent glass does the trick. You can see where things are, and especially in small dark places, the transparency creates lightness and brightness.

Stone makes a great counter, bringing warmth and personal color choice. One caution: It can discolor and hold stains.

Tile, whether ceramic or stone, will add color and durability to a kitchen. But try to avoid it on horizontal work surfaces, where its grout joints are hard to keep clean. Tile is best used as a backsplash or wall finish behind a sink or a stove.

9. Good kitchens need good lighting

If they have not been recently remodeled, most kitchens suffer from bad lighting. The common kitchen-lighting scheme is one light in the center of the ceiling and maybe a light over the sink. That's not enough.

THERE SHOULD BE THREE TYPES OF LIGHTING IN THE KITCHEN:

- **General ceiling lighting** provides light for passage and overall clarity.
- **Task lighting** over counter or under upper cabinets highlights specific work zones.
- **Mood lighting** changes the kitchen from a workplace to a place for meals, from simple suppers to fine dining or a social gathering.

   These uses can all be achieved by recessed lights or by a combination of recessed, surface-mount, pendant, cable, or track lighting. Each type of lighting should be switched separately with light levels controlled by dimmer switches.

10. The kitchen window isn't what it used to be

A window centered over the kitchen sink is fine, but it isn't the driving design force that it once was. The new window view is the kitchen itself (photo on p. 87) and all that is going on: the kids eating or playing, friends or family helping, guests relaxing or just enjoying the layers of light and complexity from the other windows within sight. Use this concept to create places within the kitchen that people want to occupy.

A COOKING WALL. Modular burners can be arranged in the traditional front/back relationship, or turned sideways to make a cooktop that is one burner deep.

Opening Up a Small Kitchen

BY JERRI HOLAN

Remodeling a small kitchen without adding square footage can be frustrating: too many tasks to fit into a limited space. However, a small kitchen can function well and include interesting elements if you open the kitchen to larger spaces and keep the layout simple.

Make it feel spacious

The first step toward making a small kitchen feel larger and more open is to improve its relationship with any adjoining rooms and outside spaces.

A kitchen surrounded by four solid walls can feel downright claustrophobic. To improve the space, you can open the walls between the kitchen and any supporting rooms, such as a dining room, a breakfast nook, or a family room. By opening the wall and allowing the sight lines to expand beyond the kitchen, you create the perception of more space without the cost of creating more square footage.

Depending on the circumstances, the wall might be removed entirely or be replaced with a peninsula countertop, a high counter, or a half-wall. Even a simple pass-through window helps if other options are not feasible.

A popular solution when space is at a premium is a peninsula that serves both the kitchen and an adjacent space. This allows open sight lines between the two rooms and adds counter space and storage on both sides.

A separate high counter above a transitional counter requires more space but replaces a table in a highly efficient manner. If the high counter will be a breakfast bar for morning coffee, it should be 12 in. to 15 in. wide. Bump the width to 18 in. to 24 in. if it will be the place for all your informal meals. (A counter-height peninsula can be used as a primary eating area by adding 6 in. to 12 in. to the typical 24-in. counter depth.)

Regardless of depth, make sure it's long enough for the number of people using it. Each person should have at least 24 in. of space, although 30 in. will be more comfortable.

Pay attention to the transition

Once the kitchen is opened up, you can detail the opening depending on how you wish to treat the transition from the kitchen to the adjoining space. If you remove a wall to connect the kitchen with another room, part of the enlarged space can be dedicated to food preparation and part to eating, socializing, reading, or watching TV (depending on whether the kitchen now adjoins a dining area, a living area, or a family room). A design element at the ceiling—an arch, a beam, a series of lights, a

REMOVE WALLS TO IMPROVE SIGHT LINES

THIS SMALL KITCHEN HAD TOO MANY DOORS, a dysfunctional range area, and a pantry that was too deep to be usable. Removing the wall between the kitchen and the dining room was the best way to enlarge the kitchen without adding space.

With an archway and a half-wall separating the kitchen from the dining area, the two rooms are perceived as one large room, greatly improving the relationship between the spaces. The high counter serves as a staging area for formal dinners and as an informal place to hang out at other times, keeping diners out of the small kitchen while still encouraging them to converse with the cook.

An additional window over the sink and open archways instead of doors enhance the spacious feeling. Using a smaller range made room for counter space on each side of the stovetop and a safer, more comfortable cooking arrangement.

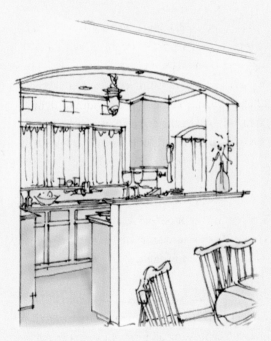

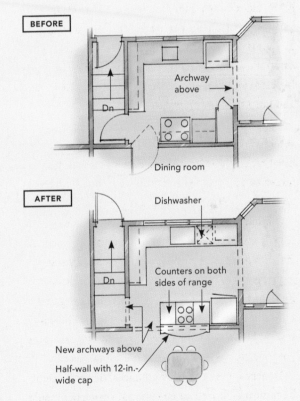

BEFORE

Archway above

Dn

Dining room

AFTER

Dishwasher

Dn

Counters on both sides of range

New archways above

Half-wall with 12-in.-wide cap

change in ceiling height—can define the two areas as effectively as a peninsula. An overhead element such as an arch above a transition counter helps to link the two spaces by repeating elements in one or both of the rooms.

Sometimes drawing a distinction between the two spaces with a half-wall makes sense. Extending 8 in. to 12 in. higher than the countertop, a half-wall screens the kitchen counter without taking up as much floor space as an eating counter (drawing on p. 95). To display vases of flowers, the half-wall's cap should be between 8 in. and 12 in. wide; to hold serving plates, plan on 10 in. to 12 in. Remember that the cap is a transitional element, so the material, the shape, and the style should relate to both spaces.

Add natural light

Take advantage of exterior walls by adding windows and doors. When you can see the landscaping, it becomes part of your kitchen. If a garden or yard borders the kitchen, add a French door or two to allow access and big views.

If a door isn't possible, add as many windows as you can. When exterior-wall space is limited and you have to choose between an extra upper cabinet and a window, choose the window. Corner windows

DIRECT FOOT TRAFFIC AWAY FROM WORK AREAS

THIS SMALL KITCHEN suffered from too many circulation routes, which disrupted its three main activity areas. Also, the dining room was rarely used.

The solution was to combine the two rooms into one spacious family room/kitchen that suits an informal lifestyle. The large new peninsula counter defines the main circulation route to the new deck, and it separates and marks the transition between family-room and kitchen activities. Opening the rear wall with a gang of windows and French doors incorporates the backyard. A cozy corner fireplace enhances both kitchen and family-room functions.

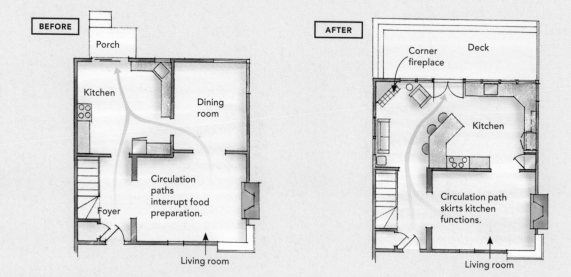

are especially effective for opening views and outside relationships. Even if there's no view, a translucent or stained-glass window can brighten the space with natural light and lend an airy feeling to a tight room.

Simplify the space

Maximize kitchen square footage by relocating functions not directly related to preparing and eating meals. The more regular or square a kitchen's floor plan, the more functional its space will be. For example, many older homes have laundry areas or closets between the kitchen and the backyard ("before" floor plan below). Moving the laundry to a small closet adds space and reduces traffic through the kitchen while gaining an exterior wall for windows and doors.

Make sure circulation patterns through the kitchen aren't disruptive. This might mean eliminating some doorways and relocating others. If you must have multiple doorways in the kitchen, try to group them in one area to confine circulation to one or two routes. For example, relocate a back door next to the dining-room door to consolidate foot traffic. Rooms that aren't related to the kitchen shouldn't connect to the kitchen.

TAKE ADVANTAGE OF EXTERIOR WALLS

THIS SMALL KITCHEN had little natural light, an awkward circulation path to the deck, and a laundry room with great garden views. Not only did the kitchen lack counter space, but the home also lacked a dining area.

By relocating the washer and dryer upstairs, a dining room could occupy the desirable space overlooking the backyard. Three new windows and a pair of French doors complete the outdoor connection. The guest-room door was relocated, and continuous counters were installed for a functional, yet compact, kitchen.

The small peninsula's extra depth serves as a coffee counter in the morning and as a preparation/staging area for large dinners.

BEFORE

Deck

Laundry room

Guest room

Kitchen

Living room

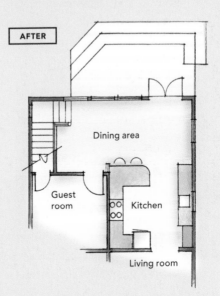

AFTER

Dining area

Guest room

Kitchen

Living room

The Energy-Smart Kitchen

BY ALEX WILSON

When it comes to electricity consumption, the kitchen is the hungriest room in the house. Kitchen appliances—including refrigerators, freezers, ranges, and dishwashers—account for nearly 27% of household electricity use. Collectively, that's more than 300 billion kilowatt hours (kwh) per year in the United States, or roughly the electricity output of 90 average-size coal-fired power plants.

Not all appliances are equally voracious, however. Refrigerators and freezers account for nearly two-thirds of kitchen energy use, with ranges, ovens, and cooktops accounting for a little over one-quarter, and dishwashers the rest. Add in the heating, air-conditioning, hot water, and lighting used in a kitchen, and this room is clearly the energy hog of most houses. Putting your kitchen on an energy diet might be one of the best things you can do to save money and resources. Like most diets, it all comes down to making informed choices.

Refrigerators are the top energy guzzlers

In a typical American home, the refrigerator accounts for about 15% of total electricity use. Assuming heat and hot water are not electric, that makes the refrigerator a home's single largest electricity consumer.

This is the case even though refrigerators have improved dramatically since the mid-1970s; today's models use about a third as much power as those from 35 years ago.

Refrigerators: style and use determine efficiency

WHAT TO AVOID:

- **Through-the-door ice and water dispensers.** Both the lost insulation and the additional cooling coils in a through-the-door ice and water dispenser increase electricity consumption.
- **Automatic ice makers.** Ice makers consume energy, although exactly how much is difficult to determine.

WHAT TO LOOK FOR:

- **The Energy Star label.** The U.S. Environmental Protection Agency confers its Energy Star label on models that are at least 20% more energy efficient than the federal minimum. Shopping for this label is an easy way to be sure the refrigerator you choose is not an energy waster.
- **Freezers on top or bottom.** Side-by-side refrigerators use more energy.
- **Manual defrost cycles.** The most energy-efficient refrigerators and freezers have manual defrost,

FRUGAL FEATURES. The most popular features with consumers—such as automatic defrosting and through-the-door ice and water dispensers—are not always the most energy efficient. Still, Maytag®'s Ice$_2$O® refrigerator meets Energy Star requirements and is equipped with two potentially energy-saving features: an alarm that alerts homeowners to a refrigerator door left ajar, and a vacation mode that saves energy by limiting automatic defrosting when the fridge isn't opened for several days.

WHERE DOES THE ENERGY GO?

KITCHEN APPLIANCES on average account for more than a quarter of household electricity use, and the appliances we use to keep food cold—refrigerators and stand-alone freezers—together are the biggest consumers. Ovens, coffeemakers, and cooktops, as a group, are the second-hungriest appliances in the kitchen, followed by dishwashers.

10%

26%

64%

TWO TOOLS TO MEASURE ENERGY EFFICIENCY

THE BLUE ENERGY STAR LABEL and the yellow EnergyGuide sticker help consumers identify energy-efficient appliances. Energy Star labeling denotes compliance with guidelines set by the U.S. Environmental Protection Agency and the U.S. Department of Energy. Appliances rated by the program include dishwashers, refrigerators, and freezers (but not cooking appliances). Although Energy Star compliance indicates an energy-efficient appliance, some models exceed the requirements more

than others (see www.energystar.gov). Unlike the voluntary Energy Star program, the EnergyGuide label is required by the Federal Trade Commission on all fridges, freezers, and dishwashers (but not on cooking appliances). The label shows the model's capacity, its estimated annual energy consumption and operating costs, and a scale that compares its efficiency to that of similar models. The Energy-Guide label helps in comparison shopping but does not indicate Energy Star compliance.

INNOVATIONS TO WATCH FOR

VACUUM-PANEL INSULATION

Thermos bottles keep coffee hot because most of the air molecules in the double wall have been removed, keeping conductive heat transfer very low. The same idea has been incorporated into flat vacuum panels. Back in the mid-1990s, Whirlpool® produced high-efficiency refrigerators that used inch-thick vacuum panels made by Owens Corning®, which had center-of-panel insulating values of R-75. The technology hasn't completely caught on, but it's currently used by KitchenAid®, a Whirlpool brand. Silica-aerogel insulation is another material that could find its way into refrigerators; it insulates better than the polyurethane foam used in most models.

VARIABLE-SPEED COMPRESSORS

Compressors account for 83% of a refrigerator's energy use, so an efficient compressor means an efficient refrigerator. Variable-speed compressors save energy by operating at low speed during low-usage periods (such as overnight) and then running faster during periods of high usage. Still mostly limited to European brands and professional-style built-ins, variable-speed compressors are used in some GE® Profile™ and Monogram® products, as well as Whirlpool's high-end built-in lines. Other manufacturers may soon follow suit.

---

a heat source, provide space for air circulation.

- **Clean the coils,** at least annually. Dust and dirt buildup on refrigerator/freezer coils reduces the heat-exchange efficiency and makes the compressor work harder. Most refrigerators now have coils that can be accessed from the front, eliminating the need to pull the unit away from the wall.

- **Turn off the condensation-control feature.** Essentially, these are heating elements under the protective shell that consume energy in two ways: by using electricity to warm the outer shell and by increasing the difference in temperature across the unit's insulation. Models with this feature usually have a switch to turn it off; do so, unless condensation becomes a problem.

- **Keep the freezer full.** Frozen food serves as a thermal stabilizer that reduces the amount of on-off cycling. If you don't have a lot of frozen food, freeze containers of water (use plastic, and allow for expansion as the water freezes) to take up the extra space. When you need ice for a cooler, you can use these frozen containers.

- **Don't keep an extra fridge in the garage.** When you buy a new refrigerator, avoid the costly mistake of keeping the old one as a backup.

Cooking options pit efficiency against cost

More efficient cooking saves energy and money directly, of course, but by keeping waste heat out of the kitchen, it also saves on air-conditioning. Although this impact might not be huge in a typical home, it can make a difference. As a rule, electric cooking appliances are more efficient than gas-fueled ones. But the relative price of natural gas versus electricity often makes natural-gas-fueled appliances a more economical choice. Gas cooktops also afford better heat control than their electric counterparts.

Because their functions are so different, it's important to consider cooktops and ovens separately, even though they might be combined in a stand-alone kitchen range.

---

although they can be hard to find, particularly among high-end models.

- **Door alarms.** Some manufacturers offer an alarm that will sound if the fridge door is left open—helping to save energy and to prevent food spoilage.

MAINTAINING HIGH PERFORMANCE:

- **Place fridges away from heat sources**—especially a range or oven but also a dishwasher. Radiant heat from these appliances warms the surface of the fridge, requiring more energy to keep the inside cool. If the refrigerator must be adjacent to

INDUCTION
Energy factor: 0.84

RADIANT
Energy factor: 0.742

ELECTRIC COIL
Energy factor: 0.737

GAS, NO PILOT Energy factor: 0.399
GAS, PILOT Energy factor: 0.156

Gas ovens draw electricity, too

With ovens, rapid heat-up and cool-down aren't as important as with cooktops, making electric ovens more competitive with gas, even for serious cooks. In fact, it is not uncommon for high-end ranges to have a gas cooktop and an electric oven. Again, electric models are more efficient: Electric ovens are 1.8 to 3.5 times as efficient as gas ovens, according to U.S. Department of Energy (DOE) data. Cost efficiency, however, largely depends on which type of fuel costs the least in your area.

Most gas ovens also use a lot of electricity while operating. In nearly all gas ovens today, when the gas burner is operating, an electric glow-bar igniter (sometimes called a "gas oven igniter") is on, drawing about 375w. Found in many self-cleaning models, the glow bar ignites the gas when the oven is turned on and reignites it as it cycles off and on during the cooking or self-cleaning process. Those 375w (or even as much as 500w in some ovens) are a significant amount of electricity. If low electricity use is a priority in your home, consider a model without a glow bar, such as ranges made by the Peerless-Premier Appliance Co. (www.premierrange.com), which operate with a pilot or a spark ignition.

Cooktops and ovens: Electric wins over gas

Cooktop efficiency is difficult to measure, and relatively little attention has been paid to it, primarily because stovetop cooking accounts for a small percentage of household energy use—about 5%, according to the American Council for an Energy Efficient Economy. My research shows that electric cooktops are the most efficient and gas the worst. Above are ranked the most common cooktop technologies in order of efficiency based on the energy factor, which is the ratio of the amount of energy conveyed to an item being heated to the device's overall energy consumption. Expressed as a decimal, it reflects the proportion of energy used that actually contributes to the cooking of food.

ELECTRIC COOKTOPS

Induction. Although induction technology initially failed to take off when introduced a decade or so ago, it's back, with more high-end induction cooktops entering the market. On an induction cooktop, electrical energy is transferred directly to ferrous-metal cookware through magnetic induction. Efficiency is the highest of any cooktop (about 84%) because the cookware is heated directly. It's also a safer way to cook: The cooking surface does not heat up, enabling photos like the one at top left, where water boils in a cutaway pan while ice cubes rest intact on the "burner's" surface. Induction cooktops also heat up and cool down quickly, providing precise controllability. Downsides include high cost and the fact that only certain cookware can be used. Cast-iron, enameled cast-iron, and some stainless-steel cookware work. Test yours to make sure a magnet sticks to it, or look for a label.

Radiant ceramic. The most common mid- to high-end electric cooktop today, it has relatively fast-heating radiant elements under ceramic glass, providing a sleek, easy-to-clean stovetop surface. Flat-bottom cookware is needed for good surface contact; older-style cast-iron pans are not recommended because burrs on the metal can scratch the glass surface. Radiant-ceramic cooktops heat faster than electric coils and are nearly equal in energy efficiency.

Electric coil. Available on low-cost ranges and cooktops, these old-fashioned open-coil elements are slow to heat up and difficult to clean but fairly efficient at transferring electric energy to the pot.

GAS (NATURAL OR PROPANE) COOKTOPS

Cooks prefer gas burners for speed and controllability, but indoor-air-quality experts often recommend against gas for health reasons. Although gas cooktops rate worst in terms of energy efficiency, they are usually more cost-efficient because the price of natural gas is typically a lot lower than electricity. Gas cooktops use only about 40% of the energy produced, and if there's a continuously burning pilot light, the overall efficiency is far lower (about 16%).

In some areas, propane is nearly as expensive as electricity per unit of delivered energy, making electric cooktops a more economical option. The efficiency of natural gas and propane is essentially the same.

Microwave ovens are tops in efficiency

First introduced as a practical kitchen appliance in 1965, microwave ovens have revolutionized cooking and offer substantial energy savings over standard ovens. They work by producing nonionizing microwave radiation (a certain frequency of radio waves) with a magnetron and directing that radiation at the food. The microwave radiation is absorbed by water, fats, and sugars, producing heat. Because the microwaves penetrate the food, heating is more rapid and requires less energy than in a conventional oven. Microwave ovens are about 5 times as energy efficient as standard electric ovens and more than 10 times as energy efficient as gas ovens.

OVEN EFFICIENCY

OVEN EFFICIENCY BY TYPE	
OVEN TYPE	**ENERGY FACTOR**
MICROWAVE	0.557
ELECTRIC (SELF-CLEANING)	0.138
ELECTRIC (STANDARD)	0.122
GAS (SELF-CLEANING)	0.054
GAS (STANDARD)	0.030

ADDITIONAL INSULATION
Self-cleaning ovens typically have more insulation than standard ovens, so if you have a choice, go for a self-cleaning model. The extra insulation keeps the outer surface of the range from becoming too hot during the self-cleaning cycle, but it also helps the oven to operate more efficiently.

A FAN
Convection ovens have a fan in the back that circulates air to maintain more even temperatures. As a result, either the cooking time or the temperature can be reduced. The energy savings from reduced gas or electricity use for cooking easily outweigh the fan's electricity use.

Increasingly, manufacturers are combining cooking functions with microwave ovens to produce a new generation of "rapid-cook" appliances. These models combine microwaves with electric grilling elements so that food can be browned as well as cooked. Quartz elements are often used to create radiant heat, though General Electric's Advantium® microwave oven (www.geappliances.com) uses a halogen-lamp element. Convection is another feature offered by the Advantium and some others, such as TurboChef®'s Speedcook Oven (www.turbochef.com). In the future, most ovens likely will include multiple heating options to speed up cooking and to serve a wider range of functions, from defrosting to reheating to grilling.

Exhaust fans are important to health

Exhaust fans add to energy consumption, but their importance with regard to kitchen air quality—and the health of your home's occupants—cannot be ignored. Chemical impurities in natural gas, along with incomplete combustion, can result in dangerous levels of carbon monoxide (CO), causing headaches and fatigue at low levels and, at high concentrations, death. Because of this concern, gas ranges should be installed with quality, outdoor-venting range-hood fans, which should be operated when the cooktop or oven is on.

Exhaust fans are most efficient when placed above the cooktop or range. Downdraft fans, which are installed at the back or in the center of a range, rely on significant airflow (and power consumption) to ventilate cooking fumes effectively. Because fumes are more easily channeled into a fan installed in a range hood, fan performance is better.

If you can't vent an exhaust fan outdoors, avoid the use of gas cooking appliances. Recirculating range-hood fans can remove odors but should not be relied on to remove combustion gases.

A significant energy-saving feature to look for in a range-hood exhaust fan is a variable-speed motor. This allows the fan to operate at a lower airflow rate

DRAWERFUL OF SAV-INGS. Compact dishwasher drawers can be highly efficient (both of these models from New Zealand manufacturer Fisher & Paykel are Energy Star compliant). An added bonus is that the integrated models, like the one pictured above, blend seamlessly into kitchen cabinetry.

when full ventilation capacity is not needed, thus saving energy and reducing noise.

Dishwashers are shaping up

Dishwashers have changed quite a bit in recent years. They use a lot less water, which translates into lower energy use for water heating. In 1978, water use by dishwashers ranged from 11 gal. to 15 gal. for a normal dishwashing cycle. By 2000, that usage had dropped to 6 gal. to 10 gal.

As water use has gone down, total energy use has also dropped, while the proportion of energy use for processes other than water heating has risen.

In 1978, 83% of the total energy use for dishwasher operation was for heating water; 10% was for motor operations; and 7% for drying. By 1994, energy use for water heating had dropped to 56%, according to a 2003 Virginia Tech report.

However, that does not mean most dishwashers are as energy efficient as they could be. Nearly all dishwashers today have booster heaters that increase the temperature of incoming water to about 140°F to improve wash performance. An integral electric element provides this heat, and it can use a lot of electricity. Recent independent testing shows that booster heaters operate throughout the dishwashing cycle, resulting in total electricity use per cycle of 2.0 to 3.5 kwh. Used an average of 215 times per year (the frequency DOE assumes), a dishwasher could easily consume more electricity annually than a refrigerator. More research is needed to determine the significance of this electricity use.

Dishwashers vary considerably in their energy use, much more so than refrigerators. For comparison, dishwashers are rated by the federal government according to their energy factor (EF), a measurement based on the energy usage for an average number of cycles (a completely different formula than the one used to rate cooking appliances). The higher the EF, the more efficient the dishwasher: The current federal standard mandates a minimum EF of 0.46; Energy Star dishwashers must meet a minimum EF of 0.65. The most-efficient dishwashers have an EF that approaches or slightly exceeds 1.0. Although the EF is used to compute the annual energy consumption and cost estimates found on the EnergyGuide label on many appliances, the EF itself might not appear there.

Dishwashers: less hot water equals less energy use

WHAT TO LOOK FOR:

- **The Energy Star label.** Energy Star-qualified dishwashers are at least 41% more energy efficient than the federal minimum. Keep in mind that some

TOP PERFORMERS. The Bosch Evolution line includes dishwashers that exceed the minimum federal energy-efficiency standard by 147%—far more than any American-made dishwasher—using approximately the same amount of energy as a dishwasher half its size.

A NEW WAY TO CLEAN DISHES. The LG SteamDishwasher™ uses only 2.8 gal. to 3.2 gal. of water in an average load.

EASY BUTTON. The "EcoAction®" button offered on some Bosch dishwashers allows homeowners to reduce energy usage by up to 25%. Activating the feature lowers the wash temperature and extends the cycle by a few minutes.

models exceed the standard significantly more than others; check the EnergyGuide label or the list of qualifying dishwashers at www.energystar.gov for high-performing machines.

- **Soil sensing.** With this technology, "fuzzy logic" is used to determine how dirty the dishes are. Water use and wash cycle are adjusted accordingly, saving significant water and energy.
- **No-heat drying.** Most dishwashers have an electric heating element and fan for drying dishes. Make sure the one you buy has a no-heat drying option, which can save a significant amount of energy.

USAGE TIPS:

- **Insulate hot-water pipes** from the water heater so that water stays hot all the way to the dishwasher and doesn't cool off as much between the different wash and rinse cycles.
- **Wash full loads only,** even if it means waiting a day or two.
- **Avoid high-temperature cycles.** Many dishwashers have a setting for more intensive cleaning in which the temperature is boosted, which can significantly increase electricity use per cycle. To conserve energy, don't use this setting.

INNOVATIONS TO WATCH FOR

STEAM-CYCLE DISHWASHERS
LG has introduced a steam-cycle dishwasher that the company claims cleans dishes better. The washing cycle uses steam higher than 200°F, apparently saving energy in the process because it uses a lot less water. You can choose different wash intensities for the bottom and top racks or a half-load option that cleans the top or bottom rack only.

DRAWER DISHWASHERS
The New Zealand company Fisher & Paykel and KitchenAid both offer drawer-type dishwashers.

They can save energy and water by allowing you to use one smaller drawer rather than a partially loaded full-size dishwasher, or by allowing two drawers to be operated at different cycles.

CONDENSATION DRYING
While most dishwashers vent moist air into the kitchen as dishes are drying, Bosch models use condensation-drying technology, which the company claims improves hygiene and saves energy.

Stay Inside the Lines

BY CHARLES MILLER

AFTER

The three transformed baths featured here show how radically a little room can be changed within the same footprint.

A bath sheds its claustrophobic character

Question: What do the words "polished," "open," and "W Hotel" have in common? **Answer:** They were all on the list of aesthetic criteria that Terilynn Perez used to describe what she wanted in her remodeled bath. Rounding out the list were "modern," "light," and "unique." A glance at the "before" photo explains the inspiration for this list. Architect Eric Dumican had one other criterion to consider as he pondered potential solutions: Don't move any walls. And oh yes, given the bath's location inside the house, windows weren't an option.

Dumican's plan for the new bath kept all the fixtures and walls in the same place, with an operable skylight over the shower funneling daylight into the room. The central lavatory space is flanked by translucent sliding doors; one leads to the shower room and the other to a walk-in closet. Made of 1-in.-

BEFORE

thick acrylic panels, the doors are sandblasted on one side. When closed, the shower-side door is a luminous plank that lights up the serene blue walls.

Methodical and orderly, rectilinear details such as the square glass tiles in the shower, the inset tile baseboards, and the powder-coated steel vanity bring polish, light, and a modern touch to this recast

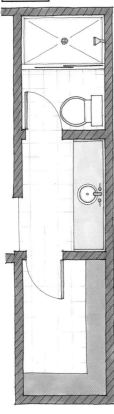

BEFORE

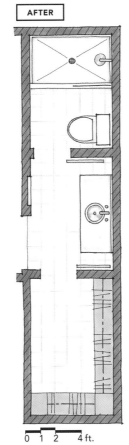

AFTER

0 1 2   4 ft.

SOURCES

PLUMBING FIXTURES
Showerhead: Taboret®, polished chrome
Shower control: Purist®, polished chrome
Toilet: Rialto®
Sink: Bolero® Round, mirror finish
Faucet: Triton widespread base with gooseneck spout, polished chrome, all fixtures by Kohler (www.us.kohler.com)

FINISHES
Paint: Benjamin Moore (www.benjaminmoore.com), Blue Seafoam
Floor/base tile: Walker Zanger (www.walkerzanger.com), D-Line, 12-in. by 12-in. ceramic, Standard White
Wall tile: Walker Zanger, Fusion, 1¼-in. by 1¼-in. glass, Mosaic Pearl

SKYLIGHT
Velux® (www.velux.com), manual operating

ROLLING DOOR
1-in. acrylic panel, sandblasted on one side only, with McMaster-Carr® I-Beam Roller Track Set (www.mcmaster.com)

DESIGN
Eric Dumican, principal; Dumican Mosey Architects, San Francisco, Calif. (www.dumicanmosey.com)

BUILDER
Abela Construction, San Jose, Calif.

COOL SLATE, WARM WOOD
Foggy-gray tile and stone are the backdrop for a splendid Douglas-fir cabinet.

AFTER

BEFORE

bath. Unlike the original blocky base cabinet, the new vanity floats above the floor, its shape echoed by the soffit above.

A tile and stone setting for a splendid cabinet

"Give it the spirit of Japanese architecture, but don't create a literal copy." That's the essence of what Wayne Lovegrove's clients requested when describing how they wanted to transform their master bath. With its sloped ceiling, generous skylight, and view of an evergreen forest, the original bath had plenty of attributes. But style and substance were not among them. The existing economy-grade materials, too-low counter, and fixtures were to be completely

replaced. To maximize investment in quality design and materials, there would be no structural or plumbing location changes.

Lovegrove's design began with the subtle organizational underpinnings that characterize traditional Japanese homes. The floor is a grid of custom-cut slate tiles centered on both the sink and the toilet. The cabinet, made of vertical-grain Douglas fir, features doors and drawers with delicate reveals between rails, stiles, and panels. The counter, raised now to a comfortable height, steps down to become the windowsill. It is a schist slab, double thick at the edges for a sense of solidity. The new bath captures the calm richness of traditional Japanese architecture without having an overt Japanese style.

THE DESIGN IS IN THE DETAILS
A shower niche that echoes the floor's grid pattern and the delicate reveals of the wood drawers show the craftsmanship that went into this remodel.

SOURCES

PLUMBING FIXTURES
Toilet: Toto® UltraMax® (www.totousa.com)
Faucet: Arwa Twin (www.arwa.ch)

WALL AND SHOWER TILE
Casalgrande Pietre Native Blue Moon series (www.casalgrandepadana.com) Decorative tiles distinguished as Decori Assortiti

DOOR AND DRAWER PULLS
Whitechapel 58CABAR5 (www.whitechapel-ltd.com)

LIGHT FIXTURE
Minka-Lavery® (www.minka.com)

DESIGN
Wayne Lovegrove, Lovegrove Design, Kenmore, Wash. (www.wlovegrovedesign.com)

BUILDER
Cieplik Brothers Construction, Tacoma, Wash.

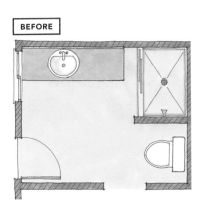

BEFORE

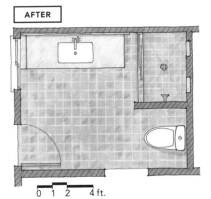

AFTER

0 1 2   4 ft.

AFTER

A bath opens up

The owners had two goals in mind when they decided to upgrade the guest bath in their 1970s ranch house. First, they wanted to lose the dated vinyl flooring, glowing fluorescent valance, and cheesy yellow tile, and fashion a bath more in keeping with their collection of Mission-style furniture. And second, they wanted a tub that made it easier to bathe the grandchildren.

Designed by Anthony Anderson of MAK Design+Build, the new bath makes the most of its modest 55 sq. ft. Anderson fixed the bathtub problem with an extra deep, drop-in tub detailed with a curb that makes a comfortable place for a grandparent to sit or lean. The tub is deep enough for the kids to splash around in a bubble bath without inundating the surrounding area. And the hinged glass splash guard swings out of the way, making access to the tub controls a lot easier than with the original sliding doors.

Instead of the chunky base cabinet in the old bath, the lavatory now sits atop a console-style quarter-sawn-oak cabinet reminiscent of a Mission-style table or desk. The custom oak-framed mirror, with raised plugs at the corners, completes the composition.

MISSION MODERN
A remodeled bath opens up with longer sight lines and calm, uncluttered finishes.

BEFORE

BEFORE

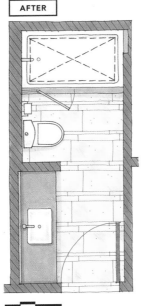

AFTER

0 1 2   4 ft.

SOURCES

PLUMBING FIXTURES
Toilet: Toto Aquia®
Shower/tub mixer and faucet:
Jado IQ (www.jadousa.com)
Soaking tub: Hydrosystems Lacey
(60 in. by 36 in.
(www.hydrosystem.com)
Sink: Kohler DemiLav®
Wading Pool®
Faucet: Kohler Purist K-14402-4

FINISHES
CaesarStone® Countertop in
Raven (www.caesarstoneus.com)
Roca Avila Tile by Laufen in Gris,
Alga, and Marron on walls; Arena
on floor (www.us.laufen.com)

HARDWARE AND LIGHTING
Hubbardton Forge®
(www.hubbardtonforge.com)

DESIGN
Anthony Anderson

BUILDER
MAK Design+Build, Davis, Calif.
(www.makdesignbuild.com)

Designing Showers for Small Bathrooms

BY BRIDGET E. CAHILL

As a bathroom designer on Cape Cod, I have plenty of opportunities to design generously sized master bathrooms in new homes without strict budgetary constraints or space limitations. More frequently, however, I'm asked to update an older bathroom to create a more comfortable and appealing space within the existing footprint. On these renovation projects, bathroom dimensions of 5 ft. by 8 ft. and 6 ft. by 9 ft. are common.

Skip the tub

To configure a full, modern bathroom in a footprint of this size, I try to get as much usable area into the shower as possible without compromising the rest of the floor plan. The best way to maximize shower space in a small bathroom is to use a tiled shower that can be customized to the available space.

Sometimes it makes sense to save money by using an acrylic or fiberglass shower unit. These drop-in units offer more showering space than a tub/shower combo and can fit in a 5-ft. by 8-ft. or a 6-ft. by 9-ft. bathroom. However, they can consume more floor space than a tiled shower, are available only in stock sizes, aren't as durable as tile, and don't offer the design options of tile.

The bathroom becomes the shower

A curbless shower—one without a threshold, door, or curtain—allows for the largest showering space within the standard bathroom footprints found in older homes. This type of shower is separated from the rest of the room visually rather than structurally. The continuous floor surface offers accessibility that will help homeowners to age in place (drawing on facing page).

While I believe this design can offer the most visual appeal, it is likely to be the most expensive option. Instead of using a shower pan, a curbless shower relies on a full mortar bed that pitches the bathroom floor toward a drain to ensure adequate drainage.

As there are no curbs or enclosures to keep water inside the shower, the bathroom becomes a wet room. The walls, then, need to be protected with at least a tile wainscot. I've found that shelving and storage compartments of acrylic, glass, or stainless steel are good alternatives to wood, which can deteriorate because of excessive moisture. Use a porcelain pedestal sink rather than a vanity, and store towels and toilet paper away from the shower area.

I usually place a built-in bench in the shower. If the shower isn't greater than 48 in. long, a bench opposite the showerhead allows you to sit in the spray. Corner benches save space, and they can serve as footrests for shaving and as storage for soaps and shampoos (drawing below). When there are two opposing showerheads, a bench centered along the wall in between is another option (right drawing on p. 114).

Walls add a sense of privacy

As trendy and appealing as a curbless shower might seem, not everyone is comfortable showering out in the open. If someone wants a greater sense of enclosure, I recommend a curbed shower.

By varying the wall heights and the materials, it's easy to change the degree of enclosure and the amount of light in a curbed shower. Properly designed, a curbed shower might not require a door (left drawing on p. 114). The curb defines the drainage area of the shower, and the walls or half-walls contain water spray. Although in very tight rooms I have designed curbed showers as small as 32 in. wide, I recommend a minimum width of 36 in. Bumping up the width to 42 in. or 48 in. provides a roomy feel without losing the sense of enclosure.

Full-height tiled walls offer the most privacy, but they restrict the usable area. A tiled wall uses up at least 5¼ in. of shower area, something to consider if showering space is limited. A tiled kneewall with an attached glass wall above allows more elbow room and lets in more light than a full-height tiled wall. A 36-in. or taller kneewall can sometimes function without an attached glass wall, increasing openness and airflow in the shower. A custom-made, full glass

CURBLESS SHOWER

DISPENSING WITH A TYPICAL SHOWER ENCLOSURE and sloping the floor to direct water to the drain creates a bathroom with clean, modern lines that can be made accessible. In the bathroom shown here, the shower area is located as far from the room entrance as possible. Placement of the sink and the toilet is crucial. If fixtures are less than 12 in. from the shower's spray area or if you want to keep an area dry, tempered-glass splash walls can shield fixtures as well as doorways from spraying water. A splash wall needs to be only as high as the showerhead and as deep as the fixture it's protecting. I try to keep the splash wall a minimum of 16 in. from the centerline of the toilet and at least 3 in. from the edge of a sink. Near doorways, I make the splash wall as deep as the door is wide.

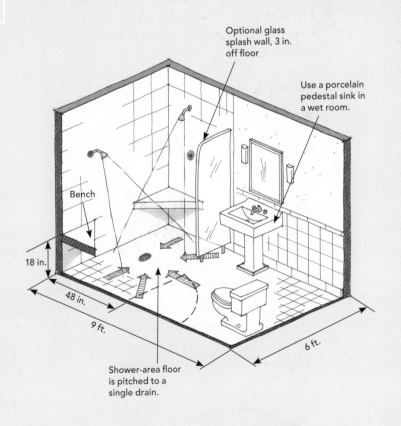

Optional glass splash wall, 3 in. off floor

Use a porcelain pedestal sink in a wet room.

Bench

18 in.

48 in.

9 ft.

6 ft.

Shower-area floor is pitched to a single drain.

KNEEWALLS, CURBS, AND GLASS KEEP WATER IN

CURBED SHOWERS allow a great deal of flexibility with the type and height of the walls and the number of showerheads. With a single showerhead, the shower doesn't require a door if the opening is out of the spray area (left drawing below). The shower isn't barrier free, however. To keep water in the shower, a curb approximately 5½ in. to 6 in. high runs across the 24-in.-wide opening. Plumbing the shower control next to the entrance lets you adjust the temperature before entering the shower spray. Controls are usually 48 in. off the floor, but 42 in.

is fine on the 48-in.-tall kneewall I'd use here. Glass panels above the kneewall contain deflected water but might not be necessary.

Multiple showerheads (right drawing below) typically require that mixing valves be plumbed on the same wall as the showerhead. Because of the extensive spray coverage, a shower door is a must. In this case, a 36-in.-tall kneewall with glass panels above maximizes light. For comfort, the bench should be at least 12 in. deep and have room underneath for feet.

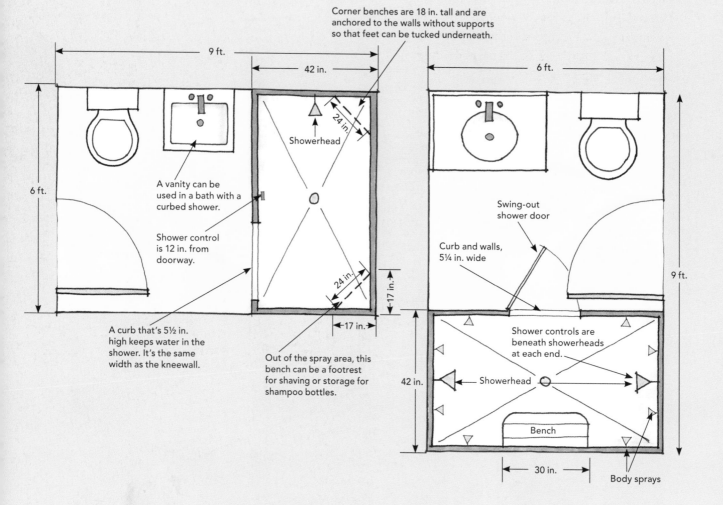

Corner benches are 18 in. tall and are anchored to the walls without supports so that feet can be tucked underneath.

A vanity can be used in a bath with a curbed shower.

Shower control is 12 in. from doorway.

Showerhead

A curb that's 5½ in. high keeps water in the shower. It's the same width as the kneewall.

Out of the spray area, this bench can be a footrest for shaving or storage for shampoo bottles.

Swing-out shower door

Curb and walls, 5¼ in. wide

Shower controls are beneath showerheads at each end.

Showerhead

Bench

Body sprays

wall keeps water inside the shower and takes up the least amount of space while maintaining an open, airy feel in the room.

Because of the many possible wall configurations, curbed showers can accommodate multiple showerheads and body sprays arranged in a variety of ways. The only restriction on horizontal sprays and showerheads is that they be directed away from any doors or seams in a glass enclosure.

Clip the corner to increase space

Small bathrooms aren't always rectangular, and designing a small, square bathroom (6 ft. by 6 ft.) to include a toilet, a sink, and a shower can be a challenge. The most efficient layout I've found for a room of this shape uses a neo-angled shower base (drawing at right). The clipped corner creates an angled opening that allows easy access to the shower between other fixtures in the room.

Neo-angled showers are curbed showers, so you can use combinations of glass and tile for the walls. If you use an acrylic shower pan, you'll have to use glass walls, and you'll be limited to off-the-shelf shower dimensions. A mortar-bed shower pan lets you use glass or tiled walls and customize the size of the shower. In a small bathroom, taking advantage of every possible inch for the shower can make an enormous difference in comfort.

ELIMINATE A SHOWER CORNER IN THE SMALLEST BATHROOMS

THE CORNERS FARTHEST FROM THE SHOWERHEAD are the least-used space in a shower. When squeezing a shower into a small, square bathroom, you can eliminate one of these corners to increase floor space in the room without impinging on leg and elbow room in the shower. Rain-shower (or sunflower) showerheads work well here because they stand out from the wall and can direct water straight down.

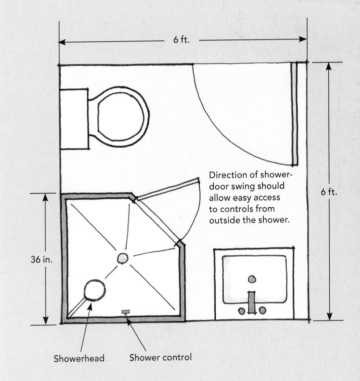

6 ft.

6 ft.

36 in.

Direction of shower-door swing should allow easy access to controls from outside the shower.

Showerhead   Shower control

Do It the Smart Way

Prep before You Paint

BY JIM LACEY

For a lot of people, painting is dreadful. They complain that it's messy and fussy and that they don't always get the results they hoped for. The truth is that most people end up with less-than-desirable results because they ignore the importance of proper preparation.

In the 20 years that I've been painting houses, I've learned how to size up quickly the results of poor prep work. The signs include paint peeling in sheets off doors and trim, mildew seeping through layers of paint, and bleeding spots on walls and ceilings— paint failures that easily could have been avoided.

At each job, I follow a basic routine that ensures a long-lasting, attractive paint job. I start by removing items from the room. Large items, such as couches, can be moved to the center of the space and covered with drop cloths. With a fresh canvas, I can begin the real prep work.

1. Drop the entire room

After the furniture is covered or removed, cover the floor with heavy-duty canvas drop cloths. Use 9-ft. by 12-ft. drop cloths near walls, 4-ft. by 5-ft. cloths under tools and paint, and a 12-ft. by 15-ft. cloth to cover a large area of flooring or furniture. Don't skimp on the drop cloths. Cheap products can allow

MUST-HAVE MATERIALS

- Stepladder
- Canvas drop cloths
- 5-in-1 tool
- Multibit screwdriver
- 2½-in. angled brush
- Acrylic caulk
- Cut bucket
- Extension cords
- Taping knives
- Paint trays
- Roller handle
- ⅜-in. roller sleeves
- Roller extension pole
- Bleach or TSP
- Rubber gloves
- Sponges
- Tinted primer
- Joint compound
- Tack cloths
- Sandpaper and sponges
- Rags
- Shop vacuum
- Auxiliary lighting

paint to seep through, and plastic drop cloths can be slippery, especially on hardwood floors.

2. Organize and stage essential tools

Keep all commonly used tools close at hand. This helps the work to go smoothly. Place these tools on their own drop cloth in an easily accessible but out-of-the-way area. Large items, such as stepladders and vacuums, also should be kept close by.

3. Light the space

Set up halogen lamps on a stand, and clamp circular incandescent lamps wherever possible. Set the lights in a position that eliminates shadows and works best with the natural light coming into the room. Adjust the lights as conditions change.

4. Remove wall and ceiling obstructions

Don't try to paint around easily removable elements such as window treatments, sconces, outlet covers, switch covers, thermostats, and recessed-light trim

rings. Large fixtures, such as chandeliers, can be covered with plastic instead of being removed. The escutcheons can be unscrewed and lowered.

5. Wash down everything

One-quarter cup of trisodium phosphate (TSP) per 2 gallons of water will remove dirt, smudges, smoke residue, and most surface grime. Pay particular attention to high-touch areas such as door jambs and areas around light switches. Bleach and TSP work best on mildew stains. Use a light hand when washing; you don't want to soak the wall. Also, wear heavy-duty rubber gloves. Allow the walls and ceiling to dry completely before moving on.

6. Assess the existing paint

Glossy finishes need to be sanded with 120-grit sandpaper, while moderate-gloss paint can be sanded with 120- to 150-grit sandpaper. Very hard surfaces may need to be prepped with a palm sander, but most often, you can get away with using a sanding sponge or sandpaper. Remove dust from the wall with a brush and a tack cloth.

7. Repair any damage and fill any gaps

Joint compound is ideal for repairing cracks, holes, or dents in both drywall and plaster walls. Use a high-quality wood filler for repairs on wood trim and doors. Sand the repairs, and remove dust from the wall with a tack cloth, a brush, and a vacuum. Any gaps that have developed between the trim and the wall or ceiling should be caulked. Acrylic caulk performs well in most applications. However, in damp areas such as bathrooms or kitchens, consider a vinyl adhesive-based caulk, such as Phenoseal® (www.phenoseal.com), for greater longevity.

8. Mask conservatively

Mask only those horizontal areas that are most vulnerable to paint splatter, like the tops of chair rails and the tops of baseboards if they're not going to be repainted. If baseboards are going to be repainted, mask the area where the wood flooring meets the baseboard.

9. Always prime walls but not ceilings

Roll primer on walls to give paint a flat, uniform base to adhere to. Ceilings don't always have to be primed because they're often in good shape and are typically painted with flat paint. Recoating flat paint is less demanding than recoating glossy paint. You should, however, spot-prime areas with repairs, such as places that had water leaks or drywall cracks. Tinting the primer to the finish color helps to improve coverage and gives a better sense of how the room will look when it's done—much better than small paint swatches, which can bleed through subsequent coats of paint and ruin the final finish. Universal acrylic primers perform better than ever and have little odor.

10. Give the wall a final sanding and cleaning

Sand all wall and ceiling surfaces with a medium-grit sanding sponge, and inspect the surface for any irregularities, such as hardened paint or primer drips. This is an ideal time to make any final touch-ups or repairs prior to painting. If you make a repair, remove the dust, and be sure to spot-prime the area before starting to paint.

An Easier Way to Hang Drywall

BY MYRON R. FERGUSON

I love working with drywall. That's not normally the sentiment you hear because, let's face it, hanging drywall is hard, dusty work. But there are ways to make it easier.

A good finished look starts with properly hung panels, which reduces the work of taping, mudding, and sanding. I try to use the biggest sheets possible to limit the number of seams I have to cover. If I'm working by myself, I can use 4-ft. by 12-ft. sheets. When I have a helper, I use 16-ft.-long sheets, if they are available at the supply store.

After I finish hanging the ceiling in a room, I hang the walls. I start where I can hang a full sheet without cutting it. Then I move to abutting walls where smaller pieces are required. This method limits the number of seams, which saves time and reduces waste. If my fastener misses a stud and finds nothing but air while I'm securing a sheet, I remove the fastener right then so there is no chance it will create a blemish on the finished wall.

Even if you are hanging just a few sheets, invest in a heavy-duty T-square to guide your cuts and a stiff-bladed keyhole saw to cut holes for outlet boxes and plumbing penetrations. Also, I use a fixed-blade utility knife called the RaspNKnife® that has a useful rasp built into the handle (www.warnertool.com).

DRIVING SOLO

I USED TO HANG DRYWALL by lifting the sheet and securing the perimeter with nails. Then, to secure the field, I had two free hands: one to hold the screw and one to hold the driver. Of course, I needed a third hand to manage the cord.

Senco's 18v DuraSpin driver

That all changed when I bought a cordless driver with collated fasteners. Senco's 18v DuraSpin driver (www.senco.com) hangs on my belt within easy reach. It weighs about the same as a corded driver, but it doesn't have a cord to contend with.

As on my corded driver, the internal clutch releases before the screw is over-driven and can break the drywall board's surface. The best feature is the collated strip of fasteners that enables me to drive screws with one hand while my other hand holds or braces the drywall. The strip holds enough 1¼-in. screws to secure one sheet.

The DuraSpin is also available in a 14v model.

HANG FROM THE TOP DOWN

POSITION THE DRYWALL directly below where it will be installed. Most settling happens where the top plate meets the studs. To prevent cracks and fastener pops, I start my screw pattern 7 in. down from the top edge. With a builder's crayon or pencil, mark each stud's location 7 in. down from the top edge **1**. Then, I use my left hand to lift and my right hand to stabilize. This way, my dominant right hand can grab the cordless screwdriver when the sheet is in place. Do the reverse if you're a lefty **2**.

When alone, lifting and fastening a sheet at the same time can be awkward. I hold up the sheet with my left hand and brace it with my shoulder while I drive the first screw **3**. I drive the bottom center screw first and then move out, first along the bottom edge, then up each stud at 16 in. on center. I use 1¼-in. fasteners for drywall thicknesses of ⅝ in. or less **4**. I lever the lower panel into place up against the upper panel's bottom edge with a rolling drywall-lifting tool (www.hydetools.com) **5**.

USE A T-SQUARE TO CUT A FULL SHEET

MAKE THE CUT IN THE PANEL'S GOOD SIDE. For safety, keep your top hand well off to the side and out of the path of the cutting blade. I use my foot to keep the bottom of the T-square in place. I start at the bottom and make the score in one motion [1]. I snap the board by lifting the center and pulling the board toward me. Then, to finish the cut, I insert my utility knife in the break and cut the paper on the back [2].

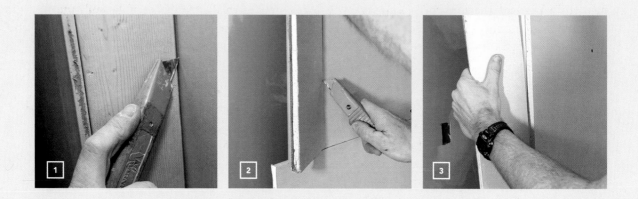

CUT THE DRYWALL IN PLACE TO SAVE TIME

IF THERE IS SCRAP LEFT IN DOOR and window openings, score the back of the sheet flush with the opening. Then break the scrap to the inside [1]. Work from the smooth side to complete the cut. With the scrap pulled toward me to create a crease, I score the paper the full length [2]. To ensure a clean edge, I push the scrap away from me to break the paper [3].

New Insulation for Old Walls

BY JUSTIN FINK

When it comes to insulating floors, walls, and ceilings, nothing compares to the blank canvas of a newly framed house. The walls are wide open, so contractors can add any type of insulation they want to achieve the best possible thermal performance.

What about the rest of us, though? Those of us living in houses built with minimal insulation or none at all? The ones who don't have the luxury of gutting their walls? The ones who work on or live in houses that hemorrhage heat in the winter and bake like an oven during the summer? What can we do to improve the thermal performance of these homes? A lot, actually.

Techniques and materials for retrofitting insulation in old walls have improved over the years. Many times, insulation can be added from the interior or exterior of the house without gutting the walls. Even so, I'm not going to sugarcoat this: Adding new insulation to closed walls is a hassle.

Pick the low-hanging fruit first

Before thinking about adding insulation to your walls, you should have already tackled your home's other major weak spots. If you haven't, you should, and your efforts should begin in the attic, where the most heat loss typically occurs. If, however, after air-sealing and insulating the attic and plugging some other common energy trouble spots your house still feels drafty and your energy bills are still too high, it's time to consider the walls.

There's a lot to consider when it comes to adding new insulation to old walls. The first step is to find out what type of insulation, if any, is already in the walls. Once that is determined, you can assess the thermal performance of the walls and then make a more informed decision about the potential benefits of an insulation upgrade. You might find that the existing insulation is astonishingly inferior and that a small outlay of cash would mean a significant decrease in your energy bills. Then again, you could be surprised to find that a high-cost retrofit will offer only a minuscule return on investment.

What's in my walls?

The first step to determining your upgrade options is to learn the type and amount of insulation, if any, in your walls. Houses built before 1930 often were left uninsulated, so you will find either empty stud bays or insulation that was added later. Houses built in the '40s, '50s, and beyond typically were insulated but often with thin batts that didn't fill the wall cavity.

WHAT'S IN MY WALLS?

Balsam wool | Urea-formaldehyde foam | Vermiculite | Fiberglass | Rock wool | Cotton batts

BALSAM WOOL (1940s)

The possibilities shown here represent the most common types of early insulation, but it's not a comprehensive list. Many of the earliest forms of insulation were driven by the local industry. If the town was home to sawmills, the surrounding houses could be insulated with sawdust. If the town was an agricultural hub, rice hulls were fairly common. What you find in your walls is limited only by the whim of the builder and the previous homeowners.

What is it? *Wool* is a bit misleading because this insulation is essentially chopped balsam wood fibers.

Positive ID: Although some installations may have been loose fill, this tan/brown insulation was most often packaged and installed in black-paper-faced batts. The tan fibers look similar to sawdust.

Health note: Balsam wool is not a health hazard, but take care when investigating this insulation; wear a dust mask. Because the paper batts are likely to be brittle to the touch, disturbing them too much may leave holes that will decrease thermal performance.

Upgrade outlook: This insulation was typically fastened to wall studs similar to fiberglass batts. Balsam wool should still yield an R-value of between R-2 and R-3 per in. if installed correctly, but the batts are likely only a couple of inches thick. Consider filling the remaining empty space in the stud cavities with blown cellulose or fiberglass. Some manufacturers of pour foam also recommend their product for this type of installation.

UREA-FORMALDEHYDE FOAM (1950 TO 1982, BUT MOSTLY IN THE LATE 1970s)

What is it? Also known as UFFI, this once-popular retrofit option is a mixture of urea, formaldehyde, and a foaming agent that were combined on-site and sprayed into wall cavities.

Positive ID: Lightweight with brownish-gold coloring, this foam is fragile and likely to crumble if touched (hence the smooth chunks shown here).

Health note: Because this open-cell foam was banned in 1982 and most of the off-gassing happened in the hours and days following installation, chances of elevated levels of formaldehyde are slim.

Upgrade outlook: Although it's rated at R-4.5 per in., UFFI rarely performs at this level. This foam is well known for its high rate of shrinkage and tendency to deteriorate if in contact with water, and it also crumbles if disturbed during remodeling.

The result is walls that likely have large voids, but this insulation isn't a good candidate for discreet removal. The best option here is to add rigid foam to the exterior to help to make up for the large air voids that are likely hidden in the wall.

VERMICULITE (1925 TO 1950)

What is it? This naturally occurring mineral was heated to make it expand into a lightweight, fire-retardant insulating material.

Positive ID: Brownish-pink or brownish-silver in color, these lightweight pellets were typically poured into closed wall cavities and into the voids in masonry blocks.

Health note: Seventy to eighty percent of vermiculite came from a mine in Libby, Mont., that was later found to contain asbestos. The mine has been closed since 1990, but the EPA suggests treating previously installed vermiculite as if it is contaminated. If undisturbed, it's not a health risk, but if you want to upgrade to a different type of insulation, call an asbestos-removal professional.

Upgrade outlook: Vermiculite doesn't typically settle and should still offer its original R-value of between R-2 and R-2.5 per in. This low thermal performance makes it an attractive candidate for upgrade, especially because it's a cinch to remove: Cut a hole, and it pours right out. But the potential for asbestos contamination makes the prep work and personal protection more of a hassle and the job more costly as a result. If cavities are not filled to the top, consider topping them off; fiberglass, cellulose, or pour foam will work if there is access from the attic.

HOW TO FIND OUT WHAT TYPE OF INSULATION IS IN YOUR WALLS

Inspector's Tricks

ELECTRICAL OUTLETS:
You often can get a peek at what's in walls by removing electrical-outlet cover plates and shining a flashlight into the space where the drywall or plaster meets the electrical box.

LOOK UP OR DOWN:
Drilling a hole up into the wall cavity from the basement or down through the top plate from the attic may be helpful. A piece of wire bent into a hook is a helpful probing tool.

CUT A SMALL HOLE:
This last resort should be done in a location that will go unnoticed once patched up. Cut a neat hole with a drywall saw—a small square or rectangle will be easiest to replace—and keep the piece to use later as a patch.

FIBERGLASS (LATE 1930s TO PRESENT)

What is it? This man-made product consists of fine strands of glass grouped together in a thick blanket.

Positive ID: Most often yellow, though pink, white, blue, and green types are used. Older products were typically paper-faced batts.

Health note: Official health information on fiberglass is ambiguous; the argument over whether it's a carcinogen continues. Even if it's not a cancer-causing material, it will make you itchy and irritate your lungs if disturbed. Be on the safe side if you plan to remove this insulation; wear gloves, long sleeves, goggles, and a respirator.

Upgrade outlook: Fiberglass has a decent thermal performance of between R-3 and R-4.5 per in., but early products were typically only about 2 in. thick. Consider filling the remaining empty space in the stud cavities with blown cellulose or blown fiberglass. Some manufacturers of pour foam also recommend their product for this type of installation.

ROCK WOOL (MOSTLY IN THE 1950s)

What is it? Rock wool is a specific type of mineral wool, a by-product of the ore-smelting process.

Positive ID: This fluffy, cottonlike material was typically installed as loose fill or batts. It usually started out white or gray, but even the white version will likely be blackened or brown from decades of filtering dirt out of air flowing through the cavity.

Health note: Research indicates that this is a safe material. It's still in use today, and it's gaining popularity among green builders.

Upgrade outlook: Rock wool is fairly dense, so it's less likely than other materials to have settled over time. If installed correctly, it should still yield a value of R-3 to R-4 per in., about the same as blown fiberglass or cellulose insulation. If anything, consider adding housewrap or a thin layer of rigid foam to the outside of the wall to air-seal the structure. If more insulation is desired, go with rigid foam.

OUT WITH THE OLD INSULATION

IF YOUR WALLS are filled with old insulation and your remodeling plans don't involve gutting the house, then you can either add rigid insulation to the exterior of the house or, in some cases, surgically remove the old insulation.

Vermiculite can be removed by drilling a hole through the wall at the bottom of the stud cavity and letting gravity empty the stud bays. In balloon-framed houses, which have wall studs that run continuously from the foundation to the roofline, blocking in the basement can be removed to access the stud cavities above.

Batts or dense fibrous insulations can be removed by cutting a "belly-band" in which a narrow strip of wall is removed about 4 ft. from the floor (this can be done from the exterior as well). With this strip of wall open, the batts can be pulled out—a homemade hook helps—and new insulation can be blown or poured into the cavities through the same openings (photo above) before being patched.

COTTON BATTS (1935 TO 1950)

What is it? Made of a naturally grown material, cotton batts are treated to be flame resistant.

Positive ID: This white insulation is dense but still fluffy. It's not as refined as cotton balls; instead, it's likely to have more of a pilly, fuzzy appearance. Although several companies manufactured cotton batts, one of the most popular seems to have been Lockport Cotton Batting. Look for a product name (Lo-K) and company logo on the batts' paper facing.

Health note: Cotton is all natural and is perfectly safe to touch, but don't remove the batts or otherwise disturb the insulation without wearing at least a nuisance dust mask or respirator to protect your lungs. Also, cotton by nature is absorbent, so if it gets wet, it will take time to dry.

Upgrade outlook: The growing popularity of green-building materials has sparked renewed interest in cotton batts. Although these modern versions of cotton batting, often referred to as "blue-jean insulation," have an R-value of R-3.5 to R-4 per in., there is some controversy over the R-value of the old versions. Some sources claim the old products perform similarly to the modern versions, and others estimate the R-value to be as low as R-0.5 per in. Considering the density of the old cotton batts, such a low R-value seems unlikely.

UPGRADE OPTIONS: FOAM

RIGID FOAM

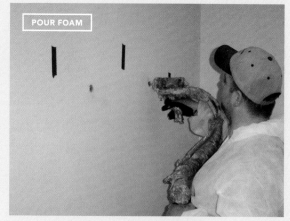

POUR FOAM

RIGID FOAM ALWAYS WORKS

It doesn't matter how the walls were built, what type of insulation they have now, or how many obstructions are hidden in the wall cavities: Rigid-foam panels installed over the exterior side of the walls are always an option. However, installation is not as easy as cutting the lightweight panels with a utility knife and nailing them to the framing, though that's part of it.

Rigid foam must be applied directly to the framing or sheathing, or on top of the existing siding, then covered with new siding. In either case, you are faced with a full re-siding job and maybe a siding tearoff. Also, depending on the added thickness of the panels, windows and doors might need to be furred out, and roof rakes and eaves extended. As long as the installation is detailed carefully, though, the result is wall cavities that stay warm and dry, allowing your existing insulation to perform its best.

Panels are available in 2-ft. by 8-ft. or 4-ft. by 8-ft. sheets and range from ½ in. to 2 in. in thickness. Vapor permeability is determined by the type of foam and the presence of a facing. Panels faced with foil or plastic are class-I vapor retarders (also called vapor barriers) and should not be used if the house has poly sheeting or an equivalent vapor retarder under the drywall. Unfaced or fiberglass-faced panels allow water vapor to pass and won't be problematic in combination with a class-I retarder.

1. Expanded polystyrene (EPS)

These white, closed-cell panels are made from the same polystyrene beads used in disposable coffee cups. EPS is the least expensive option and has the lowest R-value of the group (about R-4 per in.). Some EPS is unfaced, which makes it more fragile to handle but also allows the passage of water vapor. Unfaced EPS should be installed in combination with #15 felt paper or housewrap.

2. Extruded polystyrene (XPS)

XPS falls in the middle of the three types of rigid-foam insulation in terms of cost and performance. Easy to spot by its blue, pink, or green color, XPS is slightly more expensive than EPS and also offers better performance (about R-5 per in.). Panels are commonly unfaced, and though water-vapor transmission slows on thicker panels, all XPS panels greater than 1 in. thick are considered class-II vapor retarders, which allow water vapor to pass.

3. Polyisocyanurate (polyiso)

This is the most expensive type of rigid foam but also the best insulator (about R-6.5). Polyiso is a

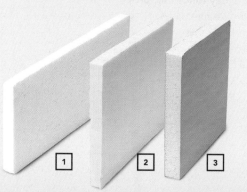

popular choice for retrofit applications because it packs more insulation into a thin package—less hassle for detailing windows and doors. All polyiso boards are faced, most with foil, which retards the flow of water vapor.

POUR FOAM IS THE MOST THOROUGH

This water- or hydrofluorocarbon (HFC)-blown mixture is injected into the wall cavity from either the interior or the exterior through two or more ¾-in.-to 1-in.-dia. holes. The foam flows to the bottom of the stud cavity, where it slowly expands upward, surrounding even the most complicated plumbing and electrical obstructions, and filling every gap to create an airtight wall assembly.

Pour foam follows the path of least resistance as it expands, so the bottoms of stud cavities (in the basement or crawlspace) need to be sealed in balloon-framed houses. Old houses with siding installed directly over the studs will likely have foam squeeze-out between siding courses, which must be removed with a paint scraper once cured.

Blowouts or distortions in drywall, plaster, or siding are also possible, although this is typically not a concern if the foam is installed by trained professionals. Still, this is the reason why most pour-foam companies don't sell directly to the public, instead relying on a network of trained installers. Tiger Foam™, on the other hand, sells disposable do-it-yourself kits to homeowners.

Although there are videos on the Internet showing pour foam being injected into wall cavities that have fiberglass insulation—compressing the batts against the wallboard or sheathing—most manufacturers do not recommend this practice. The pour foam could bond to individual strands of fiberglass and tear it apart as it expands, creating voids. Tiger Foam is the exception, but the company recommends the use of a long fill tube to control the injection.

Installation from the exterior requires removal of some clapboards or shingles. Installation from the inside is easier but requires more prep work (moving furniture, wall art, drapes, etc.). Homeowners can expect a slight odor after installation and for the day following; proper ventilation is a must.

Open-cell foams—which are more permeable to water-vapor transmission—are about R-4 per in.; closed-cell, around R-6 per in.

UPGRADE OPTIONS: BLOWN-IN

CELLULOSE

FIBERGLASS

THE MOST COMMON APPROACH

This method begins with compressed packs of dry cellulose or fiberglass, which are dumped into the hopper of a blowing machine, where they are agitated and loosened. A 1-in.- to 2-in.-dia. hose runs from the blowing machine through a hole in the interior or exterior side of the wall and is lowered to the bottom of the stud cavity. The installation process usually involves either one hole at the top of each cavity and a long fill tube that is withdrawn as the insulation fills the space, or a "double-blow" method, where two holes are used—one about 4 ft. from the floor and a second near the top of the wall.

Both cellulose and fiberglass do a good job of surrounding typical plumbing and electrical utilities routed through the wall, but the finished density of the insulation is crucial. Cellulose that's installed too loosely will settle and create voids in the wall, and fiberglass that's packed too densely will not offer the performance you paid for.

Cellulose

This insulation is made from 80% postconsumer recycled newspaper and is treated with nontoxic borates to resist fire and mold. It's a good choice because of its balance among cost, thermal performance, and environmentally friendly characteristics. Also, unlike fiberglass insulation, cellulose doesn't rely only on its ability to trap air to stop heat flow. Cellulose can be packed tightly into a wall cavity to resist airflow—a practice called "dense-packing"—yielding an R-value of R-3 to R-4 per in.

Although blowing loose-fill cellulose into attics is a pretty straightforward process (and is touted as a good do-it-yourself project), dense-packing is more complicated. As the material is blown into the cavity, the blowing machine bogs down, letting the installer know to pull back the hose a bit. This process repeats until the wall is packed full of cellulose. Although it is possible to pack cellulose too densely, the more common problem is not packing it densely enough. Most blowing machines that are available as rentals are designed for blowing loose cellulose in an open attic. These machines aren't powerful enough to pack cellulose into a wall cavity, and unpacked cellulose can settle and leave voids. The Cellulose Insulation Manufacturers Association (www.cellulose.org) recommends that dense-pack cellulose be installed only by trained professionals with more powerful blowing machines.

Finally, if soaked with water, cellulose is likely to settle, leaving voids. Then again, if there's liquid water in the wall cavity, voids in the insulation will be the least of your worries, and the least of your expenses.

SOURCES

www.certainteed.com
www.greenfiber.com
www.johnsmanville.com
www.knaufusa.com
www.owenscorning.com

Fiberglass

This loose-fill insulation is made from molten glass that is spun into loose fibers. The material is available in two forms, either as a by-product of manufacturing traditional fiberglass batts and rolls, or from "prime" fibers produced especially for blowing applications. In either case, the material is noncombustible, will not absorb water, and is inorganic, so it will not support mold growth.

Fiberglass resists heat flow by trapping pockets of air between fibers, so the insulation must be left fluffy to take advantage of the air-trapping nature of the material. The R-value (typically between R-2.5 and R-4) is dependent not only on the thickness of the wall cavity but also on the density at which the insulation is installed. For information on ensuring that the fiberglass is installed to provide the stated R-value, visit the North American Insulation Manufacturers Association (www.naima.org) for a free overview.

Because fiberglass doesn't need to be blown to such high densities, it's a more user-friendly installation for nonprofessionals. On the other hand, loose fiberglass is not as readily available as cellulose, which is often a stock item at home-improvement centers. Finally, fiberglass advocates contend that their product won't absorb water and that cellulose will—though fiberglass will still sag if it becomes wet.

Doghouse Dormers

BY RICK ARNOLD

One of the most popular ways to open the dark, cramped upper level of a house is to build one or more dormers. From a homeowner's point of view, these small additions can increase curb appeal and create more hospitable living space in the top level of a house. From a builder's point of view, dormers concentrate almost all aspects of residential framing into one small package (drawing on p. 136). If the dormer is too big, it will look out of scale with the rest of the house. The front wall of the dormer should be just large enough to fit the window (ideally, smaller than the windows on the lower levels of the house) and should leave just enough room for proper flashing where it joins the main roof. Also, a well-proportioned dormer sits beneath the line of the main-roof ridge and is set back from the facade of the house.

Like any building project, the success of constructing dormers depends on precise calculations, careful planning, and some smart assembly work. Trust me, the last thing you want is to be on the roof trying to figure out why the wing wall won't fit while a rain cloud hovers overhead, waiting to take advantage of that big hole in the roof.

Over the years, I've built a number of dormers, improving the process each time. I've finally settled on a system that enables me to figure all the dormer measurements precisely, cut and assemble most of the pieces on the ground (or in the attic), and put off cutting a hole in the roof until the last minute—no blue tarp needed.

This system is safer because it reduces the amount of time I'm measuring and building on the roof, and it also minimizes the number of trips to the ground to make cuts. My system also lowers the level of stress that comes with having a roof that's open to the elements for an extended period of time. The trade-off is that all the measurements have to be as accurate as possible. Many of the calculations build off one another, and a sloppy measurement in one step throws off the math in the many steps that follow. It sounds daunting, but most of the components of a doghouse dormer can be found by dividing the framing components into a series of triangles, and then calculating the missing dimensions.

Check the existing pitch on-site

I always start a dormer project by verifying the pitch of the existing roof. I don't want to assume that I know the pitch, then cut and build all the dormer components only to discover that the dormer doesn't fit correctly. Trusting the plans is tempting, but you might end up missing an abnormality like the 7⅛-in-12-pitch roof on this project.

The most accurate process is to measure the total rise and total run from inside the attic. This project included an attic so the rafters, the subfloor, and the main ridge all were exposed. This made it easy to get precise rise and run measurements. If the framing had not been exposed, I would have cut back the drywall at the proposed dormer opening and measured the roof pitch there. That said, I prefer to have the rafters exposed so that I can take the largest set of measurements possible. The longer the two sides of the triangle (rise and run) that you are measuring, the more accurate the numbers will be.

ASSEMBLING COMPONENTS ON the ground and cutting the roof at the last minute provide a low-stress route to a high-value remodeling project.

Determine the wing-wall dimensions

Once I know the pitch of the existing roof, I need to calculate one of the two sides that make up the dormer's triangular wing wall. I begin with the height of the front wall, which often is driven by the window height.

On this project, the homeowner wanted the dormer window to be about 3 ft. 6 in. tall. That would require a rough opening of 3 ft. 7½ in. to allow for window installation. As a rule, I keep dormer-window openings at least 6 in. above the main roof, leaving room for proper flashing, and about 6 in. below

the top plate of the front wall so that the top of the window lines up near the bottom of the dormer's soffit (see p. 138). Adding the numbers, I end up with a front-wall height of 4 ft. 7½ in. Now I can combine the height of the wing wall with the pitch of the roof and simply solve for the missing pieces.

Dormer roof is based on the available space

To figure the size of the dormer roof, I have to determine how much room I have between the top of the dormer walls and the top of the existing roof ridge.

IT'S LIKE BUILDING A SMALL HOUSE WITH ANGLED WALLS

A DOGHOUSE DORMER concentrates almost all aspects of residential framing into one small package. The foundation for this rooftop addition consists of LVL trimmer rafters that extend from the main-roof ridge to the top of the house's wall and headers that span between trimmers. The window's rough opening is centered in the dormer's front wall.

A CONSTRUCTION CALCULATOR HELPS TO MINIMIZE THE MATH

To make things easier, construction calculators allow you to work with quantities and components

that you encounter on the job site. Measurements are entered in feet and inches; labeled keys enable you to input and calculate rise, run, pitch, and other useful dimensions. It's much faster than relying on longhand equations. Construction calculators are available at most hardware stores and lumberyards, or through online sources like www.calculated.com.

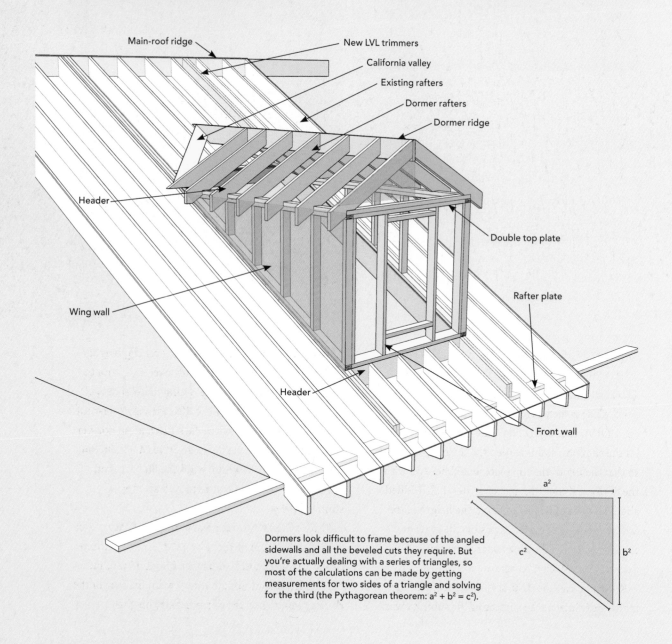

Dormers look difficult to frame because of the angled sidewalls and all the beveled cuts they require. But you're actually dealing with a series of triangles, so most of the calculations can be made by getting measurements for two sides of a triangle and solving for the third (the Pythagorean theorem: $a^2 + b^2 = c^2$).

MEASURE THE BIGGEST TRIANGLE TO FIND THE PRECISE PITCH

I CAN USE A SPEED® SQUARE or framing square to find the roof pitch, but measurements from such a small area can be misleading. To get the most accurate pitch, I measure the largest possible rise and run. On this project, I measured from the top of the roof ridge to the attic subfloor, and from the outside edge of the rafter plate to a plumb line down from the roof ridge. Subtracting the height above plate (HAP), as shown below, gives me the correct rise.

ON THE CALCULATOR
Enter 10 ft. ½ in.; press Rise.
Enter 16 ft. 11½ in.; press Run.
Press Pitch, and get 7 ⅛ pitch, or 7 ⅛ in. of rise for every 12 in. of run.

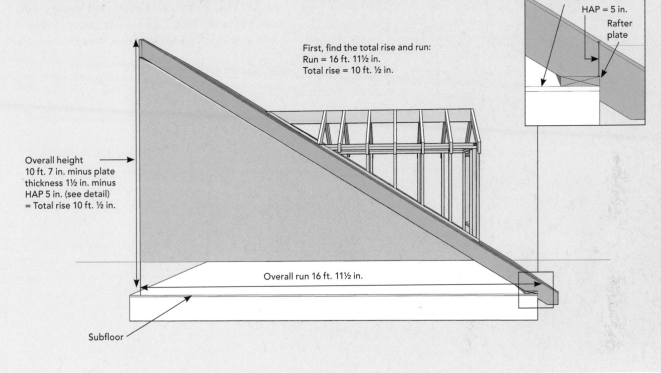

First, find the total rise and run:
Run = 16 ft. 11½ in.
Total rise = 10 ft. ½ in.

Subfloor
HAP = 5 in.
Rafter plate

Overall height
10 ft. 7 in. minus plate thickness 1½ in. minus HAP 5 in. (see detail) = Total rise 10 ft. ½ in.

Overall run 16 ft. 11½ in.

Subfloor

A dormer-roof ridge that comes too close to the existing main-roof ridge will look out of proportion and will be harder to flash and shingle properly.

For this project, the ceiling height was limited in the attic by a series of collar ties, which were 7 ft. 6 in. off the subfloor, so I installed the dormer wing walls so that the top of the top plate would be level with the bottom of the existing collar ties. I also added about an inch of wiggle room to the height of the dormer ceiling; experience has taught me that it's unusual to find old collar ties that are perfectly level and in line with each other.

Knowing that the distance from the top of the main-roof ridge to the surface of the subfloor was 10 ft. 7 in., I subtracted the existing ceiling height of 7 ft. 6 in. and was left with just over 3 ft. from the wing-wall top plates to the existing main-roof ridge.

The plans for this project called for a dormer-roof pitch of 6-in-12. I always make sure that the dormer ridge intersects the existing roof at least 8 in. below the existing main ridge to avoid the flashing and aesthetic problems of trying to intersect two shingled ridges.

I knew from previous calculations that the overall width of the dormer (including the ½-in. sheathing on each side) would be 6 ft. 1 in. I divided that number in half, then used it to find the dimensions of the dormer rafters and the dormer-ridge height.

DECIDE ON WINDOW SIZE, THEN CALCULATE WING-WALL DETAILS

ON THIS PROJECT, the homeowner wanted the dormer window to be about 3 ft. 6 in. tall. That would require a rough opening of 3 ft. 7½ in. to allow for window installation. I always keep the window opening at least 6 in. up from the roof to leave room for flashing, and in this case, about 6 in. down from the top plate of the front wall so that the top of the window lines up near the bottom of the dormer's soffit. I ended up with a front-wall height of 4 ft. 7½ in. As shown below, once you know the front-wall height and the roof pitch, it's not difficult to calculate exact dimensions for all wing-wall framing members.

ON THE CALCULATOR
Top and bottom plates

Knowing the height of the front wall, I also have the height of the adjoining wing wall. This height, combined with the roof pitch, gives me the length of the wing-wall top plates and bottom plate.

Enter 4 ft. 7½ in. front-wall height; press `Rise`.

Enter 7⅛ in. `Pitch`; press `Run`, and get 7-ft. 9½-in. **wing-wall length.**

Press `Diag`, and you get 9-ft. ¾-in. **bottom-plate length.**

Press `Diag`, and you get a 30.7° plumb cut. Round this to an even 30°.

Press `Diag` again, and get a 59.3° level cut. Round this to an even 60°.

Refer to the top left detail drawing to see how the wing-wall top plate and the wing-wall double plate need to be shortened because of corner overlaps and bevel cuts.

Infill studs

Each of these will have a bevel cut on the bottom, 60° in this case. I use the calculator's R/Wall (rake wall) function to determine the different stud lengths.*

Enter 4-ft. 2¾-in. **front-wall stud length**; press `Rise`.

Enter 7⅛ in. pitch; press `Pitch`.

Press `R/Wall`. (Screen displays selected stud spacing, 16 in. on center in this case.)

Press `R/Wall` repeatedly to display descending stud lengths.

*You might have to press `Conv` first to use the `R/Wall` function.

Front-wall studs

From the finished height of the front wall (4 ft. 7½ in.), subtract 3 in. for the double plate and the top plate, and 1¾ in. for the thickness of the angled bottom plate (bottom left detail). This yields a front-wall stud length of 4 ft. 2¾ in.

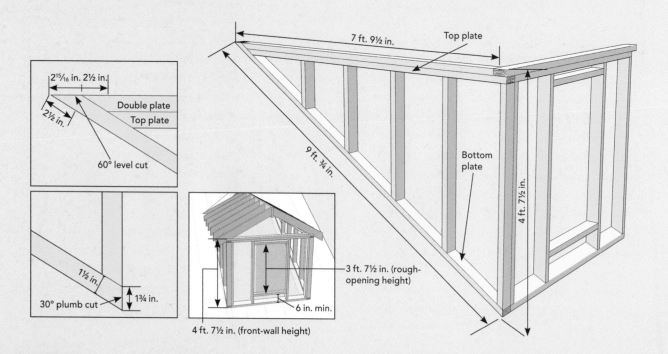

2¹⁵⁄₁₆ in. 2½ in.

Double plate

Top plate

2½ in.

60° level cut

1½ in.

30° plumb cut

1¾ in.

3 ft. 7½ in. (rough-opening height)

6 in. min.

4 ft. 7½ in. (front-wall height)

7 ft. 9½ in.

Top plate

9 ft. ¾ in.

Bottom plate

4 ft. 7½ in.

DORMER ROOF IS BASED ON THE AVAILABLE SPACE

To FIND THE SIZE OF THE DORMER ROOF, I have to consider how much room I have between the top of the dormer walls and the top of the existing roof ridge. For example, on this project, I had collar ties that were going to remain in place, which set the attic-ceiling height at 7 ft. 6 in. above the subfloor (see the top right drawing below). I also make sure that the dormer ridge intersects the existing roof at least 8 in. below the existing main ridge to avoid the flashing and aesthetic problems of trying to intersect two shingled ridges.

ON THE CALCULATOR

1. Find the location of the dormer ridge

Before I can lay out the dormer rafters, I need to find the distance between the sheathed wing walls. The easiest way to do this is to take the length of the front-wall top plate (6 ft.) and add in the thickness of the wing-wall sheathing (½ in. on each side). This gives a finished width of 6 ft. 1 in.

Enter 6 ft. 1 in. ÷ 2, press `=`, and you get 3 ft. ½ in.; this is the **total run of dormer rafters**, but this number needs to be adjusted by subtracting half the thickness of the dormer-roof ridge: 3 ft. ½ in. – ¾ in. = 2 ft. 11¾ in.

2. Calculate the dormer-ridge height

I wanted a 6-in-12 roof pitch on the dormers, so I used that combined with the run I found above to determine the adjusted length of the dormer rafters and the height of the dormer ridge:

Enter 2 ft. 11¾ in.; press `Run`.

Enter 6 in.; press `Pitch`.

Press `Diag`, and get 3 ft. 4 in. (**length of the dormer rafter**).

Press `Rise`, and get 1 ft. 5⅞ in. (**unadjusted dormer-ridge height**).

3. Lay out the dormer rafter

I start by making a plumb cut that reflects the 6-in-12 pitch of the dormer roof (see the bottom drawing below). Next, I measure 3 ft. 4 in. from the long point of that cut and mark a line plumb with the wing wall to indicate the heel cut of the rafter bird's mouth. The seat cut is perpendicular to the heel cut and is equal to the width of the top plate and sheathing—in this case, 4 in. (3½-in. top plate + ½-in. sheathing).

With the bird's mouth marked, I find the HAP of 4⅛ in. I add this number to the rise I found in the calculations above (1 ft. 5⅞ in.) and get a top-of-ridge height of 1 ft. 10 in. above the dormer walls—still falling well below the main ridge.

4. Find the dormer-ridge length

I already know that the wing walls are 7 ft. 9½ in. long, so I just need to find the length that the ridge extends past the wing walls before meeting the existing roof. I do this by using another small triangle:

Enter 1 ft. 10 in.; press `Rise`.

Enter 7⅛ in.; press `Pitch`.

Press `Run`, and get 3 ft. 1¹/₁₆ in.

Add 7 ft. 9½ in.; press `=`; you get 10 ft. 10⁹/₁₆ in., which is the **total length of dormer ridge**, straight cut to long point, with a 60° cut.

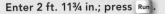

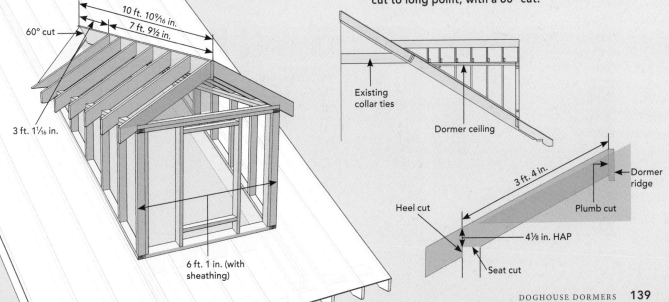

60° cut
10 ft. 10⁹/₁₆ in.
7 ft. 9½ in.
3 ft. 1¹/₁₆ in.
6 ft. 1 in. (with sheathing)

Existing collar ties
Dormer ceiling

3 ft. 4 in.
Dormer ridge
Plumb cut
Heel cut
4⅛ in. HAP
Seat cut

INSTALL TRIMMERS AND HEADERS, THEN CUT THE HOLE

I CAN PERFORM ALL THE WORK UP TO THIS POINT, including cutting all the components for the dormer and assembling the walls, without opening the existing roof. This way, unless I have to strip off the entire roof to be reshingled, the rest of the procedure, including dry-in, takes only about four hours from start to finish. This procedure minimizes risk of exposure to the elements.

MEASURE FOR THE NEW DORMER HEADERS
I first draw a level line across the rafter at the desired height 1 . In this case, I'm matching the underside of the collar ties. Then, starting from the inside end of that mark, I square up to the underside of the sheathing. Then I move the square toward the ridge, marking the 1½-in. thickness of each header piece 2 . The last line I draw is the inside edge of the first top header, which is also the cutline. To mark for the bottom header, I first put a nail into the sheathing at the last line I just drew, hook my tape to the nail, and measure along the underside of the sheathing the length of the wing-wall bottom plate. Next, I plumb down that line along the face of the rafter 3 . The inside edge of the dormer wall is 3½ in. in (toward the ridge) from this plumb line. Then I measure back (toward the eave) the thickness of the doubled-up 3-in. header and draw a plumb line to indicate the cutline for the lower header. I transfer these cutlines to all the rafters to be cut.

4 **INSTALL THE TRIMMERS.** We removed or bent back any protruding nails that might get in the way before sliding the LVL trimmer into place through the exposed eaves. Slightly beveling the leading edge of the trimmer made it easier to rotate into place.

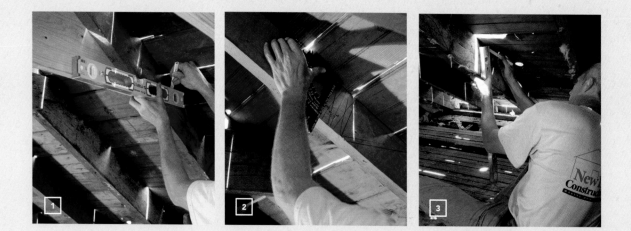

5 **DOUBLE 2X HEADERS COMPLETE THE ROUGH FRAMING.** Once the rafters are removed, I install two-piece headers at the top and bottom of the opening. A couple of temporary cleats support the newly cut rafters and keep the LVL trimmers spaced evenly until the double headers are put in place.

6 **THE SAFEST WAY.** Standing inside on the subfloor and cutting through the roof is easier and safer than standing on the roof and cutting down into the attic.

7 **TRUE UP THE OPENING.** I run a stringline along the inside edge of the trimmers and make any necessary adjustments to get them straight and plumb. Then I nail through the existing roof sheathing and into the new framing to keep everything lined up.

THE PAYOFF: PARTS GO TOGETHER QUICKLY

IF THE CALCULATIONS WERE ACCURATE, the front wall and the two wing walls should fit each other and the existing roof without any major hitches. The dormer rafters and ridge should be carried up in pieces and assembled in place.

Wing walls go up first. It takes two workers to lift the assembled walls into place 1 . Make sure to keep the inside face of the wing wall flush with the edge of the new trimmers 2 . Drop the front wall between the wing walls 3 .

FLASH THE TOP CORNERS. I apply a large square of roofing membrane (approximately 18 in. sq.) to a difficult area that is almost impossible to flash after the dormer roof has been assembled. I leave the lower and outer edges of the release sheet intact so that later I can tuck the rest of the flashing and felt paper under this flap to seal the dormer-flashing system together.

FOUR RAFTERS HOLD THE RIDGE. Nail opposing rafters to the plates at the front and back of the dormer, then install the ridge board and the remaining rafters.

MEASURING, CUTTING, AND INSTALLING THE CALIFORNIA VALLEY

A CALIFORNIA VALLEY is calculated and cut to sit on top of the sheathing of a roof rather than connecting directly to the underlying framing. The length of the California valley is the hypotenuse **(A)** of an imaginary triangle that lies flat on the existing roof **(shown in blue)**. Just as in the previous parts of the dormer, my goal is to find this missing hypotenuse by plugging in the lengths of the other two sides **(B and C)** that make up the completed triangle.

- **Side B:** Based on the measurements I used to find the adjusted run of the dormer rafters, I know that the distance from the outer edge of the sheathed wing wall to a line that's plumb with the near face of the dormer ridge is 2 ft. 11¾ in. I also have to add in the distance to the point that the rafter intersects the roof plane **(shown in green)**.

Enter 4¼ in.; press Rise .

Enter 6 in.; press Pitch .

Press Run , and get 8¼ in.

Add 2 ft. 11¾ in. + 8¼ in.; press = , and get 3 ft. 8 in.

- **Side C:** I still need to find one of the legs of this triangle, so I have to create a second triangle **(shown in orange)** in which side (C) is a shared dimension.

I know the height of the dormer ridge **(D)** is 1 ft. 10 in., and I know the pitch of the existing roof is 7⅛-in-12, so I use my calculator to find **(C)**.

Enter 1 ft. 10 in.; press Rise .

Enter 7⅛ in.; press Pitch .

Press Diag , and you get 3 ft. 7¹⁄₁₆ in.

Adjust for a flush fit. I now have the two legs of the triangle **(B and C)** that I need to solve for the missing hypotenuse **(A)**, but first I have to adjust their lengths so that when the California valley is installed, the edge of the 2x stock won't stick up past the top edges of the dormer ridge and the rafter tail.

Reduce top (ridge) end of valley

Enter 1½ in.; press Rise .

Enter 7⅛ in.; press Pitch .

Press Run , and get 2½ in.

Reduce lower (rafter tail) end of valley

Enter 1½ in.; press Run .

Enter 7⅛ in.; press Pitch .

Press Diag , and get 1¾ in.

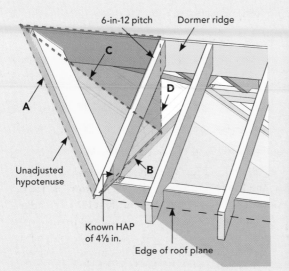

6-in-12 pitch   Dormer ridge

C

D

A

B

Unadjusted hypotenuse

Known HAP of 4⅛ in.

Edge of roof plane

Enter 1¾ in.; press Rise .

Enter 6 in.; press Pitch .

Press Run , and get 3½ in.

Adjusted length of side B:
3 ft. 8 in. – 3½ in.; press = , and get 3 ft. 4½ in.

Adjusted length of side C:
3 ft. 7¹⁄₁₆ in. – 2½ in.;

Press = , and get 3 ft. 4⁹⁄₁₆ in.

Side B = Enter 3 ft. 4½ in.; press Run .

Side C = Enter 3 ft. 4⁹⁄₁₆ in.; press Rise .

Side A = Press Diag : 4 ft. 9⁵⁄₁₆ in.

Press Diag 45.04 plumb cut.

Press Diag 44.96 level cut.

A quick bevel for a snug fit.
Last, the bottom of the valley needs to be beveled to sit snug against the dormer rafter. To find this plumb bevel angle, use the known main roof pitch: Enter 7⅛ in.; press Pitch .

Then press Pitch again, and get a **30° bevel angle.**

Install a Leak-Free Skylight

BY MIKE GUERTIN

I used to worry every time I installed a skylight. Even with the best installation detailing, I could still expect a storm to hit from just the right direction and drive water behind the flashing. When I discovered self-adhering membranes, my worrying days ended. Now I follow a series of simple steps that hasn't failed in more than 15 years' worth of installations. The key to success is integrating the membrane and the flashings with the shingles to direct water back to the surface of the roof. Although the project shown here is a retrofit, I would flash it the same way on a new house.

Center the skylight

This project called for adding two 22-in.-wide skylights (for 24-in. on-center framing) into rafters spaced 16 in. on center. To support the opening and tail rafters, I sistered the inside face of the existing rafters to close the overall opening down 3 in. more. Then I positioned the skylight up the roof plane so that the opening would be centered on the interior room's ceiling. I framed the skylight openings from the inside, as shown in the drawing on p. 148.

Cut the opening one layer at a time

With the rough opening framed, I locate the skylight on the roof by standing inside and driving screws up through the sheathing and the shingles at all four corners. Then I can go out and snap chalklines between the screws to mark the location.

To start the hole, I strip back the roof shingles, beginning three courses above the top of the skylight. To free the third course, I pull the nails at the center and at the course above. A carefully inserted thin flat bar breaks the shingles' self-adhesive strip and wedges up under the nails. It's easier to separate

drawing on p. 148.

THINGS TO CONSIDER WHEN FRAMING SKYLIGHTS

BUILDING CODES
Check local building codes to verify framing details.

STANDARD SIZES
Many skylights are sized to fit between rafters/trusses 16 in. or 24 in. on center, and need only a header installed between the two.

ROOF TRUSSES
Don't cut trusses without consulting an engineer.

the self-adhesive strip when the shingles are cool. In hot weather, I break the seal early in the morning before the sun has hit the roof. I remove full shingles to the next joint left and right of the skylight opening rather than cutting them in the middle.

Once the upper course of shingles is done, successive courses are easier to remove because the nails are exposed; just pull the nails and separate the self-adhesive strip. I remove shingles until I reach the course whose top edge is within 2 in. above or below the bottom line of the skylight opening. I save the shingles I've pulled to reuse around the skylight.

Next, I snap chalklines between the screws to outline the skylight location, then remove the screws. Inside, I staple plastic over the skylight opening to contain the dust. Then I go back to the roof, where I use a circular saw to cut the roof sheathing.

After I've swept the roof, I separate the glass portion of the skylight from the frame and install the frame per the manufacturer's instructions. I prefer to remove the glass from the frame to reduce the skylight's weight and to reduce the chance of

scratching the glass, and to make it easier to run the self-adhering membrane to the top of the frame.

Seal the frame to the roof

Despite the layers of underlayment, shingles, and flashing, the self-adhering membrane is the final line of defense against leaks. Applied meticulously around the skylight frame, the membrane collects water that gets beneath the metal flashing and redirects it to the shingle surface below the skylight.

The key is to lap the self-adhering membrane over the top edge of the shingle course that runs along the bottom of the skylight. Without this step, water that reaches the membrane will empty onto the roof underlayment and have to travel the length of the roof slope beneath the shingles until it reaches the eave. Along the way, the water will encounter hundreds of nail holes that it could leak through.

Skylights are easy to install

Reshingling and flashing are the simplest parts of the process. The base flashing wraps around the bottom

(Continued on p. 150)

REFRAME, STRIP, AND CUT

SKYLIGHT OPENINGS sometimes need additional modifications. In this example, the center rafter was cut out to create a space wide enough for the skylight. The amount removed included the thicknesses of both headers to be added. The rafters on each side of the space must be doubled from ridge to plate if the tail rafter (the remnant below the skylight) is more than 3 ft. long. In this case, the extra rafters were added to the inside to reduce the rough opening's width. Finally, headers were installed above and below the skylight's position.

1. STRIP BACK THE SHINGLES FIRST
Unless the entire roof is being replaced, shingles must be removed carefully so that after the skylight is attached, they can be reintegrated properly with the self-adhering membrane and metal flashing.

2. FOLD BACK THE UNDERLAYMENT
Once you've located the skylight's position and stripped back the shingles, snap a set of chalklines on the roofing underlayment and remove that section. Next, make 3-in.-long horizontal cuts at the bottom and 6-in.-long diagonal cuts at the top that splay out about 3 in. Then fold away the underlayment flaps. Integrate these flaps into the flashing later.

3. SEAL OUT GRIT
Tape the leading edge of the shingles with housewrap tape to keep sawdust and grit from getting under the roofing.

4. CUT THE HOLE
To keep sawdust and roof debris from falling into the house, staple a sheet of poly over the skylight opening from inside before cutting the sheathing.

5. INSTALL THE SKYLIGHT FRAME
Most frames mount to the roof deck with metal brackets screwed to both the skylight and the roof framing.

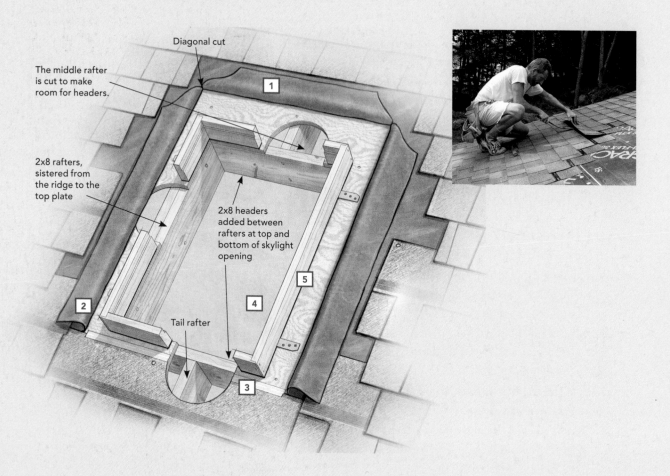

Diagonal cut

The middle rafter is cut to make room for headers.

2x8 rafters, sistered from the ridge to the top plate

2x8 headers added between rafters at top and bottom of skylight opening

Tail rafter

SLICE, WRAP, AND PROTECT WITH A WATERTIGHT SEAL

ALTHOUGH METAL STEP FLASHING is the primary weather barrier between the skylight frame and the roof shingles, self-adhesive membrane, when applied first, makes a watertight seal that also self-heals around nail penetrations. I cut 9-in.-to 12-in.-wide strips of membrane for each side of the skylight (there should be a minimum of 5 in. adhered to the roof) and make each one about 12 in. longer than the skylight edge.

1. START AT THE BOTTOM
Center the membrane, and align it with the edge of the frame. Remove the top half of the release sheet, and press the strip onto the frame. Then remove the second half of the sheet, and stick the membrane to the top edge of the shingle below the skylight. Trim the membrane just above the self-adhesive strip on the shingle course so that it won't be exposed when base flashing and shingles are reinstalled.

2. REINFORCE THE CORNERS
Make vertical cuts in the membrane at the sides of the frame ½ in. to ¾ in. from the corner. Press the narrow strip around the corner, and let the ears fold down onto the roof. Because the skylight corners are potential leak points, back up this vulnerable area with small patch pieces of membrane 1½ in. to 2 in. wide. Make them bow-tie shaped so that they have more surface area that can bond to the

skylight frame. Apply the strip firmly along one edge first, then stretch it through the corner before bonding to the other edge.

3. CREATE SIDE GUTTERS
Run membrane strips up the side of the frame, and let them overlap the underlayment by 1 in. to 2 in. After adhering the strip to the frame, fold back the underlayment, bond the membrane to the underside of the underlayment, and fold the two layers back toward the frame. Apply a small patch of membrane across the top of the fold, just above the frame.

4. THE HEAD MEMBRANE GOES ON LAST
Run the head membrane across everything at the top, trimming and reinforcing the corners in the same manner as the bottom membrane.

INSTALLATION TIP. After I cut strips of self-adhering membrane, I dry-fit them in place, then flip them over and score the release sheet along the fold line. Now I can stick the membrane to one surface and apply the other half when it's in place.

To make a gutter that directs water down and away from the frame, the side membrane is bonded to the underside of the underlayment, then folded back toward the skylight frame.

Bow-tie patches stretched around the corners reinforce areas susceptible to leaks.

The underlayment is trimmed to the edge of the membrane after the two are bonded.

INTEGRATE THE METAL FLASHING WITH THE ROOF

ONCE I'VE BROUGHT THE SHINGLE COURSES back to the bottom of the frame, I install the base-flashing piece, then begin to alternate between the step flashing and the shingles up along the frame. This skylight was a fixed frame, so the gasket was built into the window frame. If the skylight is operable, the gasket is separate, and I tuck the top edge of the flashing beneath the gasket first, then attach the step flashing with short nails or screws to the side of the skylight frame. I position the bottom edge of each step flashing above the self-adhesive strip of the shingle below.

1. BASE FLASHING
After bringing the shingles back up to the bottom of the frame, secure the base flashing to the frame with short nails or screws.

2. STEP FLASHING
Beginning at the bottom of the frame, weave the step flashing into the shingle courses.

3. HEAD FLASHING
Once the head flashing is nailed off, overlap its upper flange with the underlayment and seal the seam with strips of membrane.

Trim the shingles above to leave a 2-in. space above the head so that it won't collect debris.

Trim the shingles ½ in. from the sides of the skylight frame.

of the curb, the step flashing is integrated into the shingle courses along the sides, and the head flashing caps the top. I slip the top edge of the flashing under the skylight gasket, then secure the base flashing to the frame with short nails or screws at the top corners. When replacing shingles, I don't drive nails through the step flashing; their rigidity prevents the last several inches of shingle from lifting up.

With the head flashing nailed in, I slip the last couple of shingle courses beneath those still in place, lifting up the shingles to hammer the nails. Most important, I keep in mind that I have to renail the courses above the skylight. It's a place that's easy to forget at the end of a long day spent working on the roof.

WITH THE CURBS FLASHED, fasten the window to the frame. This skylight was a fixed frame, so the counter-flashing was part of the window frame. Don't forget to remove the protective plastic sheet before you descend the ladder.

Wiring a Small Addition

BY CLIFFORD A. POPEJOY

I t's amazing how electrical-code requirements have evolved for the wiring in bedrooms and bathrooms, the rooms that make up a master suite. These safety requirements are intended to protect against electrical fire in the bedroom when we're asleep and vulnerable, and against shock and electrocution in the bathroom where electricity and water can be an extremely dangerous combination.

When I started working on this 350-sq.-ft. master-suite addition, I received an electrical plan that met minimum code requirements in most instances and exceeded them in others. After going over the plan and examining the existing electrical system, I explained to the homeowners how I would integrate the new and old wiring, meet all the code requirements, and add a few upgraded features that would improve the comfort and convenience of their new master suite.

Begin by examining the old wiring

With the electrical plan in hand, the first thing I did on this job was to examine the existing wiring to determine two things: its condition and its existing capacity. In any master-suite addition wired to meet National Electrical Code (NEC) requirements, chances are you'll need to add at least two new

HOW TO READ AN ELECTRICAL PLAN

ELECTRICAL PLANS SHOW APPROXIMATE LOCATIONS for outlets, lights, fans, and smoke detectors. They also show how fixtures and outlets should be switched. Using the legend, you can decipher more information, including the type of light fixture or outlet to install. Before installing boxes or fixtures, make sure the plan meets local code requirements. Then, walk around and place the boxes and fixtures on the floor near their approximate locations. This will help you to identify problems with the plan. On this project, I made changes to bring the plan up to code, to make the

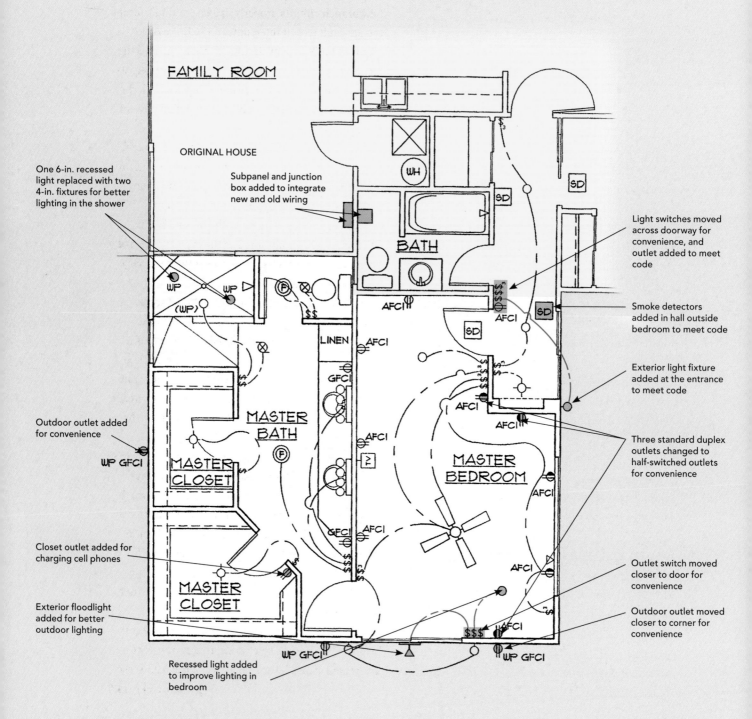

One 6-in. recessed light replaced with two 4-in. fixtures for better lighting in the shower

Subpanel and junction box added to integrate new and old wiring

Light switches moved across doorway for convenience, and outlet added to meet code

Smoke detectors added in hall outside bedroom to meet code

Exterior light fixture added at the entrance to meet code

Outdoor outlet added for convenience

Three standard duplex outlets changed to half-switched outlets for convenience

Closet outlet added for charging cell phones

Outlet switch moved closer to door for convenience

Exterior floodlight added for better outdoor lighting

Outdoor outlet moved closer to corner for convenience

Recessed light added to improve lighting in bedroom

FAMILY ROOM

ORIGINAL HOUSE

BATH

LINEN

MASTER BATH

MASTER CLOSET

MASTER CLOSET

MASTER BEDROOM

addition more convenient, and to make an art niche more attractive. What you won't find on an electrical plan is a breakdown of circuits or information on where to run cable (see the following pages).

LEGEND

$	Single-pole switch
$3	Three-way switch
⏚	120v standard duplex outlet
⏚	120v standard duplex outlet, half-switched
⏚ GFCI	Ground-fault circuit interrupter
⏚ AFCI	Arc-fault circuit interrupter
⏚ WP	Weatherproof receptacle
⊗	Exhaust fan
⎓	Surface-mounted incandescent light
○	Recessed incandescent light
⊢○	Wall-hung incandescent light
○○○○	Light bar
SD	Smoke detector
Ⓕ	Fluorescent light fixture
▽	Telephone jack
TV	Cable-TV outlet
⊼	Floodlight

circuits. I knew that here, though, I would want to add more.

The main electrical panel was at the far corner of the house, and the existing subpanel was in bad condition. It didn't have a separate equipment-grounding conductor, which meant that there was no place to hook up the grounding wires from the new branch circuits properly; it also wouldn't accept the arc-fault circuit interrupter (AFCI) breaker, required for bedroom circuits. These issues and the fact that the subpanel was failing, causing the lights to blink, simplified the decision to replace both the subpanel and the feeder cable that supplied power from the main panel.

If you decide to add circuits to an existing panel (main or sub), the first thing you should do is figure out what power is supplied by the panel (what the highest actual loads are) and compare it to the panel's capacity as marked on the panel label. If the panel is in good condition, has the capacity and the open breaker spaces, and will accept the necessary breakers, you're all set.

The electrical plan for this job included some features that exceed code minimums, including three-way-switched outlets in the bedroom and three-way switches for the ceiling-fan light. It also left out a few requirements, including an outlet and a smoke detector in the hallway immediately outside the bedroom and an exterior light fixture near the east-facing entry door.

The homeowners suggested two additional outlets: one outside for outdoor tools and appliances, and one in the master closet for charging cell phones. I suggested two additional exterior light fixtures, one by each entry door; changing the 6-in. can light in the shower to two 4-in. lights; installing an additional recessed light in the bedroom; and putting in a phone line at the cable-TV outlet for TiVo (not shown on plan).

The power for a master-suite addition rarely can be pulled from existing circuits. Bathrooms require at least one dedicated 20-amp circuit that can serve

(Continued on p. 157)

USE A SUBPANEL TO UPDATE AN OLD ELECTRICAL SYSTEM

ADDING A SUBPANEL is sometimes the best way to integrate new wiring with an old electrical system. For this addition, a new subpanel was installed to replace an old, failing subpanel in a poor location.

HERE ARE SOME OTHER CIRCUMSTANCES WHERE A SUBPANEL CAN SAVE THE DAY.

- If the main panel doesn't have enough open breaker spaces for the new circuits.
- When AFCI breakers aren't available for an older electrical panel.
- If it's a long way from the new wiring to the main panel. Pulling one feeder cable would be more convenient than pulling several branch-circuit cables.
- If you expect to need more circuits in the same part of the house in the future.

It is easier to fish one feeder cable from the main panel to the subpanel and a few metal conduits to a junction box in the attic than to run separate branch-circuit cables from the main panel to the addition. Locknuts fasten conduit to the panel; branch-circuit wires are pulled in later.

In the attic, a large junction box directs traffic. The 12-in. by 12-in. by 8-in. box houses splices that extend existing circuits. The box also directs the cables for the new branch circuits into the conduit that runs to the subpanel. Junction boxes may be in an attic or basement but must be accessible.

INSTALL OUTLET AND SWITCH BOXES FIRST

ACCORDING TO THE NEC, no point along an undisturbed wall in a room may be more than 6 ft. from an outlet, and any section of wall more than 2 ft. long must have an outlet. Also, consider convenience when locating outlets and switches. The right height is as important as the right location. A good rule of thumb is to put outlets at 18 in. (from the subfloor to the top of the box) and switches at 48 in. Don't forget telephone jacks and cable-TV outlets during rough-in. Installing the boxes before pulling wire makes it clear where the cables should be run.

ALIGNING A BOX. Face-nailing boxes (photo above left) are quick to install; the depth is set as soon as the box is fastened to the stud. Most boxes that fasten to the side of a stud have nibs that set the depth so that the face of the box is flush with ½-in. drywall (photo above right).

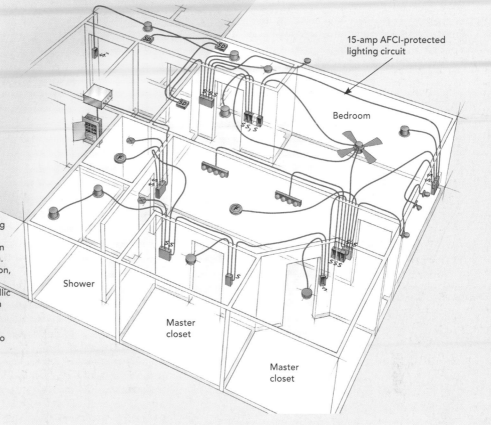

15-amp AFCI-protected lighting circuit

Bedroom

Shower

Master closet

Master closet

LIGHTING CIRCUIT

One AFCI-protected lighting circuit covers all the lights, fans, and smoke detectors in the bedroom and bathroom. In slab-on-grade construction, as shown here, the 15-amp circuit uses 14-ga. nonmetallic (NM) cable run only through the attic and walls. Power is run to each switch box first and then from each switch to the device it controls.

BLOCKING FOR TRIM. When hanging a box next to a doorway or window opening, use 2x blocking as a spacer so that the cover plate won't conflict with the casing.

COMBO BOX. This box has a line-voltage side and a low-voltage side. It's quick to install and lessens the clutter behind the TV, where these days you need power, a cable outlet, and a telephone jack.

HORIZONTAL OUTLETS. If limited space between a backsplash and a mirror in the bathroom calls for the outlets to lie on their sides, a 4-in. square box and a single-gang plaster ring do the trick.

STURDY FAN BOXES. If the plan calls for a ceiling fan, install a fan-rated box. This saddle-style box slips over 2x blocking. It is sturdy and offers enough space to splice a three-way switch.

ADJUSTABLE HANGERS. Use adjustable brackets for ceiling fixtures. A round (4-in.-dia.) fixture box on a telescoping hanger bracket makes it easy to position most ceiling fixtures between trusses or joists.

DRILL HOLES WITH WIRE RUNS AND STAPLING IN MIND

THE NEC REQUIRES NONMETALLIC CABLE (such as Romex®) to be secured within 8 in. of a box without clamps or 12 in. of a box that has clamps, and every 4½ ft. A cable running through a horizontal hole is considered secured. Run only two 14-2 or 12-2 cables or one 14-3 or 12-3 cable through each hole that will be draft- or fire-sealed to satisfy code requirements intended to protect against heat buildup and damage to the electrical insulation.

ATTIC RUNS. Drill one ¾-in. hole in the top plate for each switch in every box. Individual holes make pulling the cables a lot easier, and smaller holes let you get away without installing nail plates (above left).
CABLE DISPENSER. Pulling cable through the holes is easy when the cable feeds neatly. Available at electrical-supply houses, wire dispensers pay it out without kinks, snags, or damage to the cable. Leave plenty of extra cable to work with before stapling the run to the framing (above right).

RECEPTACLE CIRCUITS

The electrical code didn't regulate the number of outlets allowed on these circuits. It did demand specific types of breakers or outlets for certain areas. AFCI-protected circuits for both the bedroom receptacle and lighting outlets and GFCI-protected circuits for the bathroom outlets were required. Twelve-gauge cable is run through the attic to the first, or home-run, box and through the walls between outlets. On the east wall (the green circuit), five outlets are half-switched (the top of the outlet is controlled by a switch) for lamps and similar appliances.

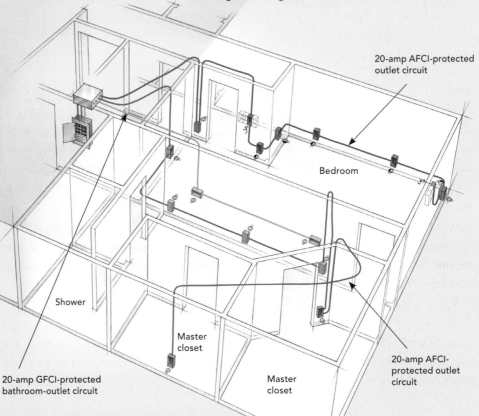

20-amp AFCI-protected outlet circuit

Bedroom

20-amp AFCI-protected outlet circuit

Shower

Master closet

Master closet

20-amp GFCI-protected bathroom-outlet circuit

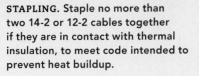

STAPLING. Staple no more than two 14-2 or 12-2 cables together if they are in contact with thermal insulation, to meet code intended to prevent heat buildup.

OUTLET RUNS. Run the outlet cables well above the boxes. You can eyeball the row of holes between receptacle boxes, but make sure they are about 1 ft. above each box. This way, you can staple the cable before it enters the box without bending it sharply, which can damage the insulation.

CABLE CLIPS. One clip can do the job of many staples. When running multiple cables to one box, it can be difficult to staple all the cables to the framing within 8 in. of the box. Cable clips can be nailed to the stud and can alleviate the need for stapling. These are great for several parallel horizontal runs, too. Install the clips with the arms pointing up to provide space between several cables and satisfy code.

either one bathroom's outlets, lights, and fan, or only the outlets for all the bathrooms in the house. The latter option is a poor choice; a hair dryer alone can max out a 20-amp circuit. Here, I added one circuit for just the two bathroom outlets.

The NEC has no requirement that governs how many circuits are needed for general-use outlets and lights in residential bedrooms. For receptacles in commercial buildings, there is a requirement to assume 180 volt-amps (watts) of demand per standard duplex outlet. This translates to 10 outlets on a 15-amp circuit or 13 on a 20-amp circuit. I like to use it as a rule of thumb in houses as well.

Including the outdoor outlets, the bedroom here has 13 receptacles. One 20-amp circuit might have been OK, but I wanted plenty of power available for

large tools and appliances at the two outside outlets, so I separated the outlets into two 20-amp circuits. Finally, one 15-amp circuit supplies power to the bedroom and bathroom lighting (including fans and smoke detectors). Together with a dedicated circuit for a hot-water booster (not shown on plan), I pulled five new circuits. This is more than twice as many circuits as required by the NEC, with plenty of power to supply the additional lights and outlets without causing future overloading problems.

Avoid a shock in the bathroom

Outlets in the bathroom must have ground-fault circuit interrupter (GFCI) protection because of their proximity to water sources. GFCIs trip when they detect current leaking out of the circuit, which can cause shock or electrocution. This can be done with a GFCI breaker in the panel or with GFCI outlets in the bathroom.

To me, GFCI outlets make more sense than GFCI breakers because they are more convenient to reset when they trip. And they will trip sooner or later, if not because of dangerous current leakage, then because of humidity and dust allowing current to leak between the prongs of an appliance plug or even across the face of the outlet.

The NEC also requires that a bathroom have an outlet within 36 in. of the sink. This bath had two sinks, and although one outlet would have satisfied code, it wouldn't have been convenient. Instead, the plan called for two receptacles above the backsplash. The first in line was a GFCI outlet, and it protected the downstream outlet as well.

In this case, because of a large mirror above the counter, there wasn't enough space for vertically oriented outlets. I used 4-in.-sq. deep junction boxes with plaster rings so that I could install the outlets horizontally. The deep boxes also gave me plenty of room for the bulky GFCI and the 12-ga. wires.

Precautions for safe sleeping

Per the NEC, all circuits supplying power inside a bedroom, hallways, and other living areas (except kitchens and bathrooms) must have AFCI protection for fire safety. This is provided by a special circuit breaker that recognizes certain arcing or sparking and cuts the power.

To meet this AFCI-protection requirement, the panel where the circuit originates has to have an arc-fault breaker available for use in it. Older panels may not be compatible with AFCI breakers. I won't use any breaker in a panel unless it is listed by Underwriters Laboratories (UL) for use in that panel. The listing means the breaker has been designed and tested to work in the panel. It's not just a matter of physical fit; the listing is a guarantee that the breaker and panel will work together even under extreme conditions.

Smoke detectors are required by the National Fire Code, not by the NEC. Whatever the source of

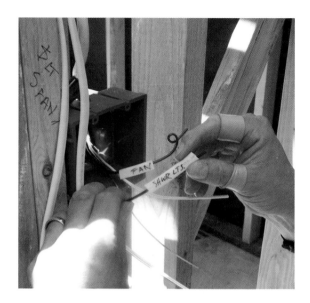

LABEL EVERYTHING. For multigang switch boxes, make sure that each wire is labeled. Remove the paper from scraps of the cable jacket to label the wires for each switch.

the requirement, wiring for interlinked hardwired smoke detectors with battery backups is required in all new construction. Although this requirement has several aspects, the most basic mandate is for a smoke detector in each bedroom and one in the area outside bedrooms. I installed one additional smoke detector beyond that shown in the plan, at the far end of the hallway leading to the new master suite. Besides offering better protection, this unit will make it easier to extend the linked-detector circuit to the rest of the house in the future.

It's up to you to research codes

The electrical-code requirements here are from the 2008 NEC. Many jurisdictions use earlier versions, and some make amendments to it. For instance, some cities require AFCI protection only for bedroom-receptacle outlets. Others limit the number of outlets allowed on a branch circuit. It's up to you to find out which version of the NEC is being used in your area and whether any amendments have been adopted. This information should be available in writing.

Add Character with a Box-Beam Ceiling

BY CHRIS WHALEN

Box-beam ceilings are a great way to add personality, elegance, and character to an otherwise ordinary space. In a room with an oddly placed structural beam, box beams can make sense of the unbalanced ceiling. Furthermore, the hollow beams can house recessed lighting and provide a chase for wiring. Whether the beams are painted or stained, the layout principles are the same, and the joinery and design can be as simple or as elaborate as you want.

A recent restoration that my company undertook provided an excellent opportunity for a box-beam ceiling: a 1970s breezeway connecting a 19th-century Queen Anne Victorian to its detached garage. The box beams and custom wall paneling helped to convert this cold breezeway into an inviting entertainment room, a cozy place to enjoy the fireplace, the wet bar, and the entertainment center.

You don't need a perfectly shaped room

Although square or rectangular rooms are the most likely candidates for box-beam ceilings, almost any room shape will work, even circular or triangular rooms. The key is to create a symmetrical layout. The breezeway is roughly rectangular, with a small bump-out in the ceiling on one end. We eliminated the bump-out by adding a soffit to one end of the room.

A typical box-beam installation usually includes some sort of perimeter band that the box beams butt into. Because banks of tall windows ran along the sidewalls, we chose to run the window head-casing assembly (which extended to the ceiling) continuously around the room, thus using it as the band. The head casing had a curved face, so the beam ends needed to be scribed and cut to fit tightly against the profile.

The grid created by the beams should be either rectangular or square. We designed a square grid that lined up with other details in the room. Along one wall is a fireplace with flanking bookcases. Dividing this space with two beams centered the fireplace nicely and visually separated the bookcases. Placement of the perpendicular beams was determined by the space between the first two; adjusting the soffits made the grid roughly square.

There are many ways to make a box beam

The size of the perimeter band determines the height of the box beams. We could have aligned the bottom of the beams with the bottom of the band, but because the ceilings in this breezeway are about a

COMBINE BASIC STOCK AND MOLDINGS FOR AN ATTRACTIVE DETAIL

THE BUILT-UP BEAM is anchored to backing cut from 2x6 framing lumber. A quirk joint formed by rabbeting the sides and slipping the bottom between them makes a tight-fitting, attractive, relatively simple joint. Cove molding provides a graceful transition between the sides and the ceiling. This simple joinery is typical of the Craftsman style.

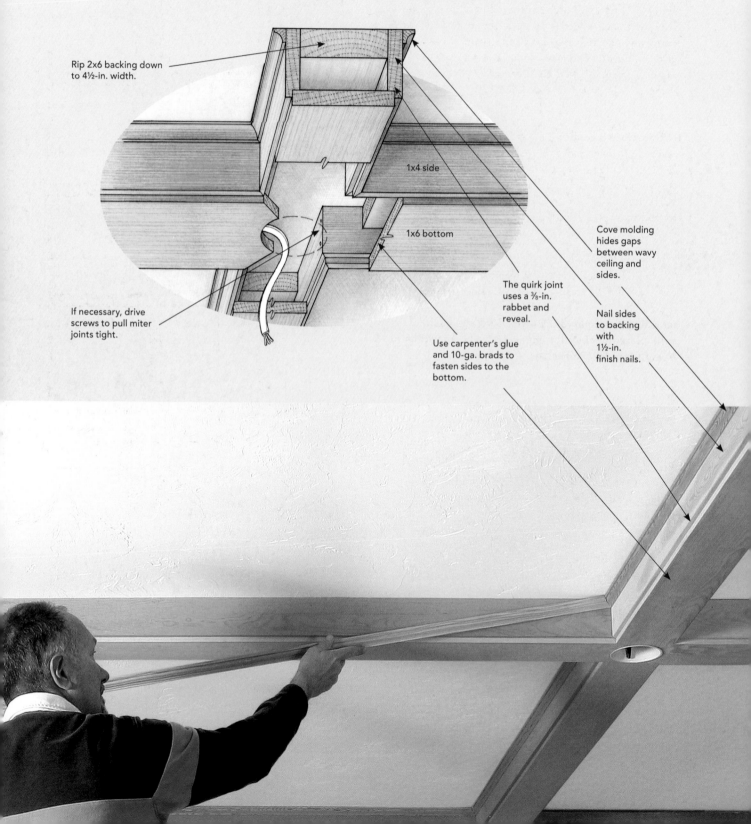

Rip 2x6 backing down to 4½-in. width.

1x4 side

1x6 bottom

Cove molding hides gaps between wavy ceiling and sides.

The quirk joint uses a ⅜-in. rabbet and reveal.

Nail sides to backing with 1½-in. finish nails.

If necessary, drive screws to pull miter joints tight.

Use carpenter's glue and 10-ga. brads to fasten sides to the bottom.

START WITH A SYMMETRICAL LAYOUT

BOX-BEAM CEILINGS need a symmetrical layout grid, which can be hard to plan in a room with bump-outs. Although you can't change the shape of the room, you can change the shape of the ceiling with a dropped soffit. The author started the layout at the fireplace, which is the focal point of the room, and adjusted the soffit's placement to get a grid composed of square panels. You also can use the golden-rectangle dimensions of 1:1.62 as a grid if squares don't fit your space or taste.

STEP 1: FOCAL POINT DICTATES THE LAYOUT

The fireplace is centered on the wall, so the author divided the ceiling into three sections. Two or four sections would have put a beam running through the center of the fireplace. Starting with the focal point provided the on-center width of the panels for rough-layout purposes.

STEP 2: USE THE PANEL WIDTH TO DETERMINE THE SOFFIT PLACEMENT

The author multiplied the panel widths (83 in. in this case) until he landed just short of the end of the room. Four panels ended around 1½ ft. from the far wall. He calculated the exact openings and the soffit placement by subtracting actual beam widths from the overall dimensions.

STEP 3: DEVISE AN ASSEMBLY STRATEGY

There are three types of panels in the project featured here: corners, sides, and centers. Each type of panel has different parts and different assembly requirements. The edge panels must be cut, fit, and installed one piece at a time, whereas the center sections can be assembled on the floor and installed whole.

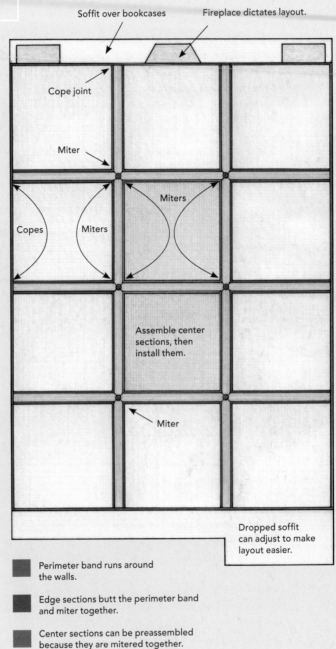

Soffit over bookcases

Fireplace dictates layout.

Cope joint

Miter

Copes

Miters

Miters

Assemble center sections, then install them.

Miter

Dropped soffit can adjust to make layout easier.

Perimeter band runs around the walls.

Edge sections butt the perimeter band and miter together.

Center sections can be preassembled because they are mitered together.

foot and a half lower than the 10-ft. ceilings in the Victorian house, we were nervous about making the room too short and top-heavy. Instead, we chose 1x4s for the sides of the beams and used a 1x6 for the bottom.

There are several ways to assemble the box beam itself. Our design, which relies on rabbet joints and a simple cove molding, manages to convey Craftsman-style detail with simple joinery.

Because the ceiling in this breezeway was plywood, attaching backing was a breeze, so to speak. We used construction adhesive and screws to hold ripped-down 2x6s in place. Without a plywood ceiling, you could attach the backing to ceiling joists in

INSTALL THE EDGE SECTIONS ONE PIECE AT A TIME

BECAUSE THE PERIMETER SECTIONS butt against the profiled band, these sections must be installed one piece at a time. After getting a tight fit on the cope joints, fit the miters with shims and screws.

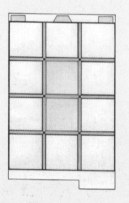

COPING FLAT STOCK TO A PROFILE. Scribe the profile with a compass, cut it with a jigsaw, and then back-bevel with a disk grinder. Fine-tune the fit with a rasp.

MARK THE SIDE FOR ITS MITER CUT. A straightedge extends the layout line from the backerboard. This is the miter's long point.

NAIL THE SIDES IN PLACE. Use 1½-in. finish nails behind where the cove molding will be. Make sure that the mitered end is at the same elevation as the other side pieces, or fitting the bottom pieces will be difficult.

CLIMB-CUT WITH CARE TO REDUCE SPLINTERING

Moving the router from right to left is called climb-cutting because the bit's clockwise rotation pulls, or climbs, into the workpiece. Rabbeting an edge with a climb cut and then a cleanup cut will produce a crisp joint, but climb-cutting can be dangerous. Grip the router firmly, and test your technique on scrap first.

USE SHIMS, GLUE, AND COUNTERSUNK SCREWS. After gluing and shimming the miter joints together, carefully drill a countersink hole to squeeze the joint tight with 1-in. drywall screws.

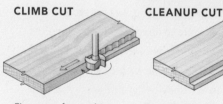

CLIMB CUT

First pass of router bit establishes a clean bottom, but side cut will be ragged.

CLEANUP CUT

Second pass of router bit establishes a clean side cut.

ASSEMBLE THE MIDDLE SECTIONS

BECAUSE THE JOINTS are all miters, the middle sections can be assembled on the floor and installed as a unit. Biscuits, glue, and brads keep the miter joints tight.

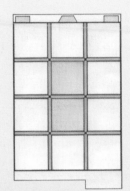

HOLD THE BISCUITED MITERS TIGHT WITH GLUE AND BRADS. One-inch brads act as miniature clamps while the glue dries. Applying glue to biscuit joints is easier with a roller bottle made for tongue-and-groove wood flooring.

one direction and rely on heavy-duty drywall anchors (or toggle bolts) and construction adhesive in the other. I like to hold the backing away from grid intersections a few inches to make fitting the inside miter joints easier.

Mill and cut the stock all at once

There are a lot of cuts, rabbets, and copes to make in a ceiling, and I save time by doing them all at once. After totaling the footage of beam sides and bottoms I need, I plow the rabbets using a router and a ⅜-in. bearing-guided rabbeting bit. Next, I cope all the ends of the pieces that will fit against the curved

perimeter band (numbering them as I go). Last, I cut the miters at the inside corners.

To eliminate chipping and blowout while routing the sides, I use a technique called climb-cutting, which is done by running the router backward (right to left) along the stock. Climb-cutting can be dangerous because with the router bit spinning clockwise, the cutting edge strikes the wood first and causes the router to climb (or jump) along the board toward you. On the first pass, though, climb-cutting creates a clean edge that resists tearout on the second pass (left to right).

Once the sides are rabbeted, I rough-cut them to length and fit them to the perimeter band with a cope joint. Normally, a cope joint is used to mate two pieces of stock with the same profile. To cope flat stock to a profiled piece, I scribe the profile, cut it with a jigsaw, then grind a back cut with a disk grinder. Touch-up can be done with a rasp.

Once coped, the other end of the box-beam side can be mitered to final length. Remember, the unrabbeted face is the finished face and will be the short point of the miters.

Install edge parts singly

Box-beam ceilings have one, two, or three different types of sections: corners, sides, and centers. The corners and sides need to be installed one piece at a time because the cope joints must fit tightly before the miters can be cut.

The center sections consist of four pieces that are mitered together. These mitered assemblies can be built on the floor and raised into place in one piece. I strengthen the miter joints with biscuits and glue before nailing them with 1-in. brads.

It's impractical to biscuit-join the miters of the perimeter parts, so I use glue, drywall screws (drill pilot holes with a countersink bit), and shims to align them properly. When installing the beam sides in place, the rabbeted bottom edges must be flush and level with each other; otherwise, the beam bottoms won't align with each other, which will cause problems at the intersections. There always will be small discrepancies between the bottom pieces, but they can be resolved with an orbital sander. If your ceiling has humps or bumps, you may need to scribe the sides to the ceiling or hold them down to keep them in alignment.

A few choices for bottom joints

After the side pieces are installed, it's time to insert the 1x6 bottoms between them. You can deal with the intersecting bottoms in several ways: They can be square-cut and butted together tight for a seamless look, or the edges can be eased, thereby accentu-

ating the joints. Another option is to cover the butt joints with a rosette.

For this installation, we chose the most difficult and trickiest method: a four-way miter joint at the intersections. The mitered boards need to fit tightly against each other but also to the corners of the beam sides. Most of the pieces must be fit between two stationary points (the perimeter band and the four-way miter), so there is no room for error. Because recessed light fixtures were incorporated into the beam intersections, our joints had to be perfect only up to the hole for the light.

The bottom pieces are tricky because both ends need to fit perfectly. First, get a tight fit against the perimeter band, then focus on the four-way miter. Because this band is curved in profile, I back-cut the end at a slight (5°) angle. Once this cut is made, I mark where the bottom crosses the intersecting beam and make a 45° angle cut from each edge, forming a point at the end.

Test-fit this piece, making sure it isn't too long and that it lines up with the inside corners of the beam sides, then glue and nail it in place. After assembly, the beam bottoms can be sanded smooth.

The final step in this project is to apply a small cove, quarter-round, or crown molding to cover the gap between the beams and the ceiling. We chose a part of the head-casing assembly, allowing us to continue a theme already established in the original house. The end result is the opposite of our original fears of a top-heavy ceiling. Rather than lowering the ceiling, the box beams open it up. Instead of the large, uninterrupted expanse of ceiling that used to loom low overhead, 12 individual ceiling spaces rise above the new box beams, giving the impression of a larger, more defined space.

BEAM INTERSECTIONS: SIMPLE TO SPECTACULAR

YOU CAN BUTT THE BOTTOMS OF THE BEAMS together, or you can use a four-way miter like the one in this project. Within these two methods, a few options exist.

BUTT JOINTS AND BLOCK. Hide butt joints with a block of wood to hang a light fixture from.

FENDER JOINT. Easing the edges of a butt joint highlights the simple joinery and is common in Craftsman-style woodworking.

ROSETTES. Hiding most of a difficult joint simplifies the joinery while embellishing the bottom of the beam.

FOUR-WAY MITER JOINT. This joint is the most difficult because eight different cuts need to align perfectly.

PART 5

Fix Up the Exterior

A Buyer's Guide to Windows

BY SEAN GROOM

When you roll up to a house for the first time, you can't help but notice the windows. Their size, style, and placement determine if they're appropriate to the architectural style and, to some degree, if the house will be a pleasure to be in.

For most people, that's as much thought as they give to windows. And that's too bad, because picking the right windows can lower heating and/or cooling costs, improve comfort inside the house, and improve indoor-air quality by dramatically limiting condensation.

To buy the best-performing windows for your house, though, you need to know a bit about how they work and what they need to do.

A window has four basic jobs

- The first thing a window has to do is control heat gain and loss. Technically, these temperature changes take place through conduction, convection, and radiation. As a practical matter, these temperature changes affect your comfort. If you're sitting next to a window, you'll experience conduction and convection when the glass acts as a cold radiator in the winter, and you'll experience radiation on a sunny day when you feel like an ant trapped under a magnifying glass.

- Second, a window must control solar-heat gain. I say *control* because heat gain isn't always bad. If you live in a heating climate—generally speaking, anywhere north of Oklahoma with the exception of California—you should take advantage of the free heat windows can provide.
- Third, windows need to regulate airflow. They should be airtight when closed and also offer fresh air when you want it.
- Finally, windows provide natural light and frame views both near and far.

Frame materials

The material you choose for your frame will dictate the performance, maintenance, and cost of your windows.

1. ALUMINUM $

Aluminum frames are strong, durable, inexpensive, and require little maintenance. Aluminum is highly conductive, however, leading to heat loss. To achieve even modest insulating levels, the frame and sashes must be carefully engineered with thermal breaks. Even then, they are best in mild desert climates or on impact-resistant windows in hurricane zones.

2. WOOD $$

The only choice for some traditionalists, wood offers a pick of colors (and it can be changed later on). Wood frames are moderately priced and have good insulating value and structural strength, but they're not low maintenance; they require periodic cleaning and painting, which adds to their overall cost.

3. CLAD $$$$

Windows with aluminum-, vinyl-, or fiberglass-clad wood frames are the most expensive. A clad unit offers the low-maintenance durability of aluminum, vinyl, or fiberglass on the outside and the thermal resistance and appeal of wood on the inside. Well-engineered aluminum cladding should strengthen the window. Custom colors for aluminum cladding can match any paint chip at an additional cost.

4. VINYL $

Vinyl frames are formed of extruded PVC. Multiple chambers in the frames and sashes add rigidity.

These chambers also act as insulation in the same way as the airspace between glass panes; some manufacturers fill the chambers with foam insulation to improve the frame's insulating ability. Vinyl is available in only a few colors, generally white and some variation on almond. Darker colors absorb too much heat, causing vinyl to deform and degrade. It's typically the least expensive window.

5. FIBERGLASS $$$

The best you can get if you want to maximize a frame's insulating ability, fiberglass is the least conductive material, and the frame can be insulated with foam. More expensive than aluminum, vinyl, or wood, fiberglass requires little maintenance and is durable and extremely strong. It can be extruded in low-profile frames and sashes in several colors and is paintable. Another advantage is that as the temperature changes, fiberglass expands and contracts at a rate almost identical to the glass. This helps to prevent seals along the glass from failing.

COMPOSITE $$$

Composite windows, like composite decking, are made of wood fibers (sawdust) mixed with vinyl resins. Up to 40% of the window content is recycled. Most, if not all, composite windows are sold as replacements by the Renewal by Andersen® division of Andersen® Windows. The material's trade name is Fibrex®. It looks a lot like wood, will not rot, requires little maintenance, and can be stained on the inside.

What makes a good frame?

When most people choose windows, they begin by considering the frame material. They might be predisposed to traditional wood or low-maintenance vinyl. However, according to Nils Petermann at the Efficient Windows Collaborative, the most important factor to consider is the frame's durability. This is where I'd like to refer you to an independent organization that provides unbiased durability ratings for window frames. Unfortunately, there isn't one.

You can make educated guesses about durability based on the frame material. But whether it's wood, vinyl, fiberglass, aluminum, or clad, a well-constructed window lasts longer and performs better than a poorly constructed one regardless of the relative benefits of its frame material.

The best way to get a sense of window quality is to read all the product literature you can get your hands on and to look at actual windows—a lot of them. Go to the big-box store and the local building supply, and open and close the windows on display, paying attention to how the corners are joined, how well the sashes seal, and how rigid the unit is.

On vinyl windows, look for continuous thermally welded corners. Examine the corner cutaway displays of aluminum windows for a continuous thermal break in both frame and sash. On a clad window, the cladding should have well-sealed corners and gaskets to prevent water from getting behind the cladding. Aluminum is an excellent heat conductor, so be sure that aluminum cladding doesn't contact conditioned interior air at any point.

Another way to sift through the options is to talk to reputable builders and architects in your area. Ask what windows they use and how long they have been using them. They won't stick with windows that make their clients unhappy.

Thirty years ago, when single-pane windows were the rule rather than the exception, companies looking to improve window performance focused their research on insulating glass. It was the lowest-hanging fruit. They've done such a good job that the R-value of insulated glass is good enough to make the window frame the weak link in the thermal chain. That's one reason why manufacturers list performance data for relatively large windows, say, 4 ft. by 5 ft. (When you're comparing windows, make sure the performance data are for windows of the same size.) Windows with large areas of glass yield better performance numbers because the frame is a smaller percentage of the window area. Savvy window designers understand this and tweak their windows accordingly for optimal performance. By using strong materials that permit low-profile sills, sashes, and jambs, they minimize the size of the conductive frame while being sure to incorporate materials that reduce air leakage.

Frame material can also influence how long a window stays airtight. Like most building materials, windows expand and contract with changes in temperature and humidity. When you see a window with moisture between panes, it's likely that movement between the glass and the sash broke the insulating seal. By choosing stable materials, you can reduce stress on the seal and increase the window's longevity. Fiberglass expands at the rate of glass, while aluminum and vinyl expand respectively three times and seven times more than glass. Wood moves in response to humidity changes rather than temperature.

Insulated glass reduces heat loss

Manufacturers typically refer to glass as *glazing.* Using glazing as a noun is a bit pretentious, like referring to a window as a *fenestration,* but it does

WINDOW ANATOMY

TO UNDERSTAND AND APPRECIATE HOW A WINDOW WORKS, you need to know the components that make up a basic window. While there are several types of windows besides the double-hung and casement illustrated here, the terminology used to describe each piece is universal.

WINDOWS NEED TO INSULATE

Sealed airspaces improve insulation. The more insulating spaces in the glass unit, the better the performance; triple-glazed windows are among the most energy efficient you can buy. Aluminum, vinyl, and fiberglass frames use extruded chambers both for strength and as a thermal break. Filling these cavities with foam provides additional insulation. Solid-wood frames are about as efficient as vinyl.

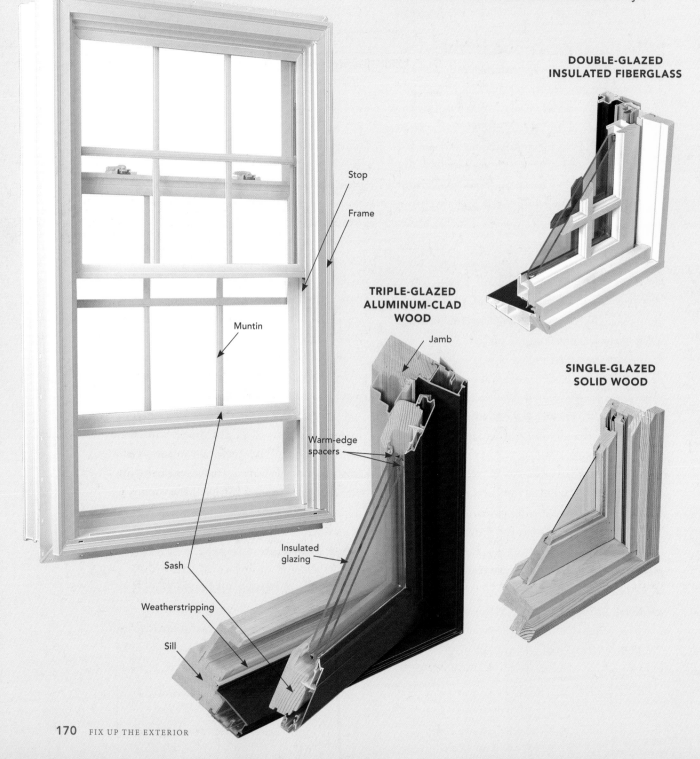

Stop

Frame

DOUBLE-GLAZED INSULATED FIBERGLASS

TRIPLE-GLAZED ALUMINUM-CLAD WOOD

Muntin

Jamb

SINGLE-GLAZED SOLID WOOD

Warm-edge spacers

Insulated glazing

Sash

Weatherstripping

Sill

WINDOW DNA: THE NFRC LABEL BY THE NUMBERS

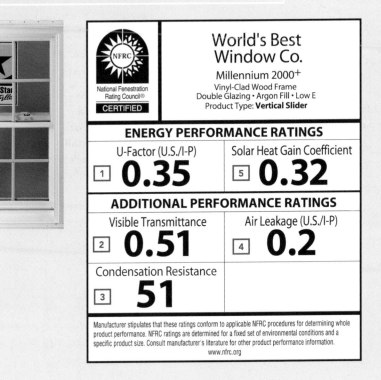

World's Best Window Co.
Millennium 2000+
Vinyl-Clad Wood Frame
Double Glazing • Argon Fill • Low E
Product Type: **Vertical Slider**

National Fenestration Rating Council®
CERTIFIED

ENERGY PERFORMANCE RATINGS

U-Factor (U.S./I-P)	Solar Heat Gain Coefficient
[1] **0.35**	[5] **0.32**

ADDITIONAL PERFORMANCE RATINGS

Visible Transmittance	Air Leakage (U.S./I-P)
[2] **0.51**	[4] **0.2**

Condensation Resistance	
[3] **51**	

Manufacturer stipulates that these ratings conform to applicable NFRC procedures for determining whole product performance. NFRC ratings are determined for a fixed set of environmental conditions and a specific product size. Consult manufacturer's literature for other product performance information.
www.nfrc.org

1. U-factor A measure of the insulating value. U-factor is the nonsolar heat flow through all parts of the window (glass, frame, and sash). A lower number means better insulation and greater performance.

2. Visible transmittance (VT) A measure of the amount of visible light that passes through the window. Values range from 0 to 1 (a higher number equals more light). However, most ratings are between 0.3 and 0.8 because they take into account the light blocked by the frame. Choose windows with higher VT to maximize daylight and views.

3. Condensation resistance A relative scale from 0 to 100 based on the window's properties. It predicts the likelihood of condensation, with higher numbers indicating less condensation.

4. Air leakage (AL) A measure of the amount of air passing through the window assembly; a source of heat gain and loss. This optional rating is expressed in cubic feet per minute through a square foot of window. Look for ratings under 0.3; lower is better.

5. Solar heat gain coefficient (SHGC) The percentage of the sun's solar heat that passes through the window. Higher numbers mean more passive solar-heating potential.

give the sense that glass assemblies in today's windows are a far cry from the single-pane windows installed in the 1970s.

Those single-pane windows have been abandoned in most heating climates because glass is a horrible insulator. A standard window today relies on an insulated glass unit (sometimes called an IG). This unit is a sealed sandwich of two or three pieces of glass with an airspace between the panes. IG units are manufactured by a few glass companies that supply the hundreds of window manufacturers in North America.

The airspace between glass panes, usually ½ in. to ⅔ in. thick, serves as insulation by reducing the transfer of heat through conduction. A single clear pane has a U-factor of 1.04, but a sealed double-pane unit has a U-factor of 0.5 (see "What's a U-factor?" on p. 172). Adding a third pane improves the U-factor to 0.3.

Replacing the air with gas improves the insulating value of the window. Manufacturers use argon or krypton gases because they're inert—chemically stable and nonreactive—and because they reduce heat loss, as they are less conductive than air. Argon and krypton also reduce convective losses because the gases are heavier than air, reducing gas movement within the insulating space.

Krypton performs slightly better than argon, but its bigger advantage is that the optimal spacing between krypton-filled panes is narrower than what's required for argon. That means less stress on the sashes, particularly in triple-pane windows.

Spacers are potential weak points

Spacers between glass panes perform three functions: They maintain a uniform separation between pieces of glass, they provide a good adhesive surface for the glass, and they create an airtight seal for the insulating cavity.

Although you should choose windows based on their overall performance ratings, the spacer, while small, substantially impacts a window's U-factor and condensation resistance.

The spacer's job is complicated by the fact that it's in contact with both the inside and outside surfaces of the window, forming a bridge between indoor and outdoor environments. Because the spacer is more conductive than the air or gas fill, it changes the temperature of a 2½-in.-wide band around the edge of the glass. As a consequence, the window's overall U-factor is affected. In smaller windows, the 2½-in. temperature band is a larger percentage of the window and has a greater effect on the window's U-factor. While spacers can be considered the Achilles' heel of all windows, a casement window performs slightly better than a double-hung of the same size because the former has less spacer area. Likewise, the thermal performance of true divided-lite windows made up of multiple IG units suffers because of all the spacer area in the window. (Simulated divided lites can also affect U-factor if the grille creates a thermal bridge between the panes.)

Spacers are made of aluminum, steel, fiberglass, foam, and thermoplastics, often in some combination. Foam spacers have the lowest U-factor, while aluminum has the highest. Today, quality windows use "warm-edge" spacers. (It's worth noting that warm-edge means only that it's less conductive than aluminum.) A good warm-edge spacer raises the interior surface temperature of the glass along the perimeter of the window. This is especially important at the window's bottom edge, which is most subject to condensation. At 0°F outside, a good spacer increases the temperature at the bottom of the inside glass pane by 6°F to 8°F. As a result, a more comfortable relative-humidity level indoors is possible during the winter without window condensation.

Coatings improve performance

Energy-efficient windows were developed during the 1970s energy crisis. When Jimmy Carter was installing solar panels on the White House and making conservation a priority, the Department of Energy's Lawrence Berkeley National Laboratory was charged with finding ways to conserve energy. Windows were among their targets. The insulating windows of that era allowed an inordinate amount of heat to escape. The lab's scientists concluded that by using existing technologies to deposit a virtually invisible metal or metal-oxide coating on the glass, insulating windows could be dramatically more efficient. This coating is transparent to visible light but blocks long- and short-wave radiation by reflecting it. Known as a low-e (for low-emissivity) coating, it's common today even on low-cost windows.

Depending on the nature of this thin coating and which window surface it is applied to, the coating can reflect heat back into the room to conserve it or

---

WHAT'S A U-FACTOR?

U-FACTOR RATES a window's insulating properties by measuring the flow of nonsolar heat through the window. You can think of it as the rate of conduction; the lower the U-factor, the less heat will flow through the window. (U-factor is the reciprocal of the more familiar R-value used to rate insulation. R-value measures resistance, so higher numbers are desirable.)

Although we tend to think of a window as primarily glass, the frame makes up 20% to 30% of the unit. U-factors are measured for the edge of the glass area, the center of the glass area, and the frame, but the important U-factor is for the entire window unit. Buying decisions should be based on this number, which appears on the National Fenestration Rating Council (NFRC) label, see p. 171.

U-factors for operable windows range from 0.14 for a super-insulating suspended-film unit to 0.5 or so for a basic double-pane window from a big-box store. Lower U-factors correlate with higher prices.

THE ROLE OF LOW-E

1. Reflects short-wave radiation to reduce heat gain.

2. Filters UV-rays that cause fading.

3. Tinted coatings, not low-e, temper visible light.

4. Reflects long-wave radiation to reduce heat loss.

filter sunlight to keep heat out. Using a coating on two different glass panes can fine-tune the amount of heat that's retained in each direction.

The measure of the amount of the sun's heat a window lets through is the solar heat gain coefficient. SHGC in shorthand, it ranges from 0 to 1, where 1 is uninterrupted heat gain. A clear-glass, two-pane insulated window has an SHGC between 0.56 and 0.68, depending on the frame material and construction. The size of the air gap, which is influenced by frame design, and the amount of light blocked by the frame and grille affect the SHGC.

A double-pane IG with two low-e coatings can achieve an SHGC of 0.33 (glass-only value). As the SHGC is minimized, the U-factor declines, which has implications for selecting windows in climates with heating and cooling seasons.

Choosing energy-saving windows

REGIONAL: A GOOD APPROACH

If you're interested in efficient windows, the starting point is an Energy Star rating. The greatest chunk of energy savings comes from good insulating properties. Energy Star performance prescriptions dictate that the colder the climate, the lower the U-factor you'll want. In southern climates, where air-conditioning dominates energy consumption, Energy Star ratings shift focus to a lower SHGC to reduce the impact of the sun.

The Department of Energy divides the United States into four climate regions (map below). Under the Energy Star program, each region is assigned threshold U-factor and SHGC ratings for a qualifying window (chart below).

LOCAL: A BETTER APPROACH

In the United States, the performance characteristics on an NFRC label (see p. 171) provide a moment-in-time snapshot of performance but don't relate anything about the long-term energy consequences and peak load demands of window choices.

To get a better-performing window than the Energy Star minimum, you need to take energy costs into account. A quick-and-dirty tool from the Efficient Windows Collaborative (www.efficient windows.org/selection.cfm) compares the energy costs for a range of windows with different performance characteristics. The cost figures are generated

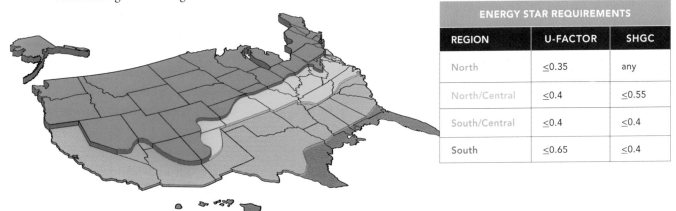

ENERGY STAR REQUIREMENTS		
REGION	**U-FACTOR**	**SHGC**
North	≤0.35	any
North/Central	≤0.4	≤0.55
South/Central	≤0.4	≤0.4
South	≤0.65	≤0.4

A BUYER'S GUIDE TO WINDOWS   **173**

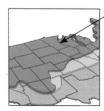

DULUTH, MINN.
Insulated fiberglass frame,
double pane with three films
U-factor = 0.09 (R-11)
SHGC = 0.26
Price = $280/sq. ft.

using RESFEN software (see "Site: Specific: The Best Approach" on the facing page) and are based on a benchmark house.

Their modeling recommends low U-factor, high-SHGC windows in the north region, the north/central zone, and the upper half of the south/central area; and low U-factor, low-SHGC windows in the southern reaches of the south/central area and in the south region.

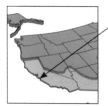

SAN FRANCISCO,
CALIF.
Insulated vinyl frame, double pane
with one film
U-factor = 0.27 (R-3.8)
SHGC = 0.47
Price = $50/sq. ft.

The most energy-efficient windows in all locations, except San Francisco and Flagstaff, Ariz., are at least triple-glazed with insulated vinyl or fiberglass frames. These windows are hard to find and expensive. The nice thing about the collaborative's website is that it shows how much annual energy expenditures rise if you opt for a readily available double-glazed window with two low-e coatings and an uninsulated vinyl or clad-wood frame. Exceeding Energy Star minimums saves money over the life of the window. (Examples shown are options exceeding Energy Star thresholds. Consult the collaborative's website or RESFEN for energy performance for your location. Prices are approximate window cost.)

Critics of Energy Star argue that in heating climates, the emphasis on insulating-value performance to the exclusion of solar heat gain misses an opportunity. By omitting an SHGC requirement in the north region, window companies can market a single low U-factor, low-SHGC glass package that meets Energy Star requirements in all regions. An

Energy Star label on low U-factor, low-SHGC windows in cold northern regions of the United States means homeowners who think they are buying energy-efficient windows are actually paying more in heating costs and adding more carbon emissions to the atmosphere than if they had purchased windows that accounted for passive solar-heating opportunities. (For some sites, a very low U-factor, such as the Duluth, Minn., example, is the best option.)

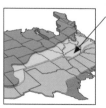

LOUISVILLE, KY.
Insulated fiberglass frame,
triple pane
U-factor = 0.23 (R-4.3)
SHGC = 0.39
Price = $80/sq. ft.

The Department of Energy is reportedly reevaluating the standard.

While insulating properties may not seem as important in the South where Energy Star thresholds are fairly high, a low U-factor helps to keep indoor temperatures cool. This reduces peak cooling loads and saves money in two ways: It reduces energy consumption in peak demand periods with higher rates, and by reducing peak loads saves on mechanical costs with a smaller air-conditioning system.

Window glass isn't the only or even the best way to block summer sun. Deciduous trees on the south, east, and west sides of a house work very well. Another strategy is the use of overhangs and shading devices.

If you need to rely on window glass to control solar gain in the South, you'll need low-SHGC, or spectrally selective, windows. They reflect short- and long-wave infrared radiation to filter out 40% to 70% of incoming heat. Sometimes known as low-e2 or low-e3, the second- and third-generation low-emissivity coatings on these windows not only reduce solar gain but also filter more than 99% of the UV-light that causes color fading.

Generally, you want a window to block solar gain but let in visible light. The window's light-to-solar-gain ratio (VT/SHGC) provides a gauge of its relative efficiency in transmitting light while blocking heat

NEW ORLEANS, LA.
Clad-wood frame, double pane
U-factor = 0.3 (R-3.3)
SHGC = 0.21
Price = $52/sq. ft.

gain. The higher the number, the more light transmitted without adding excessive amounts of heat. In a cooling-dominated climate, a ratio above 1.0 is better because light transmittance is higher than heat gain.

If glare is a problem, windows tinted bronze, green, or blue limit visible light and are spectrally selective with a low SHGC. However, because they absorb infrared radiation rather than reflect it, tinted windows radiate heat.

CANADIANS HAVE IT EASY

Windows sold in Canada have an energy rating (E.R.) that makes it easy to evaluate the trade-offs in heating-dominated climates. By weighing the amount of solar-heat gain against interior-heat loss through the window and heat loss through air leakage, the E.R. indicates whether a window is a net source of energy (positive E.R. value), energy neutral (E.R. equals 0), or a net loss of energy (negative E.R. value). If you live in a north or north/central zone in the United States or Canada and you're buying a window from a Canadian manufacturer, simply choose the highest E.R. possible.

SITE SPECIFIC: THE BEST APPROACH

Engineers and efficient-house designers use complex modeling software to evaluate the effect of window options on energy consumption. Rather than buying the same window for an entire house (as you would using Energy Star guidelines or the Efficient Windows Cooperative website), they tune the windows to optimize glass performance for each orientation.

The average homeowner or contractor can model the energy performance of a house and compare the effects of different windows with RESFEN, a free software package from the Department of Energy's

Lawrence Berkeley National Laboratory (http://windows.lbl.gov/software/resfen/resfen.html). Unfortunately, to get the most out of the program, you'll have to slog through the manual.

Generally, in heating climates, south-facing windows have a high SHGC (greater than 0.5), and east- and west-facing windows have a low SHGC (less than 0.3) to prevent solar gain in the summer.

Until recently, common wisdom was that the SHGC on north-facing windows should match east- and west-facing windows, but software modeling has shown that high-SHGC north-facing windows don't lose any energy.

Films create super windows

Another way to control the flow of heat through a window is with suspended films. These films come in two varieties: high solar gain and low solar gain.

Because these films (similar to mylar) are so lightweight and thin, as many as three films can be suspended between two glass panes. The additional insulating spaces increase the insulating ability of the window, replicating the performance of three-, four-, or five-pane windows without the weight. SeriousWindows uses this approach to create high-performance windows with both high and low solar-gain properties. The company's premium fixed window has an insulating value of R-11.1 (U-factor 0.09), nearly rivaling many wall insulations. The operable version of the window is R-7.1 (U-factor 0.14). Considering that the average insulating window is the equivalent of R-1 to R-3, SeriousWindows live up to its name.

Let the light shine in

Solar gain and insulating values aren't the only ways that windows save energy and keep you comfortable. Windows also control the view and the amount of natural light.

Daylighting, or window-placement strategies to maximize natural light, save money by reducing the need for electric lighting. Although placement is a design issue, window styles and glass properties affect the amount of light infiltration. The visible transmittance (VT) rating on the NFRC label (on p. 171) allows you to compare the amount of light that passes through windows, taking into account the light blocked by frames and grilles.

Impact-resistant glass offers protection

Although they don't affect a window's energy performance, a few options can make you safer.

Tempered glass, for example, can be specified for windows located where someone could potentially fall into one. Many of these locations are covered by code and include windows within 18 in. of the floor, next to doors, in showers or bath areas, and along decks, patios, and walkways.

If you live in a coastal area—particularly along the Atlantic and Gulf coasts, where building codes demand protection during hurricanes—or in a tornado-prone area, you can specify impact-resistant glass. Using the same technology as car windshields, a plastic sheet is laminated between two pieces of glass so that the window maintains its integrity after the glass is broken.

Window frames can also be reinforced to withstand impact. Available in three different strengths (impact zones 2, 3, and 4), the toughest windows in impact zone 4 must withstand strikes from at least two 8-ft.-long 2x4s traveling at 50 ft. per second, followed by 9,000 cycles of negative and positive pressure simulating hurricane-force winds.

Windows that keep the world at bay

Manufacturers also offer variations of pebbled, frosted, and wavy glass that add privacy to bathrooms, bedrooms, and other sensitive spaces.

If you live near a busy road, near train tracks, or under a flight path, acoustic windows can take the edge off loud or constant noise. Even if they don't readily advertise the fact, many window companies sell sound-attenuating windows. Residential "quiet"

windows are likely to be rated with a sound transmission coefficient (STC). A typical double-pane window has an STC of 25 to 27. Every increase of 10 in the STC cuts the amount of sound transmitted by half. Companies such as Milgard, Atrium, Marvin, and SeriousWindows have windows in the 40 to 47 STC range.

Self-cleaning windows reduce maintenance

For those of you who say, "I don't do windows," technology has finally caught up with your sentiment. Several big glass companies market coated glass that resists the buildup of dirt. Product names include Neat® Glass by Cardinal, Activ™ by Pilkington, and PPG's SunClean™.

By making the glass smoother and hydrophilic, rainwater collects in sheets on the surface and slides off the glass quickly, cleaning the window. Some windows include a titanium-dioxide layer that reacts with UV-light to help organic materials decompose, so dirt washes away more easily.

Window styles

1. DOUBLE-HUNG

Traditional window composed of two sashes that slide vertically. A single-hung window looks identical, but the top sash is fixed.

Pros: Available with a wide variety of grille patterns to match different architectural styles. Sashes usually tilt in for easy cleaning of the exterior.

Cons: Sashes rely on draftier sliding-style weatherstripping. The bottom edge of the upper sash is exposed to outdoor temperatures on two faces, increasing surface area for thermal bridging. Two sashes increase spacer area, increasing U-factor. Less than half the window area can be open for ventilation.

2. AWNING

Top-hinged window that usually opens outward with a crank.

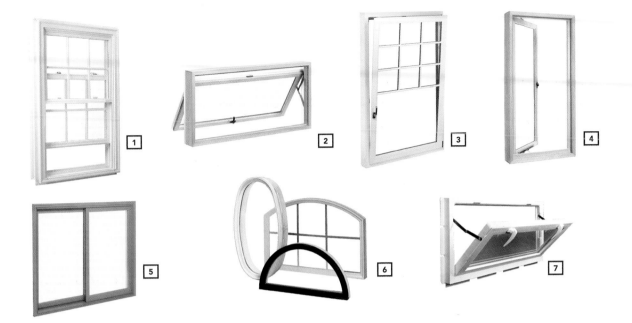

Pros: Good-sealing compression-style weatherstripping. Single glass unit and recessed sash improve U-factor. Provides ventilation while it's raining. Often used above and/or below large fixed windows for ventilation and additional daylight.

Cons: Screen on inside of window. Open window can present a hazard if installed along a walkway, deck, patio, or porch.

3. TILT-AND-TURN

Dual-action window that can swing in like a door or tilt from the bottom like a hopper window for ventilation.

Pros: Ventilation options. Secure multipoint locking. Compression weatherstripping. Large egress area and easy cleaning.

Cons: Shades and drapes can interfere with operation.

4. CASEMENT

Side-hinged window that usually opens outward with a crank. In-swing versions are available.

Pros: Compression-style weatherstripping. Single large glass unit and recessed sash improve U-factor. Largest ventilation area of any window style. Opening can be oriented to "scoop" prevailing breeze.

Cons: Screen on inside of window. Hinge design might not allow outside of window to be cleaned from inside. Open window can present a hazard if installed along a walkway, deck, patio, or porch.

5. HORIZONTAL SLIDER

The two sashes slide past one another on tracks like a sliding patio door.

Pros: Can be easier to open than other sliding styles, especially when placed over a counter.

Cons: Sliding weatherstripping and greater sash area lower U-factor and airtightness ratings.

6. FIXED

An inoperative window available in shapes that match operable windows, or as accent windows such as half-rounds to create Palladian windows and octagons.

Pros: Improved airtightness. Can be made in nonstandard, custom shapes.

Cons: Doesn't satisfy egress requirements.

7. HOPPER

Tilt-in bottom-hinged window.

Pros: Compression-style weatherstripping. Single glass unit and recessed sash improve U-factor.

Cons: Hazardous if installed at head height or lower.

Choosing replacement windows

You have three choices for replacing existing windows: a sash-only replacement; an insert-style frame and sash replacement window; or a new-construction window.

INSERT-STYLE REPLACE-MENT fits inside an existing new-construction window.

Sash-only replacement.

If the existing frames have water damage, the only choice is a new-construction window. If you're looking to improve comfort or energy performance, replacing the sashes or using a frame insert can help. They're a good choice on older homes where you want to preserve period trim, but from an energy and comfort standpoint, they're not the best option.

Replacement windows that leave the existing frame in place don't stop air leakage. If you've ever pulled out an old window, then you've seen fiberglass insulation stuffed between the window and the rough opening. Typically, the insulation is dirty. It wasn't dirty when it was put there; dirt was filtered out of the air moving through and around the window frame.

Another negative is that insert-style frame and sash replacement windows reduce the glass area because the unit fits inside the existing frame. You might be willing to live with diminished views, but are you willing to pay for that privilege every year? In a southern climate, the reduced glass area does not affect heating bills, but in northern heating climates, reducing the south-facing glass area gives away a lot of free heat.

An insert-style frame and sash replacement window is generally a bit pricier than a new-construction window. Installation costs are lower, however, because it leaves the existing trim in place and doesn't require any siding removal.

Regardless of the type you choose, replacement windows are expensive. If you're trying to save on energy expenses, new windows shouldn't be considered until you have improved the insulation and the airtightness of the rest of the building envelope.

SOURCES

There are hundreds of window manufacturers, the majority of them local companies. A sample of large national and smaller specialty manufacturers is listed here. Visit www.efficientwindows.org for a more comprehensive list.

ACCURATE DORWIN
www.accuratedorwin.com

ANDERSEN
www.andersenwindows.com

INTEGRITY®
www.integritywindows.com

JELD-WEN®
www.jeld-wen.com

LOEWEN
www.loewen.com

MARVIN
www.marvin.com

MILGARD
www.milgard.com

PELLA
www.pella.com

QUANTUM
www.quantumwindows.com

SERIOUSWINDOWS
www.seriouswindows.com

THERMOTECH
www.thermotechfiberglass.com

WEATHER SHIELD®
www.weathershield.com

Upgrade Your Entry Door

BY MATTHEW TEAGUE

O ften underappreciated but never over-looked, entry doors serve to welcome your guests, to protect against weather, and to keep out intruders. Not only does an entry door help to define the architectural elements of a house, but it also helps to distinguish the owner's style. Because prices range from $120 to the thousands, choosing an entry door involves considerations such as budget, aesthetics, and maintenance—issues based on individual need more than the construction of the door.

Many of the key components that differentiate a quality door from a lesser one, however, go unseen. Efficiency, durability, and the life of a door depend on the nuts and bolts of how a door is made. Here, I'll break down the three types of entry doors and look at the materials and techniques used in their construction. I'll also shed light on what makes a quality door and suggest where your money is best spent.

Entry doors are constructed of wood, steel, or fiberglass, each with its own attributes and draw-backs. Besides door type, there are a few things that you'll want to consider right away. For instance, pay attention to your local climate and the location of the door itself. Highly exposed entrances on the south, west, and east sides of a home receive the

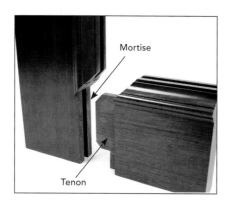

Mortise

Tenon

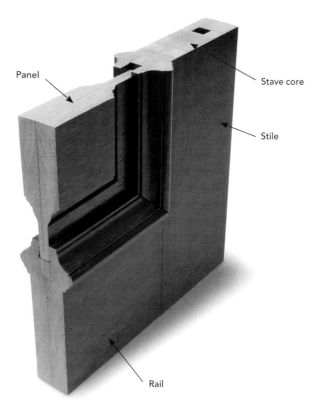

Panel

Stave core

Stile

Rail

harshest sunlight, making UV-resistance a necessity. Doors placed under eaves, porches, and other overhangs will be better protected. Most manufacturers of wood doors recommend that their doors be installed below an overhang that's at least half as deep as the distance between the sill and the eave. If you have less of an overhang, opt for a more durable door.

Wood

Although fiberglass and even steel doors attempt to mimic the look of wood, nothing matches the inviting, warm feel and heft of a well-made wood door. Available in almost any style or species and with countless glass orientations, wood doors not only offer the most traditional look but also the most options. They can be adorned with virtually any molding profile and can even be carved. Most feature frame-and-panel construction, allowing them to expand and contract with changes in humidity without sacrificing strength.

CONSTRUCTION

Although some wood doors are doweled together, those constructed with traditional mortise-and-tenon joinery fare better over time (photo above).

CORE

Most modern wood doors feature a thick veneer ($1/16$ in. is fairly standard) attached to the faces and sides of an engineered-wood core, which minimizes warping and helps to extend the life of the door. Core materials used for the stiles and rails vary among manufacturers, but better doors have stave cores (1-in. strips of wood glued together) with the same species of wood used throughout (photo above). Using the same species makes the door more stable because the expansion and contraction rates of the core and veneer are consistent.

PANELS

Panels are traditionally left unglued to prevent cracking as they expand and contract within the frame, but some manufacturers now use an elastic sealant to prevent air and water penetration in these critical areas. If energy efficiency is a concern, look for panels that have wood laminated over an insulating core. (See the sidebar on p. 184 for more on energy efficiency.)

FINISH

Wood doors can be painted, stained, or clear-coated. If you're finishing the door yourself, opt for an exterior-grade oil-based varnish or polyurethane with good UV-protection. If you stain the door, apply a minimum of two UV-protecting topcoats. Factory finishes are often a better option. They are applied under optimal conditions and generally offer better protection than those applied in the field. Also, many manufacturers finish the panels before construction so that as wood expands and contracts with the seasons, it won't expose an unfinished "tan line."

MAINTENANCE

A downside is that wood doesn't stand up well to the elements. If your door encounters excessive sun exposure or has an insufficient overhang, frequent maintenance and refinishing will be required. Depending on climate and exposure, wood doors may need to be refinished every one to three years. While a wood door can last a lifetime if cared for properly, a neglected one may last only a few years. Because the life of the door is so dependent on maintenance, most manufacturers offer only one- to two-year warranties on wood doors.

VALUE

Lower-end doors have doweled frames made of soft wood and cores of unmatched species, while pricier doors typically have traditional mortise-and-tenon construction and are the same species throughout. Stave cores represent the top of the market.

HARDWARE OPTIONS

ENTRY-LEVEL DOORS GENERALLY COME WITH standard 4-in. by 4-in. butt hinges. On heavier doors, including most wood doors, look for larger 4½-in. or 5-in. ball-bearing hinges. Spring hinges are sometimes an option on higher-end doors. They have a wound spring inside a large barrel that makes them self-closing. Adjustable hinges are another option. They're mortised into the edge of the door and allow for both vertical and horizontal adjustment so that if the door sags over time, you can move it back into alignment. With hinges, you usually get what you pay for, so splurge on the most expensive hinges your budget will allow.

Standard single-point locks work as you'd expect. The door locks into a single plate on the handle side of the door frame. Higher-end entry doors come with multipoint locking systems that secure two or more sides of the door to the frame. Some multipoint locks engage the threshold, door frame, and header, while others simply engage the jamb at the top, middle, and bottom of the door. A multipoint locking system not only makes your door more secure, but it also helps to keep the door aligned with the door frame to prevent twisting and warping. A multipoint lock also provides even pressure between the door and its weatherstripping, creating a better, more airtight seal.

HINGE PERFORMANCE. Choosing the best hinge may not seem like a big deal, but using an inferior hinge is. Select a ball-bearing hinge (left) whenever possible and an adjustable hinge (right) on heavier doors, which are more likely to need realignment over time.

HARDWARE SOURCES

BALDWIN
www.baldwinhardware.com

BALL AND BALL
www.ballandball.com

EMTEK
www.emtek.com

KWIKSET®
www.kwikset.com

SCHLAGE®
www.schlage.com

Steel

Steel doors are a good choice when budget, durability, or security takes priority over looks. Steel doors are available with a frame of wood, an engineered composite material, or less often, steel sheathed on both sides with skins of molded steel. In terms of aesthetics, steel doors come in a variety of styles, though not as many as wood doors. While a steel door might not be the first choice for a traditional home, it can look perfectly fitting on a more contemporary design.

CONSTRUCTION

Although instinct may point you toward a solid-wood frame, engineered or composite frames are more stable and less likely to warp over time. Steel frames on higher-end or safety doors are even stronger.

CORE

The foam core is made of either sheet polystyrene, which often leaves air pockets, or sprayed polyurethane foam, which expands to fill air pockets. For maximum energy efficiency, opt for sprayed polyurethane foam. Some core materials help to achieve high fire ratings, which are useful in high fire zones or multifamily housing.

SKINS

While some steel doors are embossed to mimic wood grain, few—if any—are convincing. Although some argue otherwise, it is often best to accept a steel door as just that, choosing simple patterns with minimal molding profiles. Most residential models are made of 24-ga. steel; stay away from anything thinner. Builder grades are often 26 ga., while high-end doors can be as thick as 20 ga. Dents, which are less likely on thicker-gauge steel doors, can be repaired with auto-body filler, and minor scratches can be sanded away and repainted.

FINISH

Factory finishes are available, but new doors usually arrive primed and ready to paint. Factory-applied primers are usually a durable, baked-on polyester finish—better than the average homeowner can apply in the field.

MAINTENANCE

Depending on the quality of the finish and exposure to the elements, the average steel door needs repainting every three to five years. Don't put off maintenance on a steel door: Once the surface finish becomes compromised, the steel deteriorates quickly. To prevent corrosion, repaint whenever the coating begins to crack, flake, or peel. Because corrosion is a concern, steel doors are not a good choice in any coastal environment.

In the right conditions and with proper maintenance, which is minimal, a steel door can last as long as 50 years. A midlevel steel door typically comes with a five-year warranty. Of all door materials, steel is the least expensive. Adorned with all the amenities of an entry system—door frame, sidelites, hardware, and so on—prices begin to rival wood.

VALUE

Less expensive doors have thin steel skins, sloppily applied moldings, and sheet insulation. More expensive doors have heavier-gauge steel, quality-engineered cores, and spray-foam insulation.

Fiberglass

Over the past 10 years, most door advancements have come with fiberglass because it offers the most promise for advanced performance. It's strong and won't crack, dent, or warp. A quality fiberglass door can look perfectly fitting on the front of even a traditional home. Except for custom-made wood doors, fiberglass doors are now manufactured in the same wide array of styles and with similar glass options.

CONSTRUCTION

Manufactured similar to steel doors, the frame that the fiberglass skins are applied to can be made of a wood composite, LVLs, and even steel to prevent twisting and warping. While steel frames are the strongest, composites and LVLs offer plenty of strength for almost any application. Frame joinery varies, but seldom is it a consideration because there is rarely any joint failure in a modern sheathed door.

CORE

As with steel doors, fiberglass doors are filled with a foam core that can be in either sheet or spray-on form. Again, spray-foam filled doors are superior performers.

SKINS

While you can buy inexpensive fiberglass doors with smooth faces, more innovative modern doors are textured to look like real wood. Although cheaper and earlier fiberglass graining looked inauthentic, better doors are now manufactured using molds made from actual wood doors, making them almost indistinguishable from real wood when painted or stained.

FINISH

Factory finishes are available in either paint or stain, but you also can buy doors unfinished or primed and ready to paint. As with other doors, factory finishes are applied under optimal conditions and tend to last longer than field-applied finishes. Some manufacturers—Therma-Tru®, for instance—provide stain kits to complement their fiberglass offerings.

MAINTENANCE

Keep the door clean, and restain it every two to three years with an exterior-grade finish. To strip a fiberglass door, you don't sand it. Instead, you essentially rub the stain off with chemicals and a rag. Finish scratches can be repaired by refinishing; deep scratches can be repaired with products akin to auto-body fillers. Because they're so durable, fiberglass doors come with warranties of 10 years or longer.

VALUE

Low-end fiberglass doors feature flimsy moldings screwed in place, large gaps in construction, and usually a lower efficiency rating. Costlier doors are textured using moldings from actual wood doors, which provides an authentic-looking grain effect.

ENERGY EFFICIENCY

In terms of efficiency, an exterior door works in conjunction with the door frame, threshold, and weatherstripping. While the door itself has an R-value, air penetration around the door is the biggest threat to its energy efficiency. Pre-hung doors arrive with the door and frame already hinged and properly weatherstripped, and some even come with all the hardware installed. Even so, it's important to be sure you're purchasing a door with the best performance possible.

IN THE DOOR

Fiberglass and steel doors with foam insulation are said to be as much as six times more efficient than traditional wood doors. Most wood doors are not even Energy Star-rated, but because all three types of doors are able to achieve some Energy Star qualifications, it's important to shop wisely. Although it seems counterintuitive, the most energy-efficient wood doors are usually the ones with the most glazing because low-emissivity (low-e) glass is a better insulator than wood. A basic wood door is around R-2, while the most efficient wood doors are around R-5. Fiberglass and steel doors are typically closer to R-8 but can run higher.

AROUND THE DOOR

Look for weatherstripping that fits into a kerf milled into the frame. Often called Q-Lon (a manufacturer's name), this style of weatherstripping is made of foam and is covered with a nylon jacket that springs back into shape. It's also less likely to tear or deteriorate than some other types. Q-Lon stays in place longer than adhesive-backed weatherstripping and resists compression set, which is common with some rubber products.

BELOW THE DOOR

A door sweep seals the lower door rail to the sill. Common door sweeps feature a metal channel that screws to the bottom of the door and a rubber gasket that slides onto the metal. Although they're not common, stay away from bristle-type sweeps. Because rubber gaskets may tear or become damaged over time, look for a sweep that allows you to replace the gasket without removing the door from the hinges.

Spray foam

Rigid foam

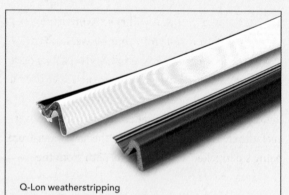

Q-Lon weatherstripping

Door sweep

The Right Way to Install New Siding

BY JUSTIN FINK

Water is lazy. It will never work hard to find its way into your house. In fact, water always will follow the path of least resistance. That's why the roofing membrane, asphalt shingles, siding, housewrap, and all the flashing details on a house are installed so that they lap over each other. They work to prevent the lazy water from being sidetracked as it follows its path from the clouds to the ground.

But houses are made of wood, and over time, wood shrinks and expands. Nails loosen, siding joints open, and finishes wear away. It eventually becomes easier for water to penetrate a home's outer layers of defense, especially the siding.

Once water has gotten through that outer layer, its potential for causing problems increases, and its potential for escaping or drying is greatly reduced. To prevent this trapped water from causing damage behind the siding, we need to give it an easy way out. It needs a place to go and a way to dry—and a vented rain screen offers both.

Yes, your siding leaks

For many people reading this, the biggest challenge will be accepting the fact that their siding leaks. So I'll be clear: It doesn't matter whether your house is clad with shakes, shingles, clapboards, vinyl, fiber cement, or stucco—your siding leaks. Water always finds a way behind siding, whether through gaps or cracks in the installation, wood movement, heavy downpours, or the heat of the sun driving moisture toward the cooler back of the siding.

But don't panic. Leaks are part of the reason that houses are built with weather-resistive barriers such as housewrap or felt paper under the siding. Even when installed correctly, though, housewrap isn't a guarantee against water problems.

Siding installed tight against housewrap isn't ideal for a number of reasons. Yes, housewrap is designed

(Continued on p. 191)

SIMPLE CONCEPT, BUT A DEBATE OVER DETAILS

THE THEORY BEHIND A VENTED RAIN SCREEN is straightforward: Water can drain, and air flowing behind the siding can intercept and dry out any moisture that has penetrated the siding. The details can be tricky, though, and there is ongoing discussion (sometimes argument) over the best way to handle crucial details. Here are answers to the most common questions.

1. HOW LARGE OF A GAP SHOULD I LEAVE BEHIND THE SIDING?

The size of the gap depends on how much water you expect and, in some cases, how much you want to alter details for trim, windows, and doors. A ⅜-in. gap is a good place to start, but even a ¹⁄₁₆-in. gap is better than none at all. A ¼-in. or ⅜-in. gap will allow many types of siding to be installed without having to fur out trim, though ⁵⁄₄ stock will be needed. The illustrations shown here use 1x3 furring strips to create a ¾-in. space.

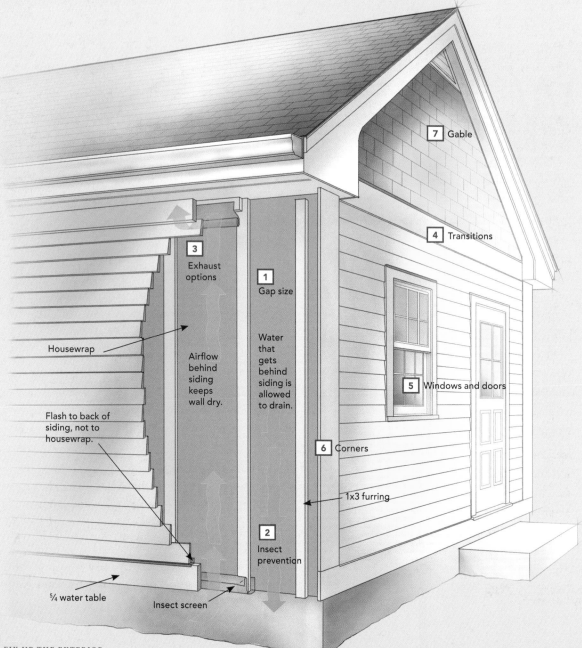

7 Gable

4 Transitions

3 Exhaust options

1 Gap size

Water that gets behind siding is allowed to drain.

Housewrap

Airflow behind siding keeps wall dry.

Flash to back of siding, not to housewrap.

5 Windows and doors

6 Corners

1x3 furring

2 Insect prevention

⁵⁄₄ water table

Insect screen

2. WHAT'S THE BEST WAY TO KEEP INSECTS FROM GETTING BEHIND THE SIDING?

The easiest way to keep insects out of the airspace is to use a corrugated vent strip with insect screen or filter fabric. It is attached at the bottom of the wall, over the housewrap, and is hidden by the first course of siding. The site-made approach is to staple up strips of insect screen over the housewrap at the bottom edge of the wall before the battens or open-weave membrane (sidebar p. 190) is installed. Then, before the siding is attached, the screen is folded up and stapled over the front face of the battens or membrane.

3. IS IT OK TO TIE THE EXHAUST INTO THE ATTIC VENTS, OR IS A FRIEZE-VENT SETUP BETTER?

This is one of the more controversial details in a vented rain-screen setup. According to building scientist Joseph Lstiburek, it doesn't matter much either way. Venting into a soffit is fine, as long as the soffit is connected to the attic ventilation. Although building scientist John Straube agrees that venting into a soffit isn't likely to be a huge deal, he prefers to see the rain screen vented at the frieze so that potentially moisture-laden air coming from behind the siding can mix with outdoor air before being drawn into the attic.

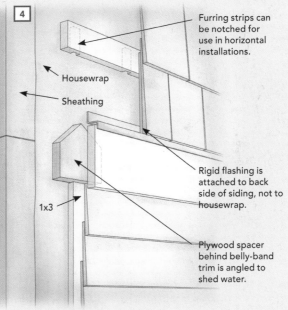

VENT AT FRIEZE

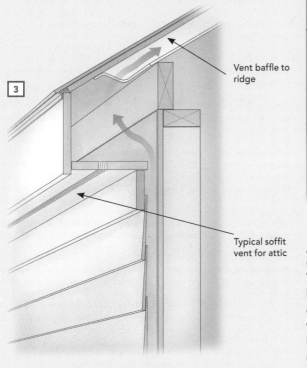

VENT INTO SOFFIT

4. ARE WOOD STRIPS THE BEST FURRING OPTION? DO THEY NEED TO BE PRESSURE-TREATED?

Best is a matter of circumstances, but wood is still a fine choice for site-made rain-screen systems. Plywood or OSB of various thicknesses can be ripped into strips and fastened over the housewrap, but most builders opt for the convenience of ¼-in. lath or 1x3 furring strips. The 1x strips (shown here) are

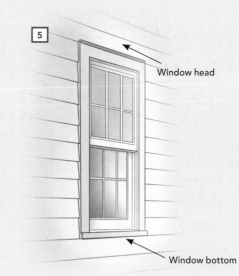

5

Self-adhesive flashing

Rigid head flashing

Housewrap tape

Self-adhesive flashing

Window

5

Window head

Window bottom

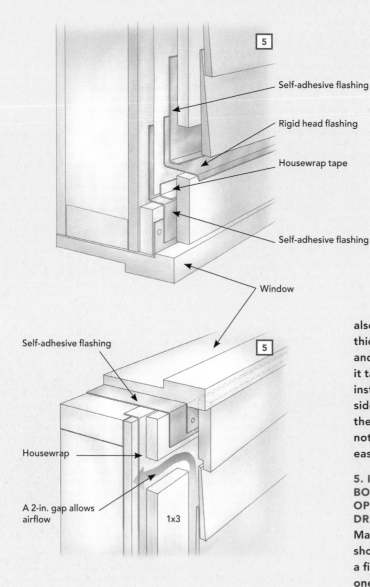

Self-adhesive flashing

Housewrap

A 2-in. gap allows airflow

1x3

5

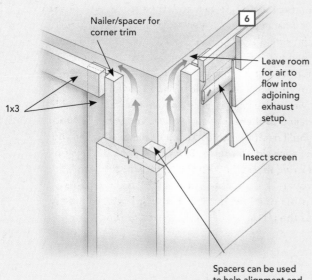

Nailer/spacer for corner trim

1x3

6

Leave room for air to flow into adjoining exhaust setup.

Insect screen

Spacers can be used to help alignment and offer solid nailing.

also common when installing siding over 1½-in. or thicker rigid foam. The strips hold the foam in place and provide solid nailing for the siding. Although it takes time, wood strips can even be notched and installed horizontally, an acceptable method behind sidewall shingles or vertical siding. Regardless of the type of wooden strip, pressure-treated stock is not necessary because the strips will be able to dry easily if they get wet.

5. IS IT NECESSARY TO VENT AT THE TOP AND BOTTOM OF EACH CAVITY, OR WILL ONE OPENING PROVIDE ENOUGH AIRFLOW AND DRAINAGE?
Many builders don't bother with exhaust vents in shorter sections of a rain-screen wall, such as below a first-floor window. According to Straube, however, one vent opening does not provide anywhere near the performance of a flow-through setup. That said, don't worry about intake/exhaust vents right at the window; just leave a gap for air to flow around the window.

6. SHOULD CORNER BOARDS BE VENTED SO THAT AIR CAN FLOW AROUND CORNERS, TOO?
According to Straube, the best approach is to isolate each face. The goal is to prevent rainwater from hitting one face of the house and being dragged around the more vulnerable corners by pressure differences. Straube also notes that a 1x3 nailed over a layer of housewrap is fine; there's no need to seal the corners with caulk or foam. You still can help these corners to stay dry by providing intake vents at the bottom of the corner boards that either tie into the attic ventilation or vent out the frieze.

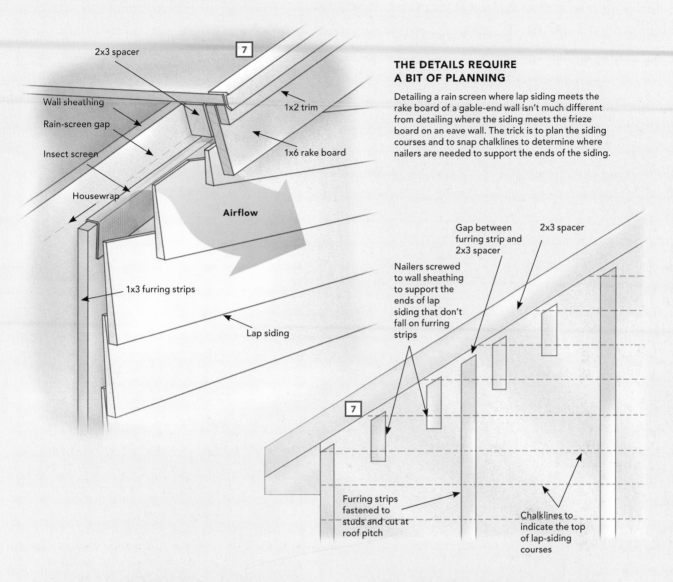

2x3 spacer

Wall sheathing

Rain-screen gap

Insect screen

Housewrap

1x2 trim

1x6 rake board

Airflow

1x3 furring strips

Lap siding

THE DETAILS REQUIRE A BIT OF PLANNING

Detailing a rain screen where lap siding meets the rake board of a gable-end wall isn't much different from detailing where the siding meets the frieze board on an eave wall. The trick is to plan the siding courses and to snap chalklines to determine where nailers are needed to support the ends of the siding.

Gap between furring strip and 2x3 spacer

2x3 spacer

Nailers screwed to wall sheathing to support the ends of lap siding that don't fall on furring strips

Furring strips fastened to studs and cut at roof pitch

Chalklines to indicate the top of lap-siding courses

7. DO RAIN-SCREEN DETAILS PROHIBIT ME FROM USING LAP SIDING ON A GABLE WALL?

Not at all. In fact, *Fine Homebuilding* editorial adviser Mike Guertin says that venting the top of a gable-end rain screen isn't much different than venting the eave overhang. The frieze board is padded off the wall to let air flow over the top of the siding, down the back side of the frieze, and out. On a gable-end wall, the rake board needs to be padded off the wall about ⅜ in. to ½ in. more than the face of the siding. Guertin recommends using a 2x3 spacer.

Staple a 4-in.-wide strip of insect screen over the housewrap about 1 in. below the rake-board spacer, then apply the vertical furring strips to the wall, leaving them about ½ in. short of the spacer. Fold the top of the screen over the furring strips, and fasten with staples.

Install the lap siding up the wall as usual. When you reach the gable level and begin cutting the ends of the siding to match the roof angle, cut each course so there's at least ½ in. of space between the siding and the rake-board spacer. To support the loose ends of the siding, screw short blocks of furring to the wall sheathing. You'll need to plan for this because the blocks need to be installed two courses ahead of the actual course that will be nailed to them. The easiest way to sort out where you'll need blocks is to snap chalklines for the top of each siding course. Blocks are needed only if no furring lines up within the last 8 in. of any siding course. Cut the top of the blocks at the same pitch as the roof, and leave a ½-in. gap between the top of the blocks and the rake-board blocking.

BATTENS, WRAPS, MATS, AND MEMBRANES

FURRING STRIPS AND BATTENS

Site-made vented rain-screen walls can be made from ripped plywood or OSB, lath strips, 1x3s, or any similar wood. Corrugated plastic battens available in thicknesses between ⅜ in. and ¾ in. are quickly becoming a popular alternative. These hollow corrugated strips allow airflow between cavities in vertical installations (under clapboards, for instance), but some can also be installed horizontally (under shingles or panel siding, for instance), providing vertical drainage. Products are typically 2 in. to 3 in. wide, vary in length from 4 ft. to 10 ft., and are installed over housewrap with nails or roofing staples.

    1. VaproBatten™
www.vaproshield.com
2. Sturdi-Strip
www.cor-a-vent.com
3. SV-3 Siding Vent
www.cor-avent.com
4. CedarVent and RafterVent
www.dciproducts.com

DRAINING HOUSEWRAPS

In areas of the country where the load on a rain-screen system is light, draining housewraps provide adequate space for drainage and ventilation. Because they still have all the qualities of a typical weather-resistive barrier, these housewraps can be used in place of standard smooth-faced housewraps, though you can expect to pay around 20% more. Some products have defined vertical channels and must be oriented to allow for drainage. Others have a nondirectional textured surface similar to the bumps on the surface of a basketball. If you are looking for a way to incorporate a modest ventilated rain screen without any changes to trim thickness, flashing details, or work habits, these are the products for the task.

    1. Hydrofilament®
www.hydrofilament.com
2. WeatherTrek®
www.berryplasticsbpg.com
3. RainDrop®
greenguard.pactiv.com
4. DrainWrap™
www2.dupont.com

FURRING STRIPS AND BATTENS

DRAINING HOUSEWRAPS

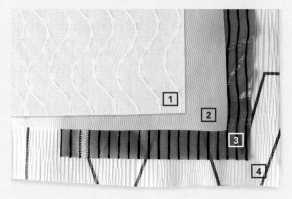

MATS AND MEMBRANES

This category is populated mostly by open-weave plastic membranes, which are almost entirely open space to provide maximum drainage. Products are sold in rolls, typically 40 in. to 48 in. wide, between 75 ft. and 125 ft. in length, and between ¼ in. and ¾ in. thick, though you can expect some compression when siding is nailed over the spongy material. The membrane is stapled over housewrap and is cut to fit around window and door openings. Products with housewrap attached to one side are also available, but don't expect to be able to peel back the plastic part of the membrane to tape housewrap seams without destroying the housewrap in the process. These membranes sell for about 60¢ to 70¢ per sq. ft.

Delta-Dry®, a semirigid plastic mat, is a bit different. It has ¼-in. dimples that provide venting on the back side and a combination of venting and drainage on the outside, under the siding. It is installed in place of housewrap, directly over the sheathing with ½-in. roofing nails or ¾-in. pneumatic staples, and is overlapped at the seams. Expect to pay about 60¢ per sq. ft.

Finally, Pactiv makes a ¼-in.-thick fanfold extruded-polystyrene drainage mat (R-1) that has ventilation channels on both sides. The rigid-foam product sells for about $3 per sq. ft. and is installed over housewrap. The manufacturer claims it offers a firmer nail base than open-weave products.

1. DC14 Drainage Mat
greenguard.pactiv.com
2. Home Slicker®
www.benjaminobdyke.com
3. Enkamat®
www.colbond.com
4. WaterWay™
www.stuccoflex.com
5. Delta-Dry
www.cosella-dorken.com

MATS AND MEMBRANES

to shed water, but it does have a weakness. Surfactants in soap and power-washing chemicals, and tannins and sugars from wood siding, can reduce the surface tension of water, allowing it to pass through the microscopic openings in the housewrap. Also, dirt can clog these openings, allowing liquid water to pass. The best way to eliminate this problem is to create a gap between the back of the siding and the face of the housewrap.

Less than an inch will do

Providing a physical gap between the back of the siding and the surface of the housewrap is like eliminating a bridge between two land masses. Remember that liquid water is lazy, so when given an uninterrupted conduit for drainage and all the appeal of gravity, it will follow that path every time. As long as that path runs straight down the back of the siding to daylight, bulk water isn't a threat.

Water drainage is only one part of the assembly, however. For a rain screen to function properly, it also must have a steady flow of air to help promote drying.

Consider ventilation

Except for vinyl, most types of siding are considered reservoir products. That is, they are like dense sponges: Even when coated with paint on all sides, they still can absorb water.

Differences in pressure (wind) and heat (sunshine) will drive absorbed water from the exterior of the siding toward the cooler back side. Unless there is enough water getting back there to drain physically or enough air leaking through the wall to help the water dry, it just sits. That's where the second part of a rain screen comes into play: the ventilation.

Located at the bottom of a wall, the same opening that allows water to drain also acts as an intake vent for air. With another vent at the top of the wall, air will constantly flow behind the siding, picking up and removing moisture on its way out.

The concept is simple, a vented rain screen is a best practice for long-lasting siding and a dry house. It's the details that seem to bog down many people.

Will Your Next Asphalt Roof Last a Lifetime?

BY SEAN GROOM

Historically, the appeal of asphalt shingles has been their low cost, both for material and installation. Early three-tab shingles, however cheap and durable, were thin and featureless. They were essentially a two-dimensional imitation of roofing slate or wood shakes. Manufacturers soon upped the ante by introducing thicker laminated, or architectural, shingles in an effort to enhance shadowlines and mimic the variability of natural materials. An improvement, perhaps, but they still don't fool anybody into thinking the shingles are anything other than asphalt.

Today the focus is on even thicker, more aesthetically convincing laminated shingles that offer much better performance and durability and that already account for 70% of asphalt-roofing sales. Now it's easy to find asphalt shingles with expected life spans of 40 to 50 years, or even longer.

Layered for better performance

By bonding multiple layers of asphalt and fiberglass (see the drawing on p. 194), manufacturers have created dimensional shingles that are thicker than three-tab shingles and offer better performance, thanks to the multiple layers of asphalt and lack of perforated tabs. Initially, the enhanced performance

on these shingles was directly related to their thickness: thicker shingle, better shingle. This is still true, but there's more. The materials themselves have gotten even better.

Improved backer mats do a better job of resisting high winds and nail pops. More important, compared to older fabrics, today's stronger mats carry more asphalt. More asphalt and better asphalt formulations have increased shingles' waterproofing ability and enhanced their stability, so they don't dry out and crack or become too soft and easily damaged. Manufacturers won't reveal any details about their asphalt formulations, but in interviews, they all acknowledge that improved asphalt mixtures have allowed them to increase the length of their warranties.

Finally, tuning the composition of the asphalt sealing strips has also improved wind resistance. The best shingles on the market are usually warranted to resist 110-mph winds with standard nailing patterns, but often, they can pass laboratory testing up to 150 mph. Look for performance standards on bundles and product literature. Shingles designed to meet the highest ASTM wind-resistance standards are labeled D3161 Class F, D6381 Class H, or D7158 Class H. But your best bet is the UL 2390 Class H certification, showing independent testing of shingles from random batches.

Thicker shingles look better and last longer

The longest-lasting products on the market are laminated shingles with lifetime warranties. These fall into two categories: dimensional shingles (the standard architectural shingle pattern) and what manufacturers call "luxury shingles." Intended to do a better job of approximating the appearance of shakes or slate shingles, luxury shingles are much thicker and can have larger exposures than dimensional shingles.

Mimicking a piece of slate or achieving the shadow-lines of wooden shingles requires a thick shingle. For example, CertainTeed's Presidential Shake™ TL

shingles are about ⅝ in. thick, and each one is made of three distinct layers of fiberglass coated in asphalt and granules. Their heft is one of the first things you'll notice—a square (100 sq. ft.) weighs 480 lb.—and is something to keep in mind if you're the one humping bundles up to the roof. (By comparison, a 30-year architectural shingle weighs about 250 lb. per square and three-tab shingles around 200 lb.)

Lifetime shingles typically use a mix of light and dark granules to enhance the shingles' depth further. Blending multiple granule shades allows the color to change slightly as your perspective changes, just as it would with a natural material. Color management on these shingles is good enough that you can use shingles from different production runs, and low-slope roll-roof products coordinate with shingles.

Companies offer algae protection for most of their shingle lines, and in most parts of the country, it's worth the small additional cost. By coating the granules in a thin layer of copper, they provide protection against blue-green algae. This airborne microorganism leaves dark streaks on roofs and is widespread across much of the country. If you've ever seen a clean swath of roof beneath a copper-flashed chimney, you have a sense of copper's effectiveness in this regard; however, the treatment is not ideal in low-rain areas or in areas with "salt fog," such as parts of Southern California, as the copper runoff can corrode aluminum gutters and flashing.

SHINGLES HAVE EVOLVED TO LAST A LIFETIME

MANUFACTURERS STILL OFFER THREE-TAB SHINGLES, but today the focus is on laminated products. Two-layer dimensional shingles, commonly known as architectural shingles, were the first step toward a more convincing roof and represent 70% of the asphalt market. More recently, manufacturers began creating lifetime-warranted luxury shingles, like the five brands shown here, with thicker two-, sometimes three-layer laminations, in the traditional architectural-shingle style, as well as more creative designs.

Fiberglass mat sandwiched between layers of asphalt

1. THREE-TAB SHINGLES
Their low cost has made them a favorite for years, and they are still available today. But these thin and featureless shingles have little aesthetic appeal, and they need to be replaced every 20 years or so.

2. DIMENSIONAL SHINGLES
Laminating two fiberglass-and-asphalt layers makes a more durable shingle that can last more than 50 years. The extra thickness and more random pattern offer some shadows and texture as well.

3. LUXURY SHINGLES
Loaded with waterproofing asphalt and composed of two or three thicker fiberglass-asphalt-granule layers, these shingles are intended to last a lifetime and to replicate traditional slates or shakes.

With an 8-in. exposure, this slate-style shingle looks best on steep roofs (9-pitch and greater). The shingle is made with two full-size laminates. The bottom layer is solid with no cutouts, the top layer has cutout tabs to replicate slates, and additional tabs are randomly applied to the top layer to increase the thickness and add the variety you'd see in a slate roof. GrandManor™ can be installed in coursing patterns or designs with CertainTeed's Carriage House™ shingle (a scalloped slate style) for a vintage slate look.

CertainTeed GrandManor
Style: Luxury, slate look
Wind-resistance warranty: 110 mph
Algae-resistance warranty: 15 years
Color options: 10

About 30% thicker than the popular 30-year version of this shingle, the lifetime model is available in eight colors nationwide, with additional colors available by region. The blend of granule colors creates a high-definition shingle with the appearance of transitioning shadowlines to enhance depth.

GAF-Elk Timberline® Prestique® Lifetime
Style: Dimensional
Wind-resistance warranty: 110 mph
Algae-resistance warranty: 10 years
Color options: 18

The crenellated design of these shingles looks skimpy, but with this triple-layer laminate, you actually end up with six layers of coverage—the most of the shingles profiled here. At ⅝ in. thick, with a 4-in. exposure and staggered lines, it's a good representation of a shake when viewed from the curb. If you like the idea of triple-laminate construction but balk at the cost and weight of the Presidential Shake TL, check out CertainTeed's Landmark™ TL. It costs about half as much, weighs a third less, and has the traditional dimensional shingle pattern.

CertainTeed Presidential Shake TL
Style: Luxury, shake look
Wind-resistance warranty: 110 mph
Algae-resistance warranty: 15 years
Color options: 10

This double-layer shingle has a granule color blend designed to add depth to each "slate" and create the appearance of shadowlines. As with many luxury shingles, special installation requirements apply. These shingles, for instance, must be installed in vertical columns rather than diagonally up the roof.

Owens Corning Berkshire® collection
Style: Luxury, slate look
Wind-resistance warranty: 110 mph
Algae-resistance warranty: 15 years
Color options: 7

Similar in appearance to CertainTeed's Presidential Shake TL, TAMKO®'s shake-look shingle is constructed of two layers, which provides four layers of coverage instead of the six found on the Presidential Shake TL. That said, the Heritage® Vintage® costs about 25% less than its competitor and shares the same UL-certified wind resistance. In fact, it had the best resistance against blow-offs in a recent *Consumer Reports* test.

TAMKO Heritage Vintage
Style: Luxury, shake look
Wind-resistance warranty: 110 mph
Algae-resistance warranty: 10 years
Color options: 7

TWO OPTIONS FOR EXTREME WEATHER

An extra layer of fiberglass on the back of these shingles prevents cracking.

Ceramic-coated granules improve solar reflectance.

IMPACT-RESISTANT SHINGLES

Houses in areas prone to hurricanes and/or strong wind gusts need a shingle with high wind resistance. And along with high winds comes a certain amount of debris in the air. Impact-resistant shingles contain a tough fiberglass base to prevent cracking when they take a hit. Tougher than the fiberglass used for the layers, this scrim is visible on the shingle bottom. Shingles with the highest impact resistance carry a UL 2218 Class 4 label and can withstand a 2-in. steel ball traveling 90 mph.

CertainTeed Landmark Special
Style: Dimensional, impact resistant
Warranty period: 50 years
Wind-resistance warranty: 130 mph
Algae-resistance warranty: 10 years
Color options: 6

Owens Corning WeatherGuard® HP
Style: Dimensional, impact resistant
Warranty period: Lifetime
Wind-resistance warranty: 130 mph
Algae-resistance warranty: 10 years
Color options: 6

COOL SHINGLES FOR HOT CLIMATES

If you use an air conditioner during most of the summer, you should consider two products that are designed to keep the roof cooler. By spraying the granules with a white ceramic coating before adding the finish color, the manufacturers of these shingles are able to improve solar reflectance.

Owens Corning Duration® Premium cool shingles
Style: Dimensional, cool roof
Warranty period: Lifetime
Wind-resistance warranty: 130 mph
Algae-resistance warranty: 10 years
Color options: 4

CertainTeed Landmark Solaris™
Style: Dimensional, cool roof
Warranty period: Lifetime
Wind-resistance warranty: 90 mph (130 mph with CertainTeed starter and hip-and-ridge pieces)
Algae-resistance warranty: 10 years
Color options: 4

SIX THINGS TO KNOW ABOUT YOUR WARRANTY

SINCE LIFETIME SHINGLES cost a good deal more than 30-year laminates, you should know what you get for the money. Aesthetic considerations aside, you get a warranty that covers labor as well as material costs for twice as long as the cheaper shingles, often a better prorated deal outside the first decade of use, and coverage for higher winds. Full warranty information can be found on each manufacturer's website, but here are the basics.

COVERAGE IS PRORATED AFTER 10 YEARS
The coverage period on a lifetime shingle is broken into two periods. If a defect is found within the first 10 years, material and labor costs (for installation only) are covered. Starting with year 11, only prorated material costs are covered, and labor is up to you. Damage related to transportation, storage, installation, or acts of God is not covered.

IS AN EXTENDED WARRANTY WORTH THE COST?
Companies focus heavily on production consistency, so manufacturing defects are pretty rare. While warranties are filled with plenty of qualifications, the fact that some brands offer extended 50-year full-material and labor coverage through certified contractors indicates that with careful installation, a lifetime shingle should be just that—with no need to pay for the extended warranty.

ALGAE MEANS A CLEANING CREW, NOT A NEW ROOF
If blue-green algae appear on algae-resistant shingles during the typical 10- to 15-year warranty period against this growth, the manufacturer will cover the cost of cleaning your roof. (Owens Corn-

ing prorates the coverage after the first year.) Don't expect a new roof or an easy battle, though. The use of qualifying phrases like "adversely affected" and "pronounced discoloration" suggest a potential claims hassle.

WIND WARRANTY REQUIRES A PROPER SEAL
The best shingles are designed and warranted to withstand winds up to 110 mph during the first 10 years. But warranties stipulate that the shingles must be exposed to direct sunlight to seal properly. If the shingles are installed in cold weather or if the roof doesn't receive adequate direct sunlight to seal the strips, the wind coverage doesn't apply. Coverage extends to 130 mph on some brands but requires a high-wind nailing pattern and the manufacturer's brand of underlayment.

WATCH OUT FOR HOT ROOFS
If you don't know how your roof was built, you need to find out before choosing a shingle. For instance, if you have an unvented, insulated roof, your shingle warranty may be void from day one.

HOME BUYERS, BEWARE OF TRANSFERS
Most manufacturers will transfer a lifetime warranty from the original homeowner to the first subsequent buyer, though coverage will be reduced to 50 years. Some manufacturers will transfer only if the house is sold within the first 10 years of the warranty period; for TAMKO, it must be within two years. Most manufacturers require written notice of the change in ownership within 30 to 60 days of the sale, and Owens Corning requires a transfer fee.

PART 6

Survive Your Remodel

A Safer Job Site

BY TOM O'BRIEN

For almost 30 years, the Occupational Safety and Health Administration (OSHA) has been ordered by Congress to "assure every working man and woman in the nation safe and healthful working conditions." Unfortunately, keeping tabs on safety is a much easier task in manufacturing plants and large commercial construction sites than on thousands of small residential job sites scattered all over the country.

Recognizing that many residential job sites could be a lot safer, the National Association of Home Builders (NAHB) has worked with OSHA to assemble an easy-to-follow booklet of minimum safety standards.

According to David Delorenzo, NAHB's director of labor, safety, and health services, the NAHB-OSHA partnership is "not about enforcement; it's about improving safety… [We're] trying to get away from the days when OSHA cited people for not having an MSDS (material safety data sheet) for motor oil. Now, motor oil hasn't killed anybody on the job site that I've seen. Let's look at the hazards, and let's figure out how to address them. That's what this is all about."

Not surprisingly, then, the *NAHB-OSHA Jobsite Safety Handbook* focuses on serious hazards, especially the big four: falls, electrocution, trenches, and falling objects, which together account for almost 90% of the deaths in construction.

Although the *NAHB-OSHA Jobsite Safety Handbook* is not intended as a substitute for the complete book of OSHA safety regulations (29 CFR 1926), according to Delorenzo: "If you're following everything in there [and you get a visit from OSHA], they're going to realize this is a safe site."

Copies of the booklet can be obtained from the NAHB bookstore (800-223-2665; www.builder books.com). The *NAHB-OSHA Jobsite Safety Handbook* is cheap insurance against disaster. Every builder should have a copy. In the meantime, here's a sampling of the book's most important safety issues.

A hard hat is no substitute for a safe job site

Employers are required by law to provide personal protective equipment such as safety glasses and hard hats. Far more important than having these devices on hand is the need for employers and employees to ensure a safe working environment. It's up to the employer to maintain an orderly, hazard-free job site and to provide adequate lighting to prevent accidents. It's also the employer's responsibility to educate workers on OSHA standards and company safety requirements.

THE RIGHT WAY TO SET UP AND CLIMB A LADDER

The base of this ladder is securely braced to prevent slipping. The worker maintains three points of contact while climbing the ladder and has plenty of extension above the roof surface to enable him to get on and off the roof easily.

The proper setup angle

For safety and ease of use, ladders should be set up at a 4:1 angle.

4 ft.

← 1 ft. →

Three-point contact: two legs, one arm

Level the ground or level the ladder

When setting up on uneven ground, take the time to establish firm, level footing . . .

. . . or attach a set of ladder levelers, which can be obtained from the ladder manufacturer.

Besides following the rules, it's up to the employees to make sure all their tools and safety devices are working properly. It's also the employees' responsibility to make sure their work never puts anyone else at risk and to report unsafe work practices.

AS TO PERSONAL PROTECTIVE EQUIPMENT:

- Hard hats must be worn whenever there is a danger of falling or flying objects (or overhead electrical shock).

- Eye or face protection must be worn when welding, cutting, and nailing (including air-nailing), and when working with concrete or harmful chemicals. Eye and face protectors are designed for specific hazards, so it's important to select the type to match the hazard.

- Safety-toe shoes are not mandatory but are encouraged when working around heavy rolling equipment or falling objects. Sneakers are not banned on the job as long as they have slip-resistant, puncture-resistant soles.

- Safety harnesses, not body belts, should be used for fall protection.

Don't prop up a ladder on a big misshapen rock

Because ladders are the most mobile and temporary devices for working above the ground, it's easy to be lax about their safe use. Serious, debilitating injuries often result from falls of 6 ft. or less. Take the time to set up a ladder properly (drawing on facing page).

- Ladders should be set up at a 4:1 angle (1 ft. out from the base for every 4 ft. of rise).

- To prevent them from slipping or falling over, ladders should be secured either at the top or at the bottom.

- When ladders are used to climb onto or off of an upper surface, they must extend at least 3 ft. above the surface (drawing on facing page).

- When climbing or working on a ladder, the worker should face the ladder and maintain three points of contact with the ladder.

- Do not set up ladders in high-traffic areas.

A SAFE AND STABLE SCAFFOLD

Adjustable base plates set on hardwood mudsills ensure stable footing. The fully planked deck, toe boards, and guardrails provide a safe, solid work surface and protect workers below from falling objects.

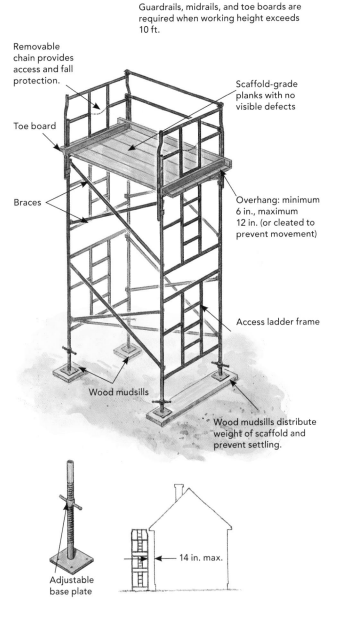

Guardrails, midrails, and toe boards are required when working height exceeds 10 ft.

Removable chain provides access and fall protection.

Scaffold-grade planks with no visible defects

Toe board

Braces

Overhang: minimum 6 in., maximum 12 in. (or cleated to prevent movement)

Access ladder frame

Wood mudsills

Wood mudsills distribute weight of scaffold and prevent settling.

Adjustable base plate

14 in. max.

Scaffolding needs good housekeeping and a firm foundation

Proper scaffold safety is as important for workers on the ground as for those above. To prevent workers from tripping and materials from falling, keep work platforms free of debris, and keep tools and materials as neatly organized as possible. For added safety, install toe boards if workers will regularly be underneath the scaffold.

WHEN ERECTING SCAFFOLDS:

- Each scaffold (drawing on p. 201) must be capable of supporting its own weight and four times the maximum intended load. (In other words, do not use pump jacks for a brick-veneer job.)

- Use manufactured base plates or mudsills made of hardwood or equivalent to level or stabilize footings. Don't use concrete blocks, bricks, or scraps of lumber.

- Fully plank a scaffold or use manufactured decking to provide a full work surface. Planking or decking must be scaffold grade with no visible defects. Manufactured decking should be inspected periodically to ensure that the end hooks are securely attached to the frame.

- Keep the front edge of the platform within 14 in. of the face of the work.

- When using planks, make sure their ends extend at least 6 in. beyond the scaffold edges, or cleat them to prevent movement. However, to prevent tipping when workers are walking on them, do not let planks extend more than 12 in. beyond the edges of the scaffold.

DO NOT:

- Place scaffolding within 10 ft. of overhead power lines.

- Swing loads near or on a scaffold unless using a tag line.

- Work from any part of the scaffold other than the platform.

- Use ladders, boxes, barrels, or other makeshift contraptions to raise your work height on the scaffold.

Fall protection is easier than falling off a roof

Fall prevention gets complicated only when great heights or steep roofs are involved. Otherwise, it's simple. Guardrails must be installed around openings in floors and across openings in walls when the fall distance is 6 ft. or more (top left drawing on facing page), and on scaffold platforms that are more than 10 ft. off the ground. Unlike a balustrade, however, an acceptable guardrail need have only a top rail (capable of withstanding a 200-lb. load) approximately 42 in. high and a midrail about half that distance.

Common-sense requirements for roof work include wearing shoes with slip-resistant soles, removing frost and other slip hazards before getting onto roof surfaces, and stopping work when storms or high winds create unsafe conditions.

ADDITIONALLY:

- Floor openings larger than 2 in. by 2 in. must be covered with material that can safely support the working load.

- Skylights and openings must be securely covered or protected by guardrails to keep workers from falling through the openings.

- When the roof pitch is between 4-in-12 and 6-in-12, a row of slide guards (drawing on facing page) must be installed along the roof eave that runs above the first three rows of the roofing material.

- When the roof pitch is between 6-in-12 and 8-in-12, additional slide guards must be installed every 8 ft. up the roof.

- A safety-harness system with a solid anchor point must be used when the roof pitch exceeds 8-in-12, or if the ground-to-eave height exceeds 25 ft.

- Impalement hazards (such as rebar) must be properly guarded or removed.

FALL PROTECTION

Guardrails prevent a tragic misstep

Guardrails must be installed on stairways, around openings in floors, and across openings in walls whenever the fall distance exceeds 6 ft. Note: Guardrail heights can vary by as much as 3 in. up or down.

Slide guards

Slide guards provide adequate fall protection unless roof pitch exceeds 8-in-12. This 7-in-12 pitch roof has properly installed slide guards. If the pitch were between 4-in-12 and 6-in-12, only the bottom row of slide guards would be required.

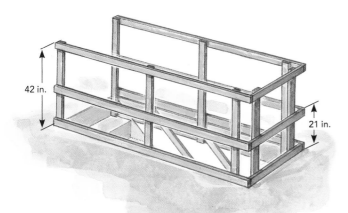

Safety doesn't have to be complicated

For this window opening, a single 2x4 nailed approximately 42 in. off the floor is all it takes to satisfy OSHA safety requirements and, more important, to prevent a tragic fall.

The bottom row of slide guards is installed above the first three rows of shingles.

Don't bury anyone who's still breathing

Workers face risk of serious injury from the heavy equipment that is used for digging trenches and from cave-ins afterward. Don't begin any excavation before contacting the local utility to find the location of underground utilities.

DURING EXCAVATION WORK:

- Keep workers away from digging equipment, and never allow workers in an excavation when equipment is in use.
- Keep the equipment and the spoils pile (excavated dirt) back 2 ft. from the edge of the excavation.
- Keep water out of trenches with a pump or drainage system, and inspect the area for soil movement and potential cave-ins.

A PROPERLY BENCHED TRENCH

To prevent a cave-in from trapping a worker against a foundation wall, the sides of a foundation trench must either be sloped back (1-ft. rise: 1½-ft. run), reinforced with shoring, or benched according to these dimensions.

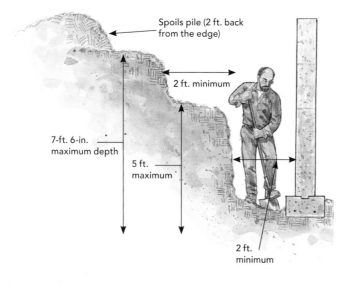

Spoils pile (2 ft. back from the edge)

2 ft. minimum

7-ft. 6-in. maximum depth

5 ft. maximum

2 ft. minimum

■ For excavations and utility trenches more than 5 ft. deep, use shoring, shields (trench boxes), benching, or sloped-back sides. Unless a soil analysis has been completed, the earth's slope must be at least 1½ ft. horizontal to 1 ft. vertical.

After foundation walls are constructed, additional precautions must be taken to prevent injury from cave-ins that could trap a worker between the excavation wall and the foundation wall (drawing above):

■ The depth of the trench cannot exceed 7½ ft. without the provision of some other cave-in protection.

■ The width of the foundation trench must be at least 2 ft.

■ No work activity is permitted to vibrate the soil while workers are in the trench.

■ Inspect the trench regularly for changes in the stability of the earth (water, cracks, vibrations, spoils pile).

Don't just tape up a damaged extension cord

In addition to overhead and underground power lines, the danger of electrocution lurks within every electrical cord on the job site. The best way to prevent electrocution is to protect all the job site's temporary power with ground fault circuit interrupters (GFCIs). This protection can be done by plugging into a GFCI-protected temporary power pole, a GFCI-protected generator, or a GFCI extension cord. It cannot be done by plugging into a household GFCI.

ADDITIONAL JOB-SITE ELECTRICAL-SAFETY MEASURES INCLUDE:

■ Use only three-wire-type extension cords designed for hard or junior-hard service (look for any of the following letters imprinted on the casing: S, ST, SO, STO, SJ, SJT, SJO, SJTO).

■ Maintain all extension cords and electrical tools in safe condition, and remove broken tools and equipment from the job site.

■ Never allow any work on hot electrical circuits until all power is shut off and a positive lock-out/ tag-out system is in place.

Protecting a House during Construction

BY GARY GILBERG

The freshly built oak staircase had become the lunchroom for the carpenters and painters. At that point in the job, it was the best seat in the house, and the general consensus held that a few sandwich crumbs wouldn't hurt the unvarnished wood. But then somebody kicked over a bottle of Gatorade; every drop spilled, staining the stair treads a lurid red.

Not all examples of construction damage are so dramatic. Often, it's as simple as a carpenter walking through a nearly finished house with his hammer swinging from his tool belt and putting a 6-in. gouge across a door panel. As a construction-project manager, I've seen lots of these incidents and have even caused a few myself. Some accidents are unavoidable, but the majority are caused by sloppy work habits and carelessness. To minimize these mistakes, I've worked with my crews and subcontractors to develop easy ways to protect our work until the owners move in. Although my focus is new construction, the same techniques apply to remodeling, where in addition to new work, you might need to protect parts of the house you're not working on.

Protect windows and doors

During the framing phase of construction, fragile items such as windows begin to arrive. First, we

SITE-BUILT BOXES PROTECT SCREENS. When the windows arrive onsite, the screens are removed for safekeeping in plywood boxes built by the apprentices.

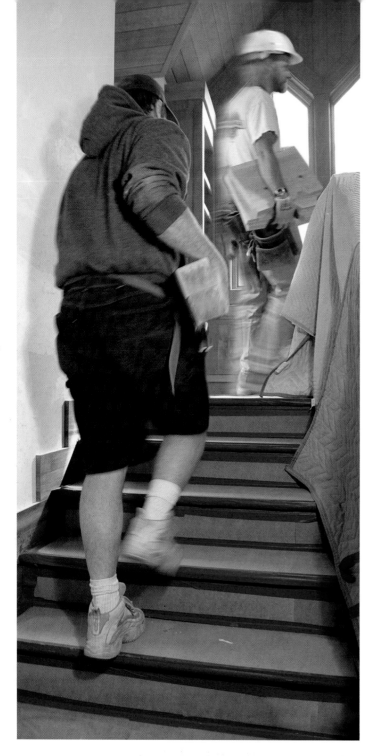

As the finish work begins, I provide drop cloths, cardboard, plastic, moving pads, tape, fiberboard, hardboard, and plywood to my crews to protect their work.

remove the screens and store them in a plywood box built by the apprentice carpenters (photo on p. 205). Windows are stacked carefully in rows along one wall of the garage; the last in each row is covered with a sheet of plywood. If the roof is still open, the windows are covered with plastic and plywood. Once the windows are installed, we staple plastic on the inside of the window framing to protect them from drywall splatter, paint overspray, and interior humidity.

After the doors are hung, we pull each door off its hinges and stack it out of harm's way, protected by a sheet of fiberboard or hardboard. We often hang a hollow-core flush door as a temporary substitute for exterior doors. In areas prone to damage, wooden door jambs are covered with cardboard or plywood. I purchase 4x8 sheets of heavy-duty cardboard from a local plywood-supply company.

French doors and large windows are marked with a large X taped onto the glass to alert everyone that the opening is obstructed with glass. When sanding door and window frames, we tape over the adjacent glass to prevent sandpaper from scratching the edge

NEVER ENOUGH PROTECTION? During a renovation, it's easy to cover everything. In this house, the staircase's treads and risers are protected with hardboard that's taped down and sealed against dirt. Railings shrouded with moving blankets won't suffer dings and scrapes. The floors are covered with hardboard; plastic taped across openings keeps dust migration to a minimum. Moving blankets and cardboard protect finishes.

of the glass panels. When we're welding or cutting steel, all nearby surfaces including glass are protected. On one job, I was cutting angle iron next to a French door and sending hot slag spinning off the blade and onto the door's glass and wooden frame several feet away. I didn't realize my mistake until weeks later when the painter showed me the pitted glass and burn marks. That lesson cost me more than $1,000.

Keep the furnace dust-free

When we're ready to fire up the furnace, we remove the plywood covers from the floor vents and replace them with plastic floor register screens (www. pro-vent.com). These screens keep debris out of the ductwork but allow heat to escape.

Drywall dust can damage the internal-combustion chambers of a forced-air furnace or boiler. Having once had to replace a dust-clogged boiler, I now turn off the boiler or furnace and cover it with plastic whenever the drywall crew is working in the mechanical room. To prevent dust from entering the forced-air unit through the cold-air return, I build a small frame of scrap 2x2, then stretch panty hose over the frame and cover the cold-air plenum with this custom filter. I vacuum the filter when it becomes clogged with dust.

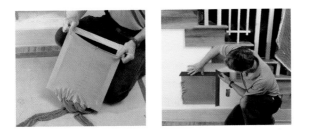

A NEW USE FOR PANTY HOSE. To prevent dust and dirt from getting sucked into the heating system's cold-air intake, the author covers a frame of scrap 2x with panty hose and tapes it into place.

PUTTING THE DOORS UNDER WRAPS. After the doors are hung, they are removed, stacked away from high-traffic areas, and protected with moving blankets and fiberboard.

Keep the finish work pristine

As the finish work begins, I provide drop cloths, cardboard, plastic, moving pads, tape, fiberboard, hardboard, and plywood to my crews to protect their work. As temporary protection, I often use rosin paper to cover finished surfaces. If it tears, I replace it promptly. I buy only the gray type; when wet, red rosin paper bleeds and can stain the surface it was designed to protect. I also save any cardboard I can reuse from my window, door, plumbing, and appliance deliveries.

While working above a fiberglass shower stall, I once dropped a piece of trim that pierced the tub floor like a javelin. I repeat that story to all my crews to remind them always to use protection when they

PROTECT DOORWAYS THAT ARE IN THE WAY. To keep door jambs free of nicks and dings, the author likes to wrap interior doorways with cardboard and blue tape. Exterior door jambs (and exposed beams) are armored with plywood.

floating mortar walls above the tub, I add a second layer of #15 felt on the bottom of the tub and sponge out the floor at the end of the day.

After kitchens and baths are installed, we cover cabinets with rosin paper, countertops with moving blankets, and bottom cabinets with fiberboard (photos on facing page). We use 3M™ long-mask blue tape when the tape will be left in position for extended periods of time. It's easier to peel off and leaves less residue than conventional masking tape, as long as you avoid prolonged sun exposure.

Wood floors and carpets need protection, too

As carpeting is installed, it is covered with 24-in.- or 36-in.-wide strips of self-adhesive polyethylene runners. Be aware that natural-fiber carpets (wool, for instance) will show a slight discoloration on those areas not covered by the polyethylene runner because the sun's ultraviolet rays are blocked by the runner. Fortunately, this minor blemish has always disappeared when the carpet under the plastic has been exposed to the sun for a few days.

Heavy-traffic rooms and hallways are covered with a layer of 6-mil plastic. Wood flooring is covered with a 32-in.-wide runner of nonslip felt pad. Wooden stairs are covered with ¼-in. hardboard that is taped in place. If the crew is using heavy tools for an extended amount of time over a wood or tile floor, I may even cover the entire floor area with ¼-in. hardboard.

I once installed a prefinished wood floor in a kitchen and loosely set down several pieces of ⅛-in. hardboard over the floor to protect it. Two months later, I pulled up the hardboard and discovered that several nails, cabinet screws, and a large accumulation of sand from the tilesetter had gotten under the hardboard and been ground into the floor. I had to refinish the entire kitchen floor. To prevent debris infiltration under the hardboard, I now tape it down with blue masking tape along the edges and heavy-duty duct tape between the sheets of hardboard.

are working over any fragile surfaces. Fiberglass tubs and shower stalls are covered with cardboard and ¾-in. plywood cut to size.

Cast-iron tubs can be covered with moving pads taped into position, then covered with plywood. We've recently tried a paint-on product called Scratch Protection (www.protectiveproducts.com). Before applying this latex coating, I tape over the drain and the overflow fittings, and then along the tub edges. I then brush or spray on the Scratch Protection, which dries into a thick, rubbery skin that can be peeled off easily or recoated as needed. Standing water can dissolve the latex, so if my tilesetter is

We vacuum as often as needed. To reduce the risk
of floor damage, tilework and interior masonry work
are scheduled before finish flooring is installed. The
mortar is mixed outside, and we put down a runner
of rosin paper for the masons to walk on; we sweep
it clean or replace it as needed. We also make sure to
cover all thresholds.

Wooden baseboards can be problematic, especially
during carpet installations. The back side of many
modern carpets is extremely coarse mesh, which
can scratch the baseboards as the carpet is unrolled,
stretched, and tucked in place. If we have a particularly expensive or delicate baseboard profile, we
cover the base with phenolic backer. I buy 4x8 sheets
of this inexpensive plastic material from a laminate-
supply house, rip it into thin strips on a tablesaw,
and tape the material in place.

CLEANING PRODUCTS: JUST IN CASE YOU MAKE A MISTAKE

ACCIDENTS HAPPEN. To clean up spills, I
start with the least invasive product available,
generally mild soap and water. If that doesn't
work, I increase cleaner strength gradually
until the stain is removed. I once saw someone melt a plastic Moen kitchen faucet by
using acetone to remove a spot, so when I use
solvents such as denatured alcohol, acetone,
lacquer thinner, or methyl ethyl ketone, I
always test them in an inconspicuous spot
first. Testing also should apply to abrasive
pads and cleansers; they can scratch plastic,
fiberglass, and some metals.

For dealing with difficult carpet stains, I
use Folex carpet-spot remover or a similar
product. Failing that, I hire a professional
steam-cleaning crew to clean the carpets.

Keep the Rain Out When Adding a Shed Dormer

BY NICHOLAS PITZ

Retrofitting a shed dormer in an occupied house can be a disruptive project. But with careful planning, intrusions such as a constant parade of workers and demolition debris can be kept out of the house. Although there's always some time when the roof is open or a wall is missing, avoiding weather damage is straightforward: Just expect pouring rain every night, and plan accordingly.

First, build the new roof

The work on this house involved replacing two small existing dormers with a large shed dormer, and the job affected almost every upstairs room. To ensure that the project was weathertight, we planned to build the new dormer's roof first, but we needed room for demolition and reconstruction under it.

We began by framing the dormer's outside wall with four posts and a long header. This approach meant we could frame the dormer roof while cutting only four small holes in the original roof. Then, after we built the new roof and removed the old dormers, we could fill in the studs and the window framing.

We marked the locations of the wall posts to correspond with where we wanted the interior partitions to fall. Then we cut out small sections of roof with a reciprocating saw to give us access to the top plate of the existing wall and installed the first corner post. When this post was carefully braced and plumbed, we used a water level to calculate the height of the other corner post to ensure that the roof was level. Once this second post was positioned and plumbed, we strung a line between the two end posts and set the remaining posts to that height, making sure the load was transferred directly to a stud below.

With the posts braced and in place, we installed the headers. At the end of the day, we covered the holes in the roof made by the new posts with aluminum flashing and plastic sheeting (top drawing on p. 212).

Tear out only what can be rebuilt that day

We framed the new dormer's roof in two sections over two days. We calculated where the new dormer rafters would intersect with the oldest section of roof, cut a 2-ft.-wide section, and removed it. This approach gave us access to the attic without having to go through the house and also provided light and ventilation to the attic where we would be working.

After the new rafters were securely in place, the sheathing and the #30 felt were installed. The next day, we repeated the performance for the rest of the dormer roof. We now had a reasonably weathertight

THE SMALL DORMERS HAD TO GO. The original house lacked space upstairs, so a big shed dormer was needed. To minimize disruption for the homeowners, access to the work zone was via ladders and scaffolds, not through the house.

lid on the work area and could begin the demolition process. To keep out rain, we protected the work site with tarps, which were layered like roofing shingles and held fast with furring strips (bottom drawing on p. 212).

Keep the work site separate from the house

The interior of the dormer was divided into four areas: master bedroom, closet, the daughter's bathroom, and her closet. It was important to complete the master bedroom quickly, so we built the front wall, sheathed it, installed the window, and had it drywalled and trimmed before some of the other sections were even started. By finishing this room first, the owners got their bedroom back quickly.

We were careful to isolate the workspace from the rest of the house. Two small existing closets were turned into walk-in closets (drawing on p. 213). Before we commenced with serious demolition of either closet, we reframed the door openings, drywalled over them, and taped the seams, planning to cut out the doorways after the dirty work was done. Having the living side of the wall closed acts as a barrier against construction while allowing the electricians and plumbers to do their work on the other side.

Even the small amount of drywall we did on the living side of the wall meant dust. We took the usual precautions. A plastic runner protected the upstairs carpet. To contain airborne dust, I tacked tarps across doorways, placed a box fan in a window as an exhaust, and vacuumed at the end of each workday. On the other side, we completed almost all the work before we cut through to install the new doors and trim.

(Continued on p. 214)

TO KEEP OUT RAIN, BUILD THE NEW ROOF BEFORE REMOVING THE OLD ONE

SUPPORTING THE NEW DORMER ROOF with one long header and four posts meant cutting only four small holes in the old roof 1. Setting and temporarily flashing the posts was the first day's work. Half of the dormer's new roof was framed and then sheathed the next day 2, and all the openings were flashed and tarped against the wind and rain. The dormer's roof was completed and sheathed, and #30 felt paper kept out the rain 3.

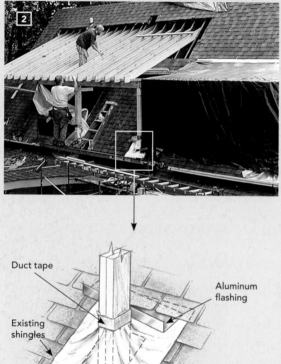

Duct tape

Aluminum flashing

Existing shingles

Plastic sheeting

DUCT TAPE AND PLASTIC FOR TEMPORARY FLASHING

Flashing is slipped under the shingles, bent, and canted at an angle to divert water around the post. Heavy plastic sheeting (6-mil poly) is slid under the flashing, wrapped around the post, and tacked down with roofing nails. Duct tape seals the poly to the posts.

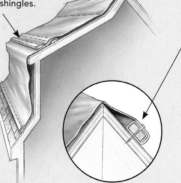

Multiple tarps can be layered like shingles.

Tarp covers the ridge and is secured with a furring strip screwed to the roof.

HAVE TARPS IN PLACE BEFORE IT RAINS

If the tarp is in the way of the work, then secure the top edge to the roof, roll up the tarp around a 1x3 furring strip, and tie the rolled-up tarp in place. When the rain starts, cut the ties.

KEEP YOUR PROJECT NEAT

TO PROTECT THE HOUSE FROM DUST AND DEBRIS, the occupied space was sealed with drywall and plastic. Also, the debris was removed (and new materials brought in) through the new dormer windows.

CONSTRUCTION SEQUENCE MINIMIZES DISRUPTION

1. Evicting the owners from their bedroom was the most intrusive part of the renovation, so this room was finished first. Its outside walls were completed and the trim put in place before demolition started elsewhere.

2. The new closet wall was framed and drywalled (including the doorway) on the occupied side, creating a solid barrier to construction fallout. Plastic sheeting would not have sealed the walls nearly as well.

3. This closet was finished quickly. The bathroom would take the most time and require the most schedule juggling, which is why it was planned to be done last.

4. Toward the end of the project, the window opening in the bathroom's outside wall was the only access to the work area. The job was finished working toward this opening, with the window installed and the bathroom paint and trim finished just before the new work was opened to the rest of the house.

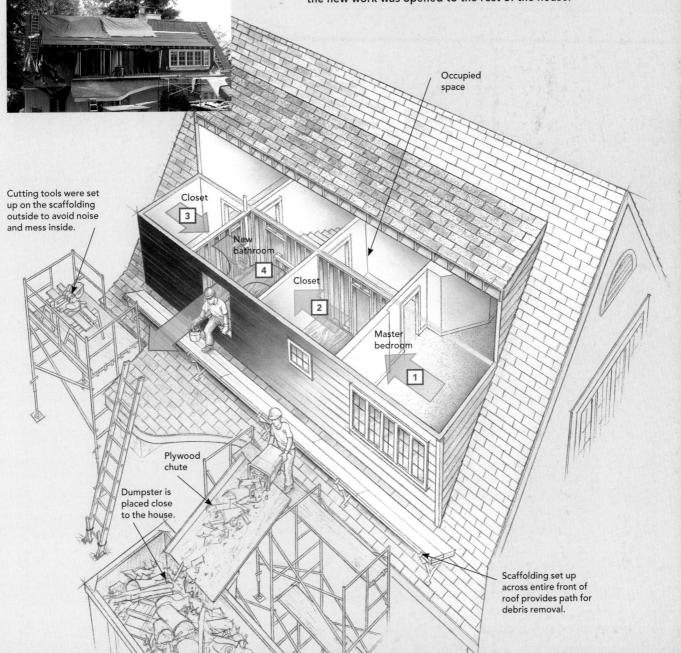

Occupied space

Cutting tools were set up on the scaffolding outside to avoid noise and mess inside.

Closet 3

New bathroom 4

Closet 2

Master bedroom 1

Plywood chute

Dumpster is placed close to the house.

Scaffolding set up across entire front of roof provides path for debris removal.

Because the bathroom door wasn't being moved, we taped it shut and put a sheet of foam insulation over it for protection. The bathroom then was gutted and rebuilt.

No muss, no fuss

Much of this job revolved around not making a mess. We planned the placement of the Dumpster so that we could build a plywood chute to it for debris removal but keep it out of the way of deliveries. We were working directly over the driveway, and we made sure we swept up carefully every night.

The bathroom's outside wall was left unframed as an access to the second floor, and consequently, little traffic went through the house. The dormer was finished toward that opening, and the day before the tile was installed in the bathroom, we finished framing the rough opening and hanging the drywall; then we installed the window and trim. The tilesetter's wet saw was set up on the scaffold outside, and his helper spent the day getting a tan and passing cut tiles through the window.

TIPS FOR ANY REMODEL

- Minimize traffic through the house.
- Scrupulously seal off the living space from the work zone.
- Use a window fan in the work zone to exhaust dust and fumes.
- Take precautions to protect the stuff that stays. If the floor stays, for instance, cover it with plywood (and tape the seams) rather than rely on a tarp.
- Clean up the work zone at the end of every day.
- To keep peace in the house, consider hiring a cleaning service halfway through the project.

Every remodeling project is an intrusive ordeal for the homeowner. The single most important aspect of our remodeling strategy was that my clients appreciated the efforts we took to protect their home and privacy.

Dust Control

BY TOM O'BRIEN

For those of us who get our hands dirty every day, dismissing dust as a minor annoyance is easy. No big deal. Nothing that a whisk broom and a Shop-Vac® can't make quick work of. But then you spend a day cleaning drywall dust out of every nook and cranny in what had been a spotless kitchen. Or maybe you have to come up with the cash to refinish a hardwood floor scratched and pitted by demolition dust. To avoid such costly, time-consuming consequences, you have to get serious about controlling dust during remodeling projects.

Keeping dust in its place requires a modest investment in time and materials, but it pays huge dividends, and not just in cost savings or goodwill. Over the years, I've become convinced that my work is more precise, better organized, and more efficient when dust is kept under control.

My dust-containment strategy has two parts. First, I isolate the work area from the occupied portions of the house to make sure that none of the dust that's generated is allowed to escape. Second, I try to cut down on activities that generate dust, and when that's not possible, I capture dust at the source using shrouded power tools combined with a tool-triggered vacuum cleaner.

PROTECT THE FLOOR FROM DUST AND DINGS

THE TYPE OF WORK AND THE TYPE OF FLOORING determine the degree of protection you need. Carpeting usually is replaced or removed during a remodeling job, but hardwood floors require several layers of defense that work together not only to seal out the dust but also to protect the surface from dropped tools, falling plaster, or dirt and debris that will leave gouges and scratches.

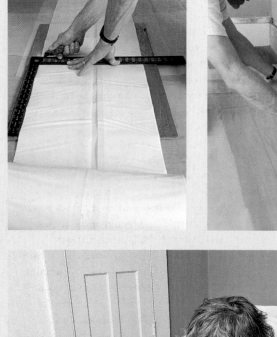

ABOVE LEFT: THE FIRST LAYER OF DEFENSE is 6-mil plastic sheeting laid over the freshly swept floor. Lap the seams between sheets about 6 in. to 12 in., and seal with 2-in. painter's tape. Cut the plastic before unfolding it, using a scrap of plywood and a framing square.

ABOVE CENTER: KEEP DUST OUT OF THE CORNERS by curling up the edges of the plastic and taping them in place with either regular or low-tack painter's tape (see p. 218).

ABOVE RIGHT AND LEFT: COVER THE PLASTIC WITH A DROP-RESISTANT MATERIAL like ½-in.-thick insulation board, Homasote®, or any other inexpensive sheathing. The author prefers ⅛-in.-thick Masonite® hardboard because it's so thin that the panels can be overlapped without being cut to fit. Once the Masonite is in place, tape the seams with duct tape to prevent the panels from shifting. If the work requires major demolition, consider covering the panels with another layer of plastic.

Floor protection comes first

I start a typical job by clearing the work area. Any items that absolutely cannot be moved are wrapped in plastic sheeting, then covered with a thick drop cloth or mover's blanket to add an extra layer of protection.

Next, I cover the floors with a layer of 6-mil plastic. I used to try to protect floors with tarps or drop cloths, but they never stayed in place and couldn't be cleaned easily. Plastic sheeting is a better choice because it can be balled up and thrown away at the end of the job, taking the dust with it.

To fashion a seamless barrier between the dust and the floor, I overlap the edges of the plastic by 6 in. or so and tape the seams with painter's tape. I turn up the edges at the baseboards and secure them with 3M #2090 blue masking tape, which is designed to be removable for up to 14 days without pulling off the paint or leaving a sticky residue. The company makes another tape that can stay stuck for 60 days without damage (#2080), but it's flimsier.

Be careful: Plastic sheeting can be slippery until it has been scuffed up by foot traffic. A few rows of masking tape laid down in high-traffic areas will help to improve traction.

Carpeting usually is replaced or removed during remodeling, but if it must be saved, I cover it with two layers of plastic. To guard against punctures during demolition or high-risk operations, I usually cover plastic with a heavy-duty tarp. After the dirty work is done, I sweep up the debris, then thoroughly vacuum the tarp before I fold it up and pack it away.

Finished hardwood floors aren't as forgiving as carpets and need more than a thin layer of plastic to guard against scratches (photos on facing page).

Install an airlock between work and living spaces

Dust control is a big challenge on jobs where the only way to get from the driveway to the work area is to pass through the living space. These setups require extra precautions and constant vigilance.

DUST IS MORE THAN A NUISANCE: PROTECT YOURSELF

WE'VE KNOWN FOR YEARS ABOUT THE DANGERS POSED BY DUSTS such as asbestos and lead. But recent medical studies show that prolonged exposure to sawdust and silica (the dust that's released when dry-cutting concrete and stone) also can have serious health consequences. Sawdust has been linked to cancer, and silica has been proven to cause a serious respiratory condition known as silicosis.

Anyone who works in a dusty environment needs adequate respiratory protection. But a paper mask held in place by a single rubber band won't cut it. Professionals routinely exposed to high levels of dust should wear a properly fitted half-face respirator that is equipped with HEPA filter cartridges.

Do-it-yourselfers or workers who aren't often exposed to dust have another choice: 3M's N100 disposable respirator is as comfortable as a paper mask, but it provides serious protection. An N100 respirator (solutions.3m.com), if it's cared for properly, can be reused for months.

N100 DISPOSABLE RESPIRATOR

HALF-FACE RESPIRATOR WITH HEPA FILTER

SPECIAL PRODUCTS HELP TO CONTAIN THE MESS

THE BASICS, such as tape and plastic, can be found at your local hardware store. Professional-grade products might have to be purchased from a retailer specializing in remodeling and personal safety. My favorite sources are Protective Products (www.protectiveproducts.com) and Aramsco (www.aramsco.com). Both companies carry many of the remodeling supplies that I use regularly.

For especially dusty jobs, I keep my clothes clean by wearing **disposable hooded coveralls** ☐1. They also can be taken off and left in the work area so that I don't track dust through the house (www.aramsco.com).

A sticky **TakMat Dirt Grabber®** ☐2 captures gritty debris from your shoes. When the mat is coated with dust, peel off the top layer to expose a fresh sheet; each mat has 30 layers (www.protective products.com).

Lightweight **Zip-Poles™ from ZipWall** ☐3 are spring-loaded and can be extended up to 12 ft. so that temporary dust curtains can be erected

and adjusted without tape or lumber. The two-part head lets you attach the plastic before lifting each pole. The basic kit includes two poles and compatible nonmarring pads (www.zipwall.com).

3M Blue Tape ☐4 is available in many lengths and widths, but the important difference lies in the tack rating. The standard blue tape (#2090) is a good all-around choice for sealing doors and attaching plastic. It can be left in place for 14 days before the adhesive becomes gummy and threatens to lift off paint or stain. The low-tack tape (#2080) is safe to leave in place for up to 60 days, but it's flimsy and doesn't work as well for taping heavy plastic (www.3m.com).

Festool's **tool-actuated vacuums** ☐5 are expensive, but they are my top choice for carpentry work. I particularly appreciate the innovations Festool has made with vacuum-connected routers and circular saws that make these tools nearly dust-free (www.festool.com).

For such a small, quiet, and lightweight unit, the **Shop-Vac Air Cleaner** ☐6 does an impressive job of capturing airborne dust before it can settle on surfaces or be inhaled by workers (www.shopvac.com).

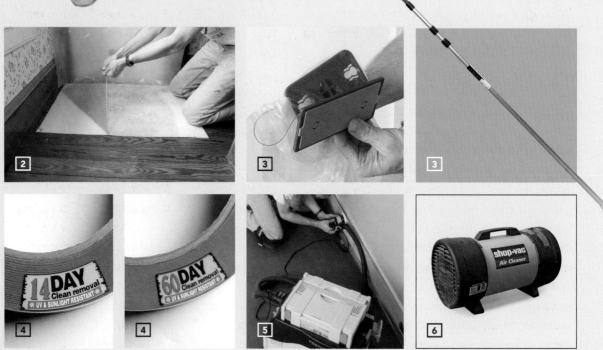

Before any work is started, I choose the only entrance to the home that any worker will be allowed to use, then lay down heavyweight drop cloths from that point to the workspace. To protect exposed floor areas, I overlap the drop cloths by at least 2 ft.

To prevent a cloud of dust from escaping every time someone opens the door to the work area, I place a fan in a window on the opposite side of the room and orient it to blow outside.

I usually close the door and seal the edges before starting to work. If the job is particularly dusty or if there is lots of traffic into and out of the room, I make an airlock using two layers of 6-mil plastic (photos on p. 220). If there is a door, it should be removed from its hinges before the dust door is built. If the temporary airlock is constructed properly, the airflow toward the fan will draw the outside layer of plastic tight to the inside layer, creating a dustproof seal, a more secure arrangement than relying on people to remember to close the door. A number of manufacturers also sell plastic zipper doors, which make it even easier to seal off the workspace—as long as you remember to zip up the zipper. DustDoor™ is a nice choice (www.dustdoor1.com).

Seal off the work area—and keep it sealed off

From a dust perspective, the ideal job is one in which you can isolate the work area from the living space simply by sealing shut an interior door. In this situation, everybody goes in and out through a separate exterior door for the duration of the project. If a bathroom is not connected directly to the work area, a portable toilet prevents a desperate but dust-covered worker from contaminating living space.

Unfortunately, not many jobs are so straightforward. When existing walls aren't located conveniently to separate the workspace from the living space, I put up a temporary plastic dust partition. Furring strips or 2xs traditionally are used to anchor the plastic to the ceiling, and these materials are still worth using if you need dust control for only one job. A longer-term investment is a system of telescoping poles that are designed especially for dust containment. This system reduces the hassle of putting up a dust barrier, even if it's just to surround an area that is likely to get particularly messy. I use the ZipWall® system, which is lightweight, portable, and easily adjustable, but other manufacturers offer similar devices.

One contractor I know saves money by using telescoping painter's poles for the same purpose. These tools lack the nonmarring two-piece top plate, but otherwise they seem to work fine.

For light-duty dust partitions, I prefer ultrathin, 3-mil painter's plastic because its featherlight weight makes it easy to put up and stretch tightly over a long distance, especially when I'm working alone. It's flimsy material, though, so if the barrier has to stand for weeks and endure heavy traffic where rips are likely to occur—or if I have to cut a doorway through the partition—I use a thicker (4 mil or 6 mil) grade of plastic.

Once the partition is in place, the edges of the plastic can be sealed to the floor, the walls, and the ceiling with painter's tape or with ZipWall's dust-sealing foam rails. In practice, though, I've learned that as long as the plastic is stretched tight, there's little room for dust to escape from the top or the bottom. If I'm not dealing with hazardous dust, I tape or seal the plastic only where it meets the wall.

I prefer not to cut holes in dust barriers, but if there's no other way to access the work area, I make a roll-up doorway using a pair of self-adhesive zippers designed for this purpose. These zipper doors can be applied to plastic-covered door frames as well.

If the house has forced-air heating or cooling, the system should be shut down for the length of the job. Otherwise, dust could be carried throughout the house, especially if a cold-air return is in the work area. During winter months or the dog days of summer, when the system must be left running, it's fine to seal off a few vents. If the work zone covers a large portion of the house or if any cold-air returns are involved, though, I consult with a heating contractor first.

CHOOSE ONE ENTRY; SEAL THE REST

WHETHER THE ROOM TO BE REMODELED has two doors or 10, you always should choose a single entry point, then seal the others until the work is complete. Doorways should be covered with sheets of plastic either taped to the trim or secured with a ZipWall or similar product. Existing doors are best sealed by applying 2-in.-wide painter's tape over the gap around the edges. (Plan by relocating any items from within frequently used closets and pantries.)

The door through which you will enter and exit the room should be sealed with a tempo-rary airlock. A window fan placed inside the room and oriented to blow outside creates enough negative pressure to keep the airlock closed and any airborne dust from escaping as you enter and exit through the airlock. Although the purpose of the fan is not to exhaust dust, particularly messy jobs will benefit from an inexpensive furnace filter attached to the fan to ensure that the shrubs outside don't become coated in dust.

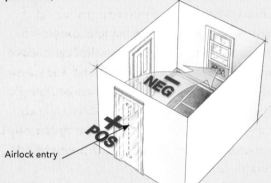

Airlock entry

A furnace filter can be attached to the window fan for messy jobs.

1

AFTER TAPING ALL SIDES OF THE PLASTIC, cut a slit down the middle, stop-ping a few inches short of the top and bottom.

2

APPLY STRIPS OF DUCT TAPE to reinforce the slit in the plastic and to keep it from widening as you walk in and out through the airlock.

3

COVER THE PLASTIC WITH A SECOND SHEET, but tape it (or anchor it with a furring strip and screws) only to the head casing so that it can hang loosely.

4

TRIM THE EXCESS OFF THE BOTTOM of the second sheet of plastic where it meets the floor, and the homemade air-lock is complete.

220 SURVIVE YOUR REMODEL

Leave the dust behind

A sneakier way for dust to break out of a tightly controlled work zone is on clothing, especially shoes. To combat this problem, I position a vacuum cleaner just inside the doorway to the work area and insist that everyone vacuum their shoes, top and bottom, before they leave the work area and walk through the house. I've also experimented with various types of disposable shoe covers, but I've found them to be a hassle to put on and take off.

For added protection, I recently started putting down a TakMat outside the door. TakMat is made with a sticky surface that grabs loose grit clinging to the bottom of shoes. I've been amazed by how quickly the mat fills up with filth.

When I'm doing especially messy work, I cover my work clothes with a disposable hooded coverall, which I can remove quickly and leave behind when I have to exit the work area. One of these suits lasts for the duration of a typical job; I try to find a convenient spot in the work area to hang the suit so that it's always at hand when things get messy.

The vacuum is important, too

It wasn't such a long time ago that performing any type of cutting operation with a portable power tool—sawing, sanding, planing, grinding, routing—was guaranteed to unleash a massive cloud of dust. These days, every major manufacturer offers some type of dust-containment system for its messiest tools. A simple dust bag is better than nothing, but the most effective tools are made with specially designed ports that capture dust at the source and whisk it away to a vacuum cleaner.

The vacuum should be a high-filtration device, such as one that's equipped with a HEPA filter; if it's not, the smallest particles of dust can get sucked into one end of the unit and then blown out the other. The vacuum also should have a tool-operated feature that switches it on and off along with the power tool.

I've had good experiences with a variety of tools and vacuums over the past 10 years or so. For dust-free carpentry work, I rely heavily on Festool products, which are designed for dust collection and are surprisingly effective. For drywall, Porter-Cable®'s dust-free sanding system remains my preferred method to keep that nasty job from getting out of hand. Now, though, you can buy joint compounds specially made to reduce the normally huge cloud of dust produced by sanding drywall joints and seams.

Dust collection doesn't require new tools, though. If I'm working with a small, one-handed tool, such as a spiral saw, I hold a vacuum hose in my free hand to suck up most of the dust before it gets away (right photo on p. 222).

Clearing the air

Technology has made controlling dust easier, but the battle is never-ending. I recently started using a Shop-Vac portable air cleaner that seems to do a good job of filtering airborne dust before it settles on surfaces, but dust continues to accumulate despite my best efforts. To prevent loose dust particles from multiplying, I sweep the floor at the end of each day and give the work area a thorough vacuum-cleaning before I pack up at the end of the week.

USE DUST CURTAINS FOR QUICK TASKS OR EXTRA PROTECTION

FOR CUTTING, PATCHING, OR SANDING A SMALL AREA, sealing and protecting the entire room may be overkill. These small jobs are best isolated with thin plastic sheeting held in place with ZipWall kits, telescoping painter's poles, or furring strips cut about an inch longer than the height of the room and pinched between the floor and ceiling. I like ZipWall best because the spring-loaded poles let me adjust the size of the enclosure easily (photo at left). The same dust curtains also are great for containing really messy jobs within an already protected room, like cutting plaster with a spiral saw, for instance (photo below).

The Remodeler's Guide to Construction Debris

BY ROB MOODY

Before I became a building-science consultant, I spent seven years as a green builder. The amount of waste generated on my remodeling sites always seemed extreme to me. Over time, I developed ways to manage the material we handled in an effort to create as little waste as possible. My approach reduced our waste stream by 40% to 60%.

In retrospect, however, I can see that my methods were elementary. As a teacher for the past four years, I've had the opportunity to work with many other builders and officials around the country, and I've learned that creating a thorough waste-management plan has the potential to reap even better financial and environmental rewards than the system I'd used. As it turns out, code officials are seeing the potential impact as well: In some areas of the country, such as Boulder, Colo., and San Mateo, Calif., a plan is required by law.

Even if your municipality doesn't require a waste-management plan, you can still benefit from one. Using thoughtful, systematic strategies to divert materials from the landfill is the simplest way to reduce tipping fees. For example, tipping fees can be significantly lower for items like "clean" woods that lack glue, paint, stain, varnish, and chemical treatment. Our local county landfill takes clean wood at $20 per ton compared with almost $43 per ton for mixed waste. You might be able to find a local stump dump—a place that produces mulch and wood chips—that will accept clean lumber scrap for even less.

There's actually a market for some waste materials. Separating valuable materials like metal can actually help to recoup some Dumpster tipping fees.

Different companies charge for waste differently. Some have time-based rental fees for Dumpsters, while others charge per ton or per cubic yard, including delivery and pickup. When you consider taking pickup-truck loads to the transfer station, make sure you take into account not only the tipping fee but also your mileage. Just as with bulk disposal to the landfill, you'll have to account for fuel charges and vehicle maintenance. Often, recycling facilities are closer to city centers for convenience, and that may or may not be convenient to a job site. Additionally, many landfill transfer stations won't accept construction and demolition debris.

Start with an inventory

To create a waste-management plan, start by estimating your waste stream by looking at the waste-hauling records from your projects. According to the National Association of Home Builders' Research Center, wood makes up the biggest stream of waste

(Continued on p. 226)

DITCH THE DUMPSTER AND SAVE MONEY

RATHER THAN DUMP EVERYTHING, divert from the landfill as much of the unusable material as possible. You'll keep tipping fees to a minimum, optimize everyone's time on-site, and in some cases even get paid for salvaging material.

Start with a written waste-management plan, which includes a site plan and a procedure for handling each material. Identify materials and estimate their weight or volume. Then present the plan to all the workers on-site. Doing so will keep the job organized, clean, and moving along efficiently.

Separate materials by type, and organize piles based on the order in which they are removed (or order in which they will be put back in or taken off-site). For a major renovation of a 2,000-sq.-ft. house (shown at right), the amount of waste generated can total 8,340 lb. Sending all that debris to the landfill will cost more than $800: $250 in labor, $209 in tipping (average $.025 per lb.), and $360 in Dumpster fees. Implementing a waste-management plan and diverting as much of the material as possible can shave nearly $300 off that figure.

1. METALS
0.07 lb. per sq. ft.
Diverted weight: 140 lb.
Cost: $7
Metals like aluminum, cast iron, and copper can be taken to a salvage yard.

2. MASONRY AND OTHER INERT DEBRIS
0.5 lb. per sq. ft.
Nondiverted weight: 1,000 lb.
Cost: $10
Use as much as possible on-site for backfill. Any debris that can't be used on-site should be taken to the landfill.

3. OTHER WASTE
0.5 lb. per sq. ft.
Nondiverted weight: 1,000 lb.
Cost: $25
Materials that can't be categorized, such as sinks

Divert the waste
Get a roll-off trash container only if absolutely necessary. By using the techniques described here, you can make it a 10-yard container instead of a 30-yard, saving space and dollars.

CHECKLIST FOR A WASTE-MANAGEMENT PLAN

- Outline the recycling and disposal resources in your area and their fee schedules.
- Conduct an inventory of materials for each job. List each item that has the potential to enter the waste stream. For each item, list in which phase of the project the item will enter your plan, followed by handling procedures.
- Estimate the weight and volume of each material.
- Determine the least expensive diversion path for each material based on resource fees, and note any labor involved in moving them off-site.
- Have subs manage their own waste, and don't have a Dumpster on-site.
- Draw a site plan that illustrates the layout of all necessary containers for each item type. Make sure that the whole team—including subs—knows the requirements and the final destination for each container.
- Offer to pay for waste management unless there is traceable trade-specific contamination.
- Inform persons from each trade what the repercussions are for contaminating waste. For example, back-charge them for it and include a liquidated-damages clause about contamination in the contract.

and glass, should be donated to a re-store or hauled to the landfill.

4. DIRTY WOOD

0.85 lb. per sq. ft.
Nondiverted weight: 1,700 lb.
Cost: $42.50
This wood has to be used or hauled to the landfill. Separate and store on-site, then haul to the landfill.

5. CLEAN WOOD

0.85 lb. per sq. ft.
Diverted weight: 1,700 lb.
Cost: $0
Much untreated, nonengineered, unpainted, unstained, unsealed, and unvarnished wood can be ground for mulch.

6. CARDBOARD

0.3 lb. per sq. ft.
Diverted weight: 600 lb.
Cost: $0
This material can be used under mulch to slow weed growth. It also can be used to protect finished flooring.

7. DRYWALL

1 lb. per sq. ft.
Diverted weight: 2,200 lb.
Cost: $22
Ground drywall can be used as a soil amendment on-site or hauled to a construction-waste recycling company.

Reach for new material last
Locate new stockpiles near the driveway and farthest from the house so that salvaged materials are used first.

Manage the day-to-day
Containers along the site entrance make recycling paper, drink, and food containers, as well as disposing of day-to-day refuse, easy for the crew.

Pull the nails
When wood is removed from a renovation, have a location designated for immediate nail pulling. Make that close to the cut station or milling station depending on the material.

Keep usable material close
Stack salvaged trim and framing lumber according to size to make pieces easy to find as needed. Locate this staging area near the house and cut station.

Have a cut station
Set up near materials and salvageables, a centralized cut station will make it easy to use and store materials within the workflow.

SOURCES

C&D MATERIAL TRADER
www.cdmaterialtrader.org

CARPET AMERICA RECOVERY EFFORT
www.carpetrecovery.org

THE CONSTRUCTION INDUSTRY COMPLIANCE ASSISTANCE CENTER
www.cicacenter.org

REGREEN
www.regreenprogram.org

REUSE ALLIANCE
www.reusealliance.org

TOOLBASE
www.toolbase.org

U.S. ENVIRONMENTAL PROTECTION AGENCY (EPA)
www.epa.gov

WHOLE BUILDING DESIGN GUIDE
www.wbdg.org

both by weight and volume (42% and 24%, respectively). This includes clean wood; painted, stained, or varnished wood; and engineered wood, such as OSB, plywood, and I-joists.

Drywall makes up 25% of job-site construction waste weight, although a lesser 11% by volume because of its high density and because it's easily stacked.

Cardboard recovery is mandated in many municipalities. Cardboard makes up 38% of construction waste by volume and 4% by weight, which is important to note if you pay for hauling by volume.

Metals have one of the highest values in recycling and can be sold to a metal yard to offset waste-management costs.

Carpet is recyclable in many locations across the country, and inert materials such as soil, concrete, block, and brick can have outlets for diversion as well.

Check with local recycling centers to see what types of plastics they accept. Vinyl is typically recyclable, as is polyethylene terephthalate (PETE, type-1 plastic) and high-density polyethylene (HDPE, type-2 plastic). Types 3 through 6 plastic can be recycled but are more difficult, and type 7 is rarely recyclable.

Solvents, paints, and adhesives must be disposed of as hazardous materials, and lead- and asbestos-containing materials have special requirements. Painted drywall and plaster are not recyclable and may contain lead, particularly if you're working in a home built before 1978. If they are free of lead or asbestos, they must be disposed of in a landfill.

Know your disposal options

Get to know the local recycling and disposal requirements for waste from new construction, demolition, and renovation. Also, look into re-stores, recyclers, haulers, and waste companies in your area. Keep a record of the weights of waste materials. This is helpful for green-building certification and for marketing your waste-diversion rate in terms of total tonnage kept from the landfill. Finally, write down your waste-management plan and make it available to employees and subcontractors.

Rick Arnold is a veteran builder and contributing editor to *Fine Homebuilding*. He is the author of *Working With Concrete* (The Taunton Press, 2003).

Bridget Cahill is a licensed contractor based on Cape Cod, specializing in the design and construction/renovation of bathrooms (www.seasidebaths.com).

Duo Dickinson (www.duo dickinson.com) is an architect in Madison, Conn. and the author of seven books, including *Staying Put: Remodel Your House to Get the Home You Want* (The Taunton Press, 2011).

Scott Donahue is an architect with RS Donahue Architect (www.rsdonahue.us) based in Emeryville, Calif.

Mark Dutka is principal at Inhouse Design Studio (www. inhousesf.com) in San Francisco.

Myron R. Ferguson (www.that drywallguy.com) is the author of *Drywall* (The Taunton Press, 2012) and a frequent contributor to *Fine Homebuilding*.

Justin Fink is a senior editor with *Fine Homebuilding*.

Gary Gilberg is a builder and the president of Quality Crafted Homes in Truckee, Calif.

Sean Groom, a *Fine Homebuilding* contributing editor, is a freelance writer in Simsbury, Conn.

Mike Guertin (www.mikeguertin. com), *Fine Homebuilding*'s editorial advisor, is a custom-home builder and remodeling contractor in East Greenwich, R. I.

Lynne Heinzmann and her husband, Chris, founded Heinzmann Architects Inc. (www.heinzmann architects.com) in North Kingstown, R. I.

Jerri Holan (www.holan architects.com) is an architect and master swimmer in the San Francisco Bay area.

Lynn Hopkins (www.lhopkins arch.com) is an architect based in Lexington, Mass.

Robert Knight (www.knight architect.com) is an architect and the president of Knight Associates in Blue Hill, Maine.

Jim Lacey is a professional painter in Bethel, Conn.

Jane K. Langmuir is a designer and former faculty member at the Rhode Island School of Design in Providence, R. I. She is one of the principal leaders of RISD's Universal Kitchen project.

John McLean is an architect in San Francisco.

Charles Miller is *Fine Homebuilding*'s special issues editor.

Keyan Mizani is a partner at eM/Zed design (www.em-zed.com) in Portland, Ore.

Rob Moody is a building-science consultant and educator with Organic Think Inc. (www.organic think.com).

Paul Murray is a second-generation master plumber and mechanical contractor in Johnston, R. I.

Tom O'Brien is a carpenter in New Milford, Conn. and a former *Fine Homebuilding* editor.

Charles Peterson is a wood-flooring expert. His latest book is *Wood Flooring: A Complete Guide to Layout, Installation & Finishing* (The Taunton Press, 2010).

Nicholas Pitz is the principal of Catamount Construction in suburban Philadelphia.

Clifford A. Popejoy is a licensed electrical contractor in Sacramento, Calif.

Fernando Pagés Ruiz, a builder with 30 years of experience, is the author of *Building an Affordable House* (The Taunton Press, 2005) and *Affordable Remodel* (The Taunton Press, 2007).

Matthew Teague is a *Fine Homebuilding* contributing writer and a professional furniture maker.

Chris Whalen is a finish carpenter and partner in Black Mountain Company (www.blackmountain company.com), a home-building, renovating, and woodworking firm in Missoula, Mont.

Alex Wilson is the founder and president of BuildingGreen in Brattleboro, Vt. (www.building green.com). His latest book is *Your Green Home* (New Society Publishers, 2006).

Dave Yates owns and operates F.W. Behler Inc., a mechanical-contracting firm in York, Pa.

All photos are courtesy of Fine Homebuilding magazine (FHB) © The Taunton Press, Inc., except as noted below:

Front cover: main photo by Charles Bickford (FHB), top photos from left to right: Charles Bickford (FHB), Justin Fink (FHB), Rob Yagid (FHB), Justin Fink (FHB), and Rodney Diaz (FHB). Back cover: top photo by Charles Miller (FHB), bottom photos from left to right: Tom O'Brien (FHB), Kenyan Mizani (FHB), and Rob Yagid (FHB).

The articles in this book appeared in the following issues of Fine Home-building:

pp. 2-5: Recovery Remodeling by Fernando Pagés Ruiz, issue 212. Left photo p. 3 by Brian Pontolilo (FHB), right photo p. 3 by Charles Miller (FHB), left photo p. 4 by Tom O'Brien (FHB), middle photo p. 4 by Roe A. Osborn (FHB), right photo p. 4 by Fernando Pagés Ruiz (FHB), left and middle photos p. 5 by Charles Miller (FHB), right photo p. 5 Fine Gardening © The Taunton Press, Inc.

pp. 7-21: 11 Essential Remodeling Strategies by Kenyan Mizani, issue 195. "Before" photos by Keyan Mizani (FHB), "After" photos by Charles Miller (FHB) except photos p. 10, p. 15, p. 16, p. 17 and p. 19 by Keyan Mizani (FHB). Drawings by Martha Garstang Hill (FHB).

pp. 22-27: How to Afford an Architect by Duo Dickinson, issue 195. Photos by Mick Hales (FHB). Drawings by Duo Dickinson (FHB).

pp. 28-37: Designing an Addition that Looks Right by Lynn Hopkins, issue 203. Photos by Lynn Hopkins (FHB) except photos pp. 29-30 by Jim Rymsza (FHB), top photo p. 31 by Charles Bickford (FHB), and top photo p. 32, bottom photo p. 36, and top right and bottom left photos p. 37 by Charles Miller (FHB).

pp. 38-40: Commentary: A contract that makes everybody happy by Robert Knight, issue 179. Photo © Artur Gabrysiak/istockphoto.com.

pp. 42-47: The Well-Designed Walk-In Closet by Lynne Heinzmann, issue 196. Photo p. 43 by Brian Pontolilo (FHB), top photo p. 46 courtesy © Rubbermaid, bottom photo p. 46 courtesy © Easy Track, photo p. 47 courtesy © EasyClosets. Drawings by Dan Thornton (FHB).

pp. 48-55: Your Perfect Home Office by Mark Dutka, issue 211. Photos by Charles Miller (FHB) except photos p. 48 and top photo p. 51 courtesy © Humanscale, far left photo p. 52 and top left photo p. 53 courtesy © Doug Mockett, middle right photo p. 52 courtesy © Belkin, photo top p. 54 by Mark Dutka (FHB), and finished office photos p. 54-55 © Ken Gutmaker. Drawing p. 49 by Bruce Morser (FHB) and drawing p. 54 by Martha Garstang Hill (FHB).

pp. 56-61: A Wood Floor that Can Survive Anywhere by Charles Peterson, issue 206. Photos by Rob Yagid (FHB).

pp. 62-68: Plumbing a Basement Bathroom by Mike Guertin with contribution by Paul Murray, issue 193.

Photos by Charles Bickford (FHB) except photos p. 63 and left photo p. 64 by Chris Green (FHB), right photo p. 64 by Mike Guertin (FHB), photo p. 65 courtesy © Liberty Pumps and photo p. 67 courtesy © Saniflo. Drawing by John Hartman (FHB).

pp. 69-75: Trimming a Basement Window by Chris Whalen, issue 189. Photos by Daniel S. Morrison (FHB). Drawings by Bob La Pointe (FHB).

pp. 76-77: A Skylight Cheers Up an Attic Bath by Scott Donahue, issue 199. Photos by Charles Miller (FHB). Drawings by Martha Garstang Hill (FHB).

pp. 79-86: How Much Will My Kitchen Cost? by John McLean, issue 183. Photos by Brian Pontolilo (FHB) except photo p. 80 by Charles Miller (FHB).

pp. 87-93: Ten Ways to Improve Your Kitchen by Jane K. Langmuir, issue 135. Photos by Charles Miller (FHB) except bottom photo p. 91 by Aaron Pennock (FHB). Drawing p. 88 by Matt Collins (FHB) and drawing p. 90 by Paul Perreault (FHB).

pp. 94-97: Drawing Board: Opening up a small kitchen by Jerri Holan, issue 201. Drawings by Jerri Holan (FHB).

pp. 98-105: The Energy-Smart Kitchen by Alex Wilson, issue 191. Photos p. 99 courtesy © Maytag Corp., 3 left photos p. 101 and photo p. 103 courtesy © General Electric, right photo p. 101 courtesy © Whirlpool Corp., photo p. 102 courtesy © Peer-less-Premier Appliance Co., photos

p. 104 courtesy © Fisher & Paykel Appliances, left and right photos p. 105 courtesy © Bosch Appliances, middle photo p. 105 courtesy © LG Appliances. Drawing by Matt Collins (FHB).

pp. 106-111: Design Gallery: Stay inside the lines by Charles Miller, issue 207. Photos by Charles Miller (FHB) except left photo p. 106 courtesy © Eric Dumican, right photo p. 108 courtesy © Wayne Lovegrove and bottom photos p. 110 courtesy © Anthony Anderson. Drawings by Martha Garstang Hill (FHB).

pp. 112-115: Drawing Board: Designing showers for small bathrooms by Bridget E. Cahill, issue 191. Drawings by Martha Garstang Hill (FHB).

pp. 117-121: Prep Before You Paint by Jim Lacey, issue 209. Photos by Rob Yagid (FHB).

pp. 122-124: Building Skills: Hanging drywall on walls by Myron R. Ferguson, issue 196. Photos by John Ross (FHB) except photo p. 122 courtesy © Senco Products.

pp. 125-133: New Insulation for Old Walls by Justin Fink, issue 206. Photos by Dan Thornton (FHB) except top left photo p. 131 by Daniel S. Morrison (FHB), photo top right p. 131 courtesy © Demilec USA, photo top left p. 129 by Andy Engel (FHB), photo top left p. 130 by John Curtis (FHB), and photo top right p. 130 courtesy © Johns Manville.

pp. 134-145: Doghouse Dormers by Rick Arnold, issue 186. Photos by Justin Fink (FHB) except photo

p. 136 by Krysta S. Doerfler (FHB). Drawings by Justin Fink and Dan Thornton (FHB).

pp. 146-150: Leak-Free Skylights by Mike Guertin, issue 204. Photos by Charles Bickford (FHB). Drawings by John Hartman (FHB).

pp. 151-158: Wiring a Master Suite Addition by Clifford A. Popejoy, issue 181. Photos by Brian Pontolilo (FHB) except top photos p. 154 by Lisa Long (FHB). Drawings by Don Mannes (FHB).

pp. 159-165: Add Character with a Box-Beam Ceiling by Chris Whalen, issue 181. Photos by Daniel S. Morrison (FHB). Drawings by Vince Babak (FHB).

pp. 167-178: A Buyer's Guide to Windows by Sean Groom, issue 203. Photos by Rodney Diaz (FHB) except photos 1-5 p. 177 courtesy © Marvin, photo 6 p. 177 courtesy © Eagle, photo 7 p. 177 courtesy © Simonton, photo left p. 178 by Randy O'Rourke (FHB), and photo right p. 178 by Joseph Kugielsky (FHB). Maps p. 173-174 © courtesy of Energy Star. Drawing p. 173 by Dan Thornton (FHB).

pp. 179-184: Choose a Quality Entry Door by Matthew Teague, issue 211. Photos by Dan Thornton (FHB) except photo p. 179 courtesy © Simpson Door, photo p. 181 courtesy © Weather Shield, and right photo p. 183 and bottom p. 184 courtesy © Therma-Tru.

pp. 185-191: Keep Siding Dry with a Vented Rain Screen by Justin Fink,

issue 213. Photos by Dan Thornton (FHB) except photo p. 185 by Rodney Diaz (FHB). Drawings by Dan Thornton (FHB).

pp. 192-197: Will Your Next Asphalt Roof Last a Lifetime? by Sean Groom, issue 214. Photos by Rodney Diaz (FHB). Drawings by John Hartman (FHB).

pp. 199-204: A Safer Job Site by Tom O'Brien, issue 130. Drawings by Rick Daskam (FHB).

pp. 205-209: Protecting a House during Construction by Gary Gilberg, issue 161. Photos by Charles Bickford (FHB).

pp. 210-214: Keeping a Dormer Addition Clean and Dry by Nicholas Pitz, issue 158. Photos by Nicholas Pitz (FHB). Drawings by Don Mannes (FHB).

pp. 215-222: Dust Control by Tom O'Brien, issue 180. Photos by Justin Fink (FHB) except product photos by Krysta S. Doerfler (FHB). Drawing by Don Mannes (FHB).

pp. 223-226: The Remodeler's Guide to Construction Debris by Rob Moody, issue 213. Photos by Rob Moody (FHB). Drawings by Martha Garstang Hill (FHB).